MASSACHUSETTS HISTORICAL REVIEW

VOLUME 13, 2011

Contents

ESSAYS

"Gifts That God Didn't Give"

White Hopes, Basketball, and the Legend of Larry Bird

JOHN MATTHEW SMITH

When Bird makes a great play, it's due to his thinking, and his work habits. It's not the case for blacks. All we do is run and jump. We never practice or give a thought to how we play. It's like I came dribbling out of my mother's womb. Magic and Michael Jordan and me, for example, we're playing only on God-given talent, like we're animals, lions, and tigers, who run around wild in a jungle. . . . Blacks have been fighting that stereotype . . . for so long, and basically it still exists.

—Isiah Thomas, 1987

THEY CALLED HIM THE SAVIOR, though he hardly looked the part. For a basketball player, he had a forgettable appearance: a lean, undefined body; pale skin; pointed nose; shaggy, blond hair; and blue eyes. The shy, introverted young man came to Boston from a hardscrabble town in rural Indiana, a place that celebrated old-fashioned values, blue-collar work, and basketball legends. The people of Boston hoped that he could revive the Celtics from the ashes of its storied past. For nearly two decades, Celtics fans had proudly entered the Boston Garden, the team's home arena, where thirteen championship banners hung from the rafters, but by the late 1970s, the home team inspired little "Celtic Pride." In 1979, Boston fans watched

---

John Matthew Smith earned his Ph.D. in history at Purdue University and currently is visiting assistant professor in the History Department at Middle Tennessee State University. His interests are American popular culture, race, sport, and twentieth-century United States history. He has published articles in the *Michigan Historical Review* and the *Journal of Sport History*.

in misery as the floundering team finished 29–53, last in its division. It made some fans wish that they were the ones hanging from the rafters.

The Celtics were one of many teams in the National Basketball Association (NBA) dealing with an image crisis in the 1970s. Stories circulated in the nation's major newspapers and magazines that players throughout the league used illegal drugs. Critics complained that the players were lazy, selfish, and greedy. In their view, the game lacked marketable personalities. With low attendance and shrinking television ratings, few teams made significant profits and advertisers showed little interest in buying airtime during the games broadcast on CBS. A perception existed among some owners, promoters, and writers that the NBA had become an undisciplined "playground" game. Some said that professional basketball had become "too black" to sell to white fans. Other observers suggested that the league needed a Great White Hope to save the sport. In 1979, it appeared that they had found their man. His name was Larry Bird.

In the 1980s, Bird became a cultural icon and, arguably, the best basketball player in the NBA. When he arrived in Boston, critics complained that he could not run very fast or jump incredibly high. But Bird was a complete player who took full advantage of his other physical assets: he had large hands, remarkable court vision, exceptional timing, and strong wrists that allowed him to shoot from any distance. He immediately became a major attraction at basketball arenas and on national television, a star who increased media attention and advertising sponsorships. In 1980, he won the Rookie of the Year award, and the following season, he led the Boston Celtics to the NBA championship. By mid decade, his success and popularity soared higher than those of any other player. During that time, the Celtics appeared in the NBA Finals for four consecutive years, winning twice. Bird captured the Most Valuable Player trophies for three of those years, from 1984 to 1986. Many coaches, players, and writers were convinced that he was the best player in the history of the game.

Although commentators, players, and fans were aware of Bird's importance to the success of the NBA, historians have neglected to explain his cultural significance. A few historians and journalists have written about the integration years of the NBA, but only Raymond Arsenault has dealt with Bird from a historical perspective, and he offers little analysis of him as a cultural icon in the post-integration era.[1] "Basketball," author John Edgar Wideman observed, "mounts competing attitudes about race onstage, where they are contested, publicly shaped, and reshaped."[2] Throughout the 1970s and 1980s, the NBA was a "showplace for American racial tension."[3] Most of the players on the court were black, while the owners, coaches, general managers, referees, broadcasters, writers, and fans were mostly white. These racial tensions were most visible when the Celtics, the whitest team of the 1980s, played against the predominantly black Los Angeles Lakers; they were the two most successful and popular teams of the decade. Some fans and writers, white and black, viewed Bird, the only white superstar of the time, as an even greater hero because he played in Boston, a city with a history of deep racial conflict between a large population of conservative whites and a relatively small black population.

Bird's popular image had a direct impact on the marketing strategies of the NBA and its sponsors, and as a result he helped shape the league's financial success during the 1980s. Throughout his career, NBA executives, advertisers, television producers, and sportswriters collectively constructed around him an image of a flawless white star in order to broaden the popularity of the league.[4] The media portrayed him as a traditional sports hero, a Horatio Alger protagonist, who overcame poverty and achieved the American dream. The image of Larry Legend was built on his white, blue-collar, Middle American roots. At a time when American politics had shifted decisively to the right, Bird was celebrated as the embodiment of traditional conservative values.

Part of Bird's legend grew out of racial mythology that claimed he overcame "gifts that God didn't give."[5] Such racial ignorance suggested that black athletes only possessed natural physical gifts—gifts that supposedly allowed them to outrun and outjump white athletes. Conversely, therefore, white athletes who succeeded allegedly did so because they could outwork and outsmart their black counterparts. Although a number of historians have examined the historical debate over alleged black athletic superiority, none has explored this question in the context of professional basketball's surge in popularity during the 1980s.[6] Throughout this decade, writers, coaches, and players romanticized Bird as a white, working-class icon who made up for his supposed lack of God-given athletic ability with hard work, ambition, and intelligence, characteristics credited to few black players. On the court, he challenged black athletic superiority and affirmed that traits supposedly intrinsic to whites should earn them a place within the sport. To many, he was a throwback to an era before integration, when players did not dunk or otherwise express their race on the court. In the context of conservative nostalgia, Bird's image reflected a vision of a purer, more innocent time when meritocracy defined achievement. The success of a white superstar changed the face of the NBA.

Ted Landsmark was running late. The twenty-nine-year-old, African American lawyer had planned to meet with Boston Redevelopment Authority officials inside Boston City Hall on April 5, 1976, at 10:00 A.M., but he could not find a parking space nearby. He never made it to the meeting. Instead, he crossed paths with the outskirts of a group of protesters, some two hundred whites from South Boston and Charlestown who were marching to the federal courthouse carrying antibusing placards, American flags, and Bicentennial banners to demand that Judge W. Arthur Garrity end busing. Hurrying along Washington Mall, Landsmark could see a group of white teens rounding the corner of city hall, when one of them shouted, "Get the nigger, kill him!" Immediately, he felt a blow to the head when one student hit him from behind, knocking his glasses off. Then a hit from the front sent him to the brick pavement. A swarming mob of fifteen to twenty youths kicked and punched him in the ribs, back, and face. Blood spilled onto his three-piece suit. When he struggled to his feet he was thrown back down again. Like a prizefighter who refuses to be knocked out, he rose again. A student with an American flag on a long, steel staff lowered it like a spear and smashed it into the black man's face, breaking his nose. A photographer from the *Boston Herald American* captured the attack in a Pulitzer Prize–winning picture that appeared on the front page of newspapers all across the country.[7] For many readers, this violent image demonstrated that Boston had become one of the most racist cities in America.

Boston's busing crises revealed deep racial and class tensions between the city's blacks and whites. Working-class and middle-class whites confronted crosstown busing of black and white students with organized resistance and violence. Historian Ronald P. Formisano has argued that the antibusing movement was "a case of reactionary populism," a white backlash that grew out of fears that blacks threatened to "take over" their jobs, neighborhoods, and schools. Fierce competition between blacks and whites for diminishing blue-collar jobs in a post-industrial city dominated by banks, insurance companies, and other service enterprises fed these tensions. Highly protective of their "turf," white ethnics demanded a return to conditions before Garrity's 1974 decision, when segregation maintained a clear separation between the city's black and white neighborhoods.[8] Boston's reputation for white hostility toward African Americans shaped how basketball fans perceived the Celtics during the late 1970s and 1980s.

Two months after white youths attacked Ted Landsmark, the Boston Celtics defeated the Phoenix Suns for their second NBA championship in three years. The team's success at that time was built largely on the talent of two white stars: John Havlicek and Dave Cowens. Havlicek was "the ideal Celtic": unselfish, disciplined, and team oriented. He won six titles in the 1960s playing with Bill Russell and two more in the 1970s with Cowens. Toward the end of Havlicek's career, *Sports Illustrated*'s Curry Kirkpatrick wrote that he was "the quintessential throwback to the old days, to the pre-trillionaire days, to the days when players cared about such trivial items as pride, teamwork, and the difference between winning and losing."[9] Writers also praised Cowens as a "6 foot 8 ½ inch everyman" who played with great intensity and hustle.[10] During the 1974 finals, an article in *Newsweek* stereotypically described Kareem Abdul-Jabbar, the Milwaukee Bucks star center and an African American Muslim, as a player who "lays back on offense and defense and waits for the action to come his way"; the same article, conversely, attributed a tireless, and implicitly white, work ethic to Cowens. Most basketball coaches believed that in order to win teams had to have a talented center. From 1958 to 1973, not a single team won a championship starting a white center.[11] But when Dave Cowens helped the Celtics win their first championship since Bill Russell had retired, he symbolized the Great White Hope—a white player who filled a black star's position and restored Celtic glory.

In the late 1970s, the Celtics fell on hard times. By 1979, Havlicek had retired, Cowens's skills had diminished, and the team had the second worst record in the entire league. While the Bruins, Boston's hockey team, consistently filled the Garden to near capacity every night, the arena was usually half empty for the Celtics. Tickets were always available and cheap. For two dollars one could buy a seat in the nosebleeds, or "nigger heaven," as bigots often called it.[12] But Boston never followed the Celtics as it did the Bruins or the Red Sox—which was the last Major League Baseball team to integrate.[13] From 1959 to 1966, the prime years of the Russell dynasty, which included eight consecutive championships, the team averaged only 6,783 fans per game in a facility that could seat about 14,000. Historian Thomas J. Whalen has suggested that "the brutal truth of the matter is that the city's majority white inhabitants felt uncomfortable paying money to see athletically gifted African Americans run up and down a basketball floor, even when they were wearing Celtic green."[14]

In the late 1970s, the Celtics, like most NBA teams, were a predominantly black team. Local critics blamed the team's demise on black players, whom they described in stereotypical terms as an undisciplined group of "ballhogs and playground freelancers."[15] Angry fans excoriated Curtis Rowe and Sidney Wicks as egotistical, selfish, and lazy, characteristics unfitting "true" Celtics. The players' dour attitudes seemed to embody the avaricious "Me

Generation." After an embarrassing 30-point loss, Rowe wondered, "What's everybody upset about? The W's and L's don't show up on the paychecks."[16] Even the team's vice president, Jeffrey Cohen, noted that "people suddenly became aware of a player's color" when the Celtics started losing.[17]

In many ways, the Celtics epitomized the racial tensions that pervaded the NBA. By the late 1970s, the best white players had either recently retired (Havlicek, Jerry West) or their careers were declining (Cowens, Rick Barry, Pete Maravich). It appeared as if the white stars had disappeared just as black players had "taken over." Some critics unabashedly complained that the league had become "too black"—too black to sell to white ticket buyers, television audiences, and advertisers. By 1979, almost 75 percent of the players were black—ten years earlier the league was 60 percent black—while more than 75 percent of its fans were white. Many white fans began to view the sport as an undisciplined style of playground basketball. More importantly, they perceived the sport "as *Black*."[18] Some whites claimed that even the best black stars lacked desire and effort. Kareem Abdul-Jabbar was accused of "going all out for no more than two or three of every 48 minutes," while the Philadelphia 76ers' Julius Erving, "who should be the game's most exciting player, is either too tired, too knee-sored, too bored" to go all out.[19] One team executive wondered, "The question is are they [*black players*] promotable? People see them dissipating their money, playing without discipline. How can you sell a black sport to a white public?"[20]

The team owners, the players, and the fans were certainly aware of race. It appeared that in some cities quotas still existed. In 1980, the Utah Jazz, the Phoenix Suns, and the Portland Trail Blazers—the three teams from the cities with the smallest black populations—had the largest number of white players. The Eastern Conference champion Philadelphia 76ers, with nine blacks and two whites, averaged a little over ten thousand fans in an arena that held fourteen thousand. A *Philadelphia Daily News* poll showed that 57 percent of fans believed that a white audience would not pay to watch black athletes. Julius Erving also maintained that race influenced fan attendance: "I would like to say race is not involved, but I'm afraid that would be naïve." A number of Philadelphians wrote letters to the editor suggesting that the NBA needed more white superstars. Cleveland Cavaliers owner Ted Stepien agreed. Before he purchased the team in 1980, he promised that half of the team would be white. "White people have to have white heroes," he said. "I respect [*black players*], but I need white people. It's in me. And I think the Cavs have too many blacks. . . . You need a blend of white and black. I think that draws, and I think that's a better team." Another Philadelphia "fan" blamed blacks for poor attendance, asserting that they did not buy enough tickets.[21] Such racist attitudes reflected the larger conservative backlash that sought to resist the social, economic, and political gains being made by black Americans.[22] Some observers noted that it was impossible to determine the number of whites who refused to watch the NBA because of its large number of black players. Nonetheless, "They're out there," maintained the *Boston Globe*'s Bob Ryan, and "probably in frightening numbers."[23]

Racism was not the only problem the NBA faced. Writers and fans compiled a litany of complaints: outside of Philadelphia, the major markets—New York, Chicago, Los Angeles, and Boston—either had poor teams or dull personalities; the eighty-two-game season was too long; there were too many fights; only the playoff games were worth watching; the players were selfish, greedy, and overpaid; and, worse yet, the *Los Angeles Times* estimated that up to 75 percent of the NBA's players used cocaine. Reports of widespread drug use in the predominantly black sport created an image crisis for the NBA. All of these issues translated into poor television ratings for CBS. In 1979, ratings for CBS's *Game of the Week* were down 27 percent from the previous year, and advertisers were not interested in a sport with poor viewership. Media commentator William Leggett pointed out that there were no dominant teams to generate national interest. Furthermore, he offered, there was simply too much college and professional basketball on television—the product was overexposed.[24] The NBA needed a rivalry, a storyline. It needed stars and heroes. It needed magic. It needed a legend.

In the fall of 1974, Larry Bird drove a garbage truck, pumped gas, painted park benches for the sanitation department, and worked for a construction company. He was just trying to get by. The high school basketball star had returned to his hometown, French Lick, Indiana, after spending less than one month at Indiana University on a basketball scholarship. On a campus sixteen times the size of his hometown, with little money in his pocket and a roommate who had a closet full of clothes and plenty of spending money, Bird felt completely out of place. He had grown up in utter poverty in the kind of small town that John Mellencamp sings about—a simple, hardscrabble town where people did not have much but took pride in their jobs. His mother often held down two or three jobs at a time, usually as a waitress, while his father battled alcoholism and struggled to hang onto various jobs. Bill collectors frequently showed up on the Birds' doorstep. With barely enough money to feed all six children and pay the rent, the Birds endured eviction on more than one occasion, and at times Larry had to live with his grandmother. With little else to do, he spent most of his time playing sports with his brothers. For Bird, like many boys in Indiana, basketball became his life. He spent countless hours shooting alone, dribbling, and practicing the fundamentals of the game. Basketball gave him an escape from the daily grind of poverty. It gave him purpose in a world that offered little else.[25]

After deciding that IU wasn't right for him, Bird worked odd jobs and played basketball at a junior college, before he received a scholarship to play for Indiana State, a much smaller school than Indiana University. The basketball program was so bad that even the students in Terre Haute paid hardly any attention. Before attending ISU, Bird was relatively unknown to most of the state's basketball fans. That all changed in his first varsity season. In 1976–1977, the country's third-leading scorer lifted the Sycamores to twenty-five wins and three losses, the best team record in school history, and a trip to the National Invitation Tournament. Out of nowhere he had become a folk hero, a "living legend, a program savior."[26] Reluctantly, the shy, introverted player agreed to appear on the cover of *Sports Illustrated*. *Sporting News* and *Basketball Weekly* put him on their covers as well. In a culture of narcissism, Bird rejected celebrity. He wanted to live a simple life, hang out with friends, drink beer, and play pool. At one point, he became so overwhelmed with media requests that he simply stopped talking with reporters. But college basketball's "secret weapon" had become more than a good local player. He was now nationally popular and a cultural icon, a promising white star from Middle America in a sport seemingly dominated by urban blacks.[27]

For many Hoosiers, the pale star embodied "Indiana's past, a reminder of times when basketball was all there was in the winter and when it was played by the best white players from small towns, boys who spent more time on the floor than in the air."[28] "In a day of shot-oriented individuals," commented a writer for *Sport*, "Larry Bird is a basketball throwback—an old fashioned, all around, team first player." In many ways, Bird's style of play evoked conservative nostalgia for basketball before integration. Writers often compared the college sensation to past white stars such as John Havlicek, Rick Barry, and Pete Maravich.[29] By his senior year, basketball officials began discussing the value of a white player to the NBA. Pat Williams, the Philadelphia 76ers' vice president, believed that Bird's race and star status made him "an asset" to the NBA. Pete Newell, chief scout for the Golden State Warriors, said, "Bird's marketability is increased by the fact he's white." An NBA executive maintained that Bird would make more money than black players because a white star was "an unusual commodity in our business."[30]

The 1979 NCAA national championship game foreshadowed how valuable Larry Bird and Magic Johnson would be to the NBA. It was the perfect story for television. Indiana State, the "disciplined, hard working team," symbolized Small Town, U.S.A., the underdog that nobody knew anything about. Michigan State represented the city game with its two black stars, Johnson and Greg Kelser. Together, these two had perfected the alley-oop dunk, in which Johnson threw the ball just above the rim for Kelser to slam it through the net. In the buildup to the championship game, the press could not get enough of "The Bird" and the "Magic Man." Johnson loved the spotlight, flashing his million-dollar smile at every photo opportunity. On the court, the six-foot-eight-inch point guard transcended the position, playing half a foot taller than most floor leaders. He could dominate a game without scoring. Johnson often snagged a rebound at one end of the court, dribbled the length of the floor, and dished out jaw-dropping, no-look passes that confused his defenders. Bird was even more valuable to his team because he did everything. The college player of the year scored, rebounded, and passed the ball better than any other forward in the country. But in the championship game, Michigan State suffocated him every time he touched the ball. The Spartans crushed the dream of an undefeated Sycamore season, running away with a 75–64 victory. The game generated more national interest than any other championship in history, registering a record 24.1 Nielsen rating. Americans wanted to see more of Bird and Magic. On March 26, 1979, a rivalry was born. Basketball fans could not wait for more.[31]

Boston eagerly anticipated Bird's arrival. Celtics president and general manager Arnold "Red" Auerbach drafted Bird with the sixth overall pick of the NBA draft in 1978, when the young player was still in his junior year, even though it would mean waiting a year to sign him. Auerbach, who had coached the Celtics during the team's dynasty in the 1960s, believed that Bird's acute court awareness, raw toughness, and sharp shooting ability would help the team. Throughout the summer of 1979, the media filed almost daily reports on the status of Bird's contract negotiations. After he signed the most lucrative rookie contract in all of professional sports, Celtics fans purchased a record six thousand season tickets before Bird played a single game.[32]

When Bird showed up at his first press conference dressed "down home casual" in a red shirt and khaki pants in a room full of tailored suits, *Boston Globe* writer Leigh Montville found him refreshingly "real." Bird seemed to say all the right things. He did not want to be the savior. He was committed to playing good team basketball and promised to give 100 percent—a stark contrast to the surly, self-absorbed Sidney Wicks. Montville wrote, "There was a pleasant, unforced humility about him that somehow came through everything he said or did. He spoke about the virtues of teamwork as if it were religion." All of the lights, cameras, and questions "did not distract him. He was the Midwestern phenom, basketball in a dusty backyard, long days in the sunshine, shot after shot going through the hoop, a picture on the wall."[33] Bostonians wanted to believe not only that Bird could save the Celtics; they also wanted to believe in what he stood for. He seemed to bring a mythic purity to the game—purity based on the image of white Middle America, where people with traditional values were rewarded for hard work and modesty.

Some commentators wondered whether Auerbach selected Bird not only to win but also to placate contemptuous fans who resented the team's disproportionate number of black players. In Bird's first training camp, *eight* of the fifteen players were white, convincing some observers that Auerbach had deliberately whitewashed the roster. His defenders claimed that those accusations were baseless, pointing out the team's progressive racial history during his tenure as head coach: in 1950, the Celtics drafted Chuck Cooper, the first black player selected by an NBA team; during the 1963–1964 season, the Celtics became the first team to play five black players at the same time; and in 1966, Auerbach selected Bill Russell as his coaching replacement, making him the first black head coach in professional sports. Still, in the late 1970s, the nadir of Celtics history, Auerbach was fully aware of the racial tensions surrounding the team, acknowledging that "in certain areas of the country, unless the team is strong, it can be hurt at the box office by a predominance of blacks." "My job," he conceded, "is to get a ball club out there the town will like." If the Celtics lost with too many black players, he explained, the fans would criticize him, but if they won with a predominantly black team, "a lot will be forgiven." Somehow, winning made Celtics loyalists forget about race.[34]

When Bird entered the NBA, there were some observers who doubted that he would save the league, let alone the Celtics. Sure, they said, he would be a good player but not one of the best players in the entire league. Some black players questioned whether the pale Hoosier was as good as he was made out to be in his press clippings. He could not jump and he was too slow—traits that translated to the popular stereotype that he was "too white" to succeed in a predominantly black sport. The notion of "white man's disease," which assumed that African Americans were inherently physically superior, implied that Bird would succeed only if he could outwork his black peers.

As the number of black athletes—especially high-profile black athletes—in professional sports surged, many observers came to express the belief that black bodies were better suited for athletics. In 1971, Martin Kane, a senior editor for *Sports Illustrated*, wrote an inflammatory essay entitled "An Assessment of Black Is Best." He claimed that there was "an increasing body of scientific opinion which suggests that physical differences in the races might well have enhanced the athletic potential of the Negro in certain events."[35] Popular magazines as diverse as *Time*, *Ebony*, *Sepia*, and the *Progressive* also featured stories on innate black athletic superiority, some of it meant to be valorizing. White and black athletes, coaches, and commentators perpetuated the myth. Jerry West, a white star for the Los Angeles Lakers in the 1960s and the team's coach in the late 1970s, believed that there were "incredible differences between black and white ballplayers. It seems that all the black guys have bigger hands, they're so much quicker, they jump higher. They seem to do everything a little bit better." Dominique Wilkins, a black star for the Atlanta Hawks during the 1980s, believed that black athletes excelled at dunking the ball because "It must be in the blood."[36]

Bird's legend grew in part out of his ability to overcome his alleged racial inferiority. To many fans, he did not look like the "typical" basketball player. He possessed an unimpressive body, lacking in muscular definition. Jim Murray wrote in the *Los Angeles Times* that "the Lord didn't give him much to work with. You don't get basketball players out of French Lick, Ind. You get them off the playgrounds. The projects. The sidewalks of New York. Or the sidewalks of Chicago."[37] While fans were attracted to Bird because of his gritty attitude and style of play, undoubtedly much of the fascination with the "Designated Savior of professional basketball" had to do with his race. One Celtics official maintained that "Bird would have been a commodity for any NBA team, but in a racially-conscious city like Boston, he is a hero."[38] Frank T. Bannister, Jr., wrote in *Ebony* that Bird gave Boston another hardworking white star to pin its hopes on—something fans had lost when Havlicek and Cowens retired. He added, "Most folks agree that any pro team in prejudiced Boston needs its share of white stars if it is to make it at the box office." As black athletes threatened white positions in professional basketball, it became increasingly clear to Bannister that white America needed "its heroes and symbols" more than ever.[39]

Bird made an immediate impact on the Celtics and the NBA. In his first season, he led the Celtics to sixty-one wins, thirty-two more than the previous season, easily the best turnaround in NBA history. He had become the NBA's major attraction. To increase the audience for its broadcasts, CBS changed the programming for *Game of the Week*, airing one national game each week instead of local matchups in different cities simultaneously. The network's first nationally televised game between the Celtics and Lakers registered an 8.5 rating, more than double the 4.0 rating of the NBA game that aired the following week.[40]

The change that registered in television ratings also had an impact at the gate. Fans all across the country clicked the turnstiles at their local arena when Bird came to town. While many clubs struggled to fill their stadiums, he helped sell out arenas in New York, Philadelphia, Indianapolis, Kansas City, and Atlanta. Cleveland's two biggest crowds of the season turned out for games against the Celtics. Boston sold out twenty-seven of their forty-one road games, a remarkable feat in light of league-wide attendance problems. Bird was also largely responsible for improving home attendance by 46 percent to a record high. The *Chicago Tribune*'s Bob Logan asserted that Bird had become a national phenomenon and that he had "turned the Celtics back into basketball's version of America's team." Bob Ryan of the *Boston Globe* predicted that the 1980 Rookie of the Year was "a year away from being the best player in America."[41]

More than anything else, Bird made his teammates better. He had great court vision, an awareness of where everyone stood on the court. The six-foot-nine-inch forward's remarkable hand-eye coordination allowed him to make passes that others would not dare, threading the ball into tight passing lanes. He would look one way and throw the ball the other. His imaginative passes created easy lay-ups for Kevin McHale and Robert Parish. All of these traits enhanced his dominance on the court, but what made him unstoppable was his ability to shoot from any distance. "If there was a key to Bird's game," David Halberstam noted, "it was those wrists. He was in many ways a wrist shooter—just a little flick of the wrist and he had his shot."[42] Bird kept the other team's defense off balance with an array of moves that included shoulder dips, head nods, and ball fakes. His opponents were most surprised by his toughness and his ability to rebound against bigger, stronger players. Quite simply, he could do it all. And as his second NBA season unfolded, most writers agreed with Bob Ryan: Larry Bird had become the best player in the game.[43]

In 1981, Bird led the Celtics to an NBA championship over the Houston Rockets, winning the series four games to two. Yet the NBA failed to provide a national stage for him during the most significant games of the season. During the finals, four of the six telecasts were broadcast on tape delay after the late local news. The previous season, when Magic Johnson had starred in the finals between the Lakers and the 76ers, the deciding sixth game was shown on tape delay in most areas of the country. Thus, over the two seasons, the NBA missed a tremendous opportunity to showcase Magic and Bird at their finest. The inability of the league to televise its most important games typified the treatment of the sport at its nadir. The NBA had not yet developed a sound marketing plan to promote its two young stars, and CBS was unwilling to show the games during primetime. The league's marketing failures hurt the individual teams: during the 1981 season, sixteen of the NBA's twenty-three teams lost money. Total attendance declined by almost a million from the year before, and teams attracted on average a little over ten thousand fans for each game, filling 59 percent of their arenas' capacity. Some observers suggested it was time to reduce the number of teams.[44]

Over the course of the decade, however, the NBA made a number of important changes that boosted the league's image and profitability. After the tape-delay failures, CBS agreed to show all games of the NBA Finals live. In return, the league started its season three weeks later than usual, avoiding a conflict with Major League Baseball's World Series. Also, a June start for the NBA Finals placed it safely after Nielson's "May sweeps," the most important ratings period for advertisers. During the regular season, CBS substantially reduced the number of games broadcast, favoring a few teams in major markets and ignoring the majority of teams. Essentially, the NBA and CBS worked together to expose the very best of its product to national audiences. This meant that most games that were aired included at least one of the three most popular teams—Boston, Philadelphia, or Los Angeles. After signing a four-year contract with CBS in 1982, the NBA also made agreements with USA, ESPN, and TBS, realizing future marketing opportunities existed on cable television.[45] Before the 1984 season, new commissioner David Stern negotiated a landmark collective bargaining agreement with the National Basketball Players Association that implemented drug testing and a salary cap. Under the agreement, the players received 53 percent of the gross revenues (comprised of gate receipts and television fees); a new salary cap was designed to create greater parity between large market and small market teams. The drug testing program made it clear to fans and advertisers that the teams—ownership and players—wanted to clean up the sport's image.[46]

The most important aspect of the NBA's growth during the 1980s was the ability of the league to build relationships with advertisers. To accomplish this, the league had to change the face of the sport. The biggest challenge was convincing reluctant advertisers to sponsor a predominantly black sport. A Madison Avenue agency representing a car company told Stern that the head of the car company would only sponsor college basketball because the profes-

Los Angeles Lakers Magic Johnson, right, knocks the ball from Boston Celtics Larry Bird, May 27, 1984, at Boston Garden. In the background is Lakers Kareem Abdul-Jabbar. AP Photo, Mike Kullen photographer.

sional game was too black. Rick Welts, vice president of NBA Properties, the league's licensing and merchandising division, recalled that race, more than anything else, prevented advertisers from sponsoring NBA games: "When I first began this job and called on Madison Avenue agencies, people would look at me like I was out of my mind. They didn't want to get involved with this *thing* called the NBA."[47] Soon after starting his new position, Stern realized that in order to change the perception of the league, the NBA and its partners had to find a way to manage racial tensions. He believed "that if everything else went right, race would not be an abiding issue to NBA fans, at least not as long as it was handled correctly." That is, Stern believed it was possible that skillful marketing could create a "colorblind" relationship between the players and fans, and his comment reflected the kind of codified language that helped "sell" a predominantly black sport to a predominantly white audience.[48]

In its campaign to remove the pervasive negative perceptions of professional basketball, the NBA took advantage of the narrative potential of television: the league would reframe the games as entertaining stories with compelling characters. In its buildup to and presentation of the games, CBS showcased the sport's biggest personalities—Bird, Magic, and Erving. Ted Shaker, executive producer of the NBA on CBS, explained that the network "began talking about the players as much or more than teams. We wanted people to tune in to see the players more than tune in to see anything else." The network determined that they were going to prop up Bird, Magic, and Erving, and show them playing against each other as often as possible. Games were no longer promoted as "The Celtics vs. The Lakers." Instead, viewers were invited to tune in to see "Bird vs. Magic." David Stern understood that the only way the NBA could grow was "by focusing on the players, their talents on the court, their talents off the court, their sense of personality."[49] In "an eighties culture driven and dominated by the production and circulation of the image," the NBA's mission was simple: market heroes.[50]

Bird's image as a white, small-town hero made him a valuable commodity to the NBA. Mike Littwin of the *Los Angeles Times* wrote, "He's, remember, the hick from French Lick. That's French Lick, Indiana. Middle America. The NBA needs Middle America to survive, the way Ronald Reagan does."[51] In a reactionary racial climate, the image of Bird as a pale, blue-collar athlete in a predominantly black sport appealed to working-class and middle-class whites who expressed frustration and resentment toward busing, "reverse discrimination," affirmative action, and "elite" liberals who seemed to support such measures—measures that arguably placed whites at a disadvantage. During the recession of the late 1970s and early 1980s, many whites worried that their American dream was slipping away while the government gave more opportunities to inner-city blacks. In this conservative narrative, Bird became a symbol for the "little guy" from Middle America whose virtues, codified as racial, lifted him to the top of his field, even where his physical capability was thought to be inferior to that of black athletes. Without any "handouts," he overcame the economic disadvantages of growing up poor and succeeded as a professional basketball player. His rags-to-riches story reminded many whites that the American dream was alive and well—that it was, in the words of Reagan, "Morning Again in America."[52]

In an age of avarice, Bird seemed unchanged by celebrity. At the end of each season, he returned home to French Lick, where he enjoyed mowing his own lawn, building his own fence, fishing, and hunting. Once in a while he could be seen having a beer at a local watering hole. He wore simple clothes: blue jeans, t-shirts, and a "Roughneck Trucking" baseball cap. One time, Bird went shopping and fell in love with a pair of $285 cowboy boots. Sure, he could easily afford them, but, he wondered, "How can I tell the people in French Lick I spent $285 on a pair of boots?"[53] He did not drive a luxurious Mercedes-Benz; instead, he rode around in an American-made Ford Bronco. While black basketball stars "Dr. J and Isiah Thomas wear furs," *Boston Globe* scribe Dan Shaughnessy wrote, "Bird wears a Republican cloth coat." The Hoosier basketball star made it clear that, like most conservatives, he did not believe in welfare. He refused to give his brothers a free ride by handing them tons of money. Bird shook his head at people "who always seem to expect something more from their employers." In French Lick, he was "brought up to work real hard every day," he wrote in his 1989 autobiography, adding, "that's why I try to give 110 percent in every game I play—*my workday*."[54]

Even Bird saw himself as a kind of blue-collar icon who lacked natural physical ability. "A lot of people who come to games work hard—six days a week, long hours," he said in 1982. "What I try to do every time is give the best I can. I like to think I give people their money's worth when they come to a game. Someone once wrote about me that I'm a blue collar basketball player that I work hard for my money. I like that."[55] Like many athletes, fans, and commentators, Bird believed in the myth that black players were more naturally gifted. "I'm not a natural talent like a [*Michael*] Jordan or a [*Clyde*] Drexler," he declared. "I have to practice and practice and practice."[56] Addressing the same idea a year later, he explained, "Some guys can compensate for their deficiencies. I am one of the fortunate ones who can. I've already proven that a white boy who can't run or jump can play this game."[57] In other words, nothing came easy for Bird. The white superstar had to work hard for everything he achieved.

By the mid 1980s, Bird had become more popular than ever before. In 1985, he graced the cover of *Time* with another white sports icon, hockey player Wayne Gretzky. A year later, he won his third consecutive MVP trophy, *Sporting News* and the Associated Press made him their Man of the Year, and the *New York Post* and the *Boston Herald* named him Athlete of the Year.[58] Advertisers and marketers exploited Bird's swelling popularity. His face appeared everywhere—on billboards and television commercials and in magazine ads. He endorsed products for Converse, Nestle, Ford, Spalding, Canon, and 7-Up. These companies wanted to sell their products using the image of Bird and his traditional values. A New York marketing firm determined that he was the most popular basketball player among fans. A representative for a celebrity brokerage firm in L.A. claimed that many companies felt "a white spokesman for middle white America is a natural advantage," making Bird all the more valuable to the NBA and its sponsors.[59]

The Bird-Magic rivalry greatly enhanced the image and profitability of the NBA. The league's strategy of showcasing Bird and Johnson paid off handsomely during the NBA Finals. Every season, from 1980 to 1989, either the Lakers or the Celtics played in the championship, and they faced each other three times during that span. The rivalry was great theater. It was Larry Legend vs. Magic, Celtic Pride vs. Showtime, Hardhats vs. Hollywood, East vs. West, and White vs. Black. David Stern averred that fans tuned in to see "the *metaphor*."[60] The Celtics and Lakers were cast in the image of their stars, "shaped to the styles and contours of their superstars, one white, one black."[61] Supposedly, the Celtics played "white basketball," a slow, methodical, and patterned style. This racial label ignored the contributions of the Celtics' black players, rendering Robert Parish, Dennis Johnson, and Cedric Maxwell invisible in the success of the team. Johnson claimed that whenever the Celtics lost the local newspapers would "use a big picture of me or Robert [*Parish*] or Max [*Maxwell*] on the front" of the sports section. "When we won they'd use Larry [*Bird*] or Kevin [*McHale*] or Danny [*Ainge*], but when we'd lose it'd be one of us."[62]

The Celtics' style of play stood in stark contrast to that of the Lakers, who emphasized a faster game that relied on quickness, mobility, and improvisation. Their disciplined fast-break offense ran opponents into the ground. The fast break was effective because of Magic Johnson's court vision, timing, and creativity. His "now you see it, now you don't" sleight-of-hand passes made it impossible for the other team's defense to stop the Lakers. Magic, along with James Worthy, Byron Scott, and Michael Cooper, created the most entertaining team in basketball. The Lakers' up-tempo style and highlight-reel plays, enhanced by instant replay, made for especially compelling television. But that national stage also fed into the racial stereotypes that shaped audience perceptions. Lakers coach Pat Riley, describing his team as "very agile, versatile, quick athletes whose instincts are to attack," characterized the players as aggressive and instinctual rather than thoughtful and disciplined.[63] The Lakers appeared to be a team of "thoroughbreds" who won because of their natural athleticism alone.[64]

Bird and Johnson competed in their first NBA Finals showdown in 1984. After the Lakers won the third game 137–104, it seemed that they would easily win the series. To slow down the Lakers, the Celtics became much more physical. They believed that the Lakers could be intimidated with force. The strategy worked. The Celtics triumphed in game seven, though Cedric Maxwell thought that when it came to "Natural talent, [*the Lakers*] had the advantage."[65] Kareem Abdul-Jabbar said, "I don't think it matters too much who has the most talent. They had the best team."[66] A number of commentators suggested that the Lakers, especially Magic, had choked under pressure. This was the same Magic who had given one of the most memorable performances seen in any NBA Finals when he was a rookie in 1980.[67] Such racially codified language suggested that the "naturally superior" Lakers should always win if the game depended on physical prowess alone. "Choking," however, implied that the "best team" possessed something the "natural" team did not: effort and mental acuity.

During the 1980s, the Celtics were the whitest team in the NBA. Over the course of the decade, the Celtics played twenty-four blacks and twenty-two whites. The Lakers, on the other hand, had forty-five blacks and fifteen whites.[68] Before the 1986 season, Celtics coach K. C. Jones cut David Thirdkill and Carlos Clark but kept Rick Carlisle. Neither Thirdkill nor Clark would have seen much playing time, but the decision to cut two black players and keep one white player made headlines. The Celtics now had an unparalleled roster of eight whites and four blacks, clearly an inversion of the racial dynamic then prevalent in the NBA. It was the whitest team since the Golden State Warriors had featured eight whites in 1970. For some fans, the Celtics represented "America's Team," while others cynically referred to the predominantly white squad as "South Africa's Team."[69] A number of white Boston writers admitted that the city had its racial troubles but refused to believe that the Celtics were a racist institution, citing the progressive history of the organization. These writers reminded readers that Jones, who had started on the integrated teams in the 1960s, was one of the few black head coaches in all of sports, and they stressed that it was his decision to keep Carlisle.[70]

It was all true. But none of these writers described the horrific racism that Russell and Jones experienced in Boston. Instead, they painted a nostalgic, feel-good picture of sports integration. More importantly, fans and commentators viewed the team through a racial lens that extended beyond the boundary lines of the basketball court. The city's ugly racial tensions lingered into the 1980s, and few blacks attended events at Boston Garden or Fenway Park. Cedric Maxwell said that the black players joked among themselves that if there was a black person in the stands "you could find him fast because he's the one yelling, 'Peanuts! Peanuts! Get your peanuts!'"[71] *Black Enterprise* writer Victoria Everett charged that "no major city so isolates its minority population from the mainstream of social activities as does Boston." In a Pulitzer Prize–winning series on job discrimination, the *Boston Globe* claimed that "Boston today is the most difficult place in America for a black person to hold a job or earn a promotion."[72] Many African Americans still lived with the haunting memory of the Ted Landsmark attack. Although there is no hard evidence that the Celtics deliberately added players to its roster because they were white, for many blacks the image of a mostly white team seemed to reflect the history of racial intolerance in Boston.

In this context, many writers argued that Bird's race enhanced his popularity. *Time*'s Tom Callahan claimed, "No city cheers a white star more enthusiastically than Boston." Bob Ryan suggested that "a lot of fans cheer extra hard when a Larry Bird puts a move on a black guy or when a Kevin McHale blocks a brother's shot."[73] Ten years after Bird retired, Ryan asserted more bluntly that "The Celtics were clearly the favorite team of blatant racists. . . . Anybody that would deny that is naïve."[74] Art Spander of the *Sporting News* maintained that "Bird gets a lot of publicity not only because of what he does, but what he is, a Caucasian in a league where the majority of the players are black. A white audience and a white press are quick to seek verification that one of theirs still belongs."[75] *Newsday*'s Les Payne criticized the white press for building him up as the greatest player ever. Payne, an African American, proposed that the "mythification" of Bird resulted from white writers who had grown "impatient with the pace at which truly outstanding white players" entered the NBA. These writers "resorted to gilding the white lilies."[76]

Many African Americans agreed with Payne. Movie producer and director Spike Lee, who critiqued Bird's image as the Great White Hope in two of his films, *She's Gotta Have It* (1986) and *Do the Right Thing* (1989), said that black people were tired of hearing that a white player was the greatest player of all time. To Lee, it seemed obvious that the Celtics purposely added white players to please white fans in Boston. He maintained that the image of the mostly white Celtics represented a desire for "white supremacy." "When I hear the name Celtics," Lee asserted, "I see the bus with black schoolchildren being overturned during the whole busing thing in Boston."[77] Andrew P. Jones, the lead organizer of a movement to allow Roxbury to secede from Boston, asserted that Boston blacks who did not cheer for the Celtics were protesting against "the exclusion of black players." A number of African Americans complained to K. C. Jones that the team needed more black players. Former Celtic Jo Jo White claimed that since 1969, when Bill Russell had retired, the Celtics "always had to have their white superstar. In Boston it's a must. And the league needs it in a place like Boston, too." Sociologist William Sampson accused referees of giving Bird favorable calls as part of "the plan to have a Great White Hope in a sport dominated by blacks."[78]

The greatest controversy over Bird's race came in the aftermath of the 1987 Eastern Conference Finals when he made a critical steal against the Detroit Pistons. With five seconds remaining in game five, and the Pistons up by one point, all-star Isiah Thomas simply had to pass the ball inbounds to secure a win at the Boston Garden. A victory by the Pistons would give the team a 3–2 series lead heading back to Detroit. Standing on the sideline near the Celtics' basket, Thomas lofted the ball toward teammate Bill Laimbeer. Bird's eyes danced as he watched the ball travel in the air. Then he lunged in front of Laimbeer and intercepted the ball. Teetering on the baseline with his heels nearly out of bounds, he turned back and fired the ball to Dennis Johnson, who streaked toward the basket and laid the ball in for a score. Celtics 108–Pistons 107. Basketball fans could not believe what they had just witnessed. Larry Bird had rescued the Celtics once again.[79]

The steal only added to the mythology of Larry Legend. The *Boston Herald* called it the "steal of the century." One teammate called him "Superman."[80] The Celtics went on to win the series in seven games. In the aftermath, commentary about what made Bird a superstar continued. Pistons rookie Dennis Rodman told writers that Bird "ain't God, he ain't the best player in the NBA," adding that the Celtic was "overrated"; finally, Rodman also surmised that Bird won three consecutive MVPs "because he's white. That's the only reason." When asked about his teammate's comments, Isiah Thomas replied, "I think Larry is a very, very good basketball player. An exceptional talent, but I'd have to agree with Rodman. If Bird was black, he'd be just another good guy."[81] Rodman's and Thomas's comments reflected the frustration of many African Americans who believed that white commentators exaggerated Bird's abilities simply because he was white. But Larry Bird was more than "just another good guy." He was clearly one of the best players of the decade, consistently ranking among the league's leading scorers, an elite shooter, a fine passer, and a clutch performer. A year earlier, when the Celtics played the Houston Rockets in the NBA Finals, Bird nearly averaged a "triple-double" (24 points, 9.7 rebounds, 9.5 assists), a virtuoso performance that demonstrated his exceptional overall ability during the most important games of the season.

Immediately, the majority of Boston and national media condemned Thomas, then one of the league's biggest stars, as racist. Michael Madden of the *Boston Globe* twisted the two black players' words, claiming that they believed "a stereotype that white players can't run or jump." Letters complaining about Thomas flooded the desks of newspaper editors all across the country. The Pistons received over one hundred calls from season ticket holders; some canceled their commitments. One *Los Angeles Herald Examiner* writer supported such actions, arguing that "the Pistons must be threatened with a boycott if Thomas isn't fired." Mike Shalin of the *Boston Herald* insinuated that Thomas made the statement to divert attention "from the real issue—that he choked" when he failed to call a time-out at the end of the game. Shalin also suggested that the black point guard "should think better," betraying his acceptance of the stereotype that black athletes were not as intelligent as white players.[82]

In response to the backlash, Thomas moved to defuse the incident. In an interview with journalist Ira Berkow, he explained that he was not criticizing Bird but trying to draw attention to the perpetuation of black stereotypes. He elaborated:

> When Bird makes a great play, it's due to his thinking, and his work habits. It's not the case for blacks. All we do is run and jump. We never practice or give a thought to how we play. It's like I came dribbling out of my mother's womb. Magic and Michael Jordan and me, for example, we're playing only on God-given talent, like we're animals, lions, and tigers, who run around wild in a jungle. . . . Blacks have been fighting that stereotype . . . for so long, and basically it still exists.[83]

Thomas made an important point. The image of Bird as the best player in the game had been built not only on his fantastic performances but also on hyperbolic statements that he had "gifts that God didn't give." Many players, writers, and commentators portrayed him as the smartest player in the game, an immeasurable characteristic. The internal logic of this stereotype, based in racial ignorance, seemed to justify the explanation that only hard work and intelligence could make a white man the best player in a "black man's game."[84]

At a press conference in Los Angeles, where the Celtics were preparing to meet the Lakers in the NBA Finals, Thomas stated that he was only joking when he said that Bird would be just another good player if he was black. Most writers refused to believe his defense, until Bird announced that he had forgiven him. Bird said, "If it didn't bother me, it shouldn't bother anyone else. If he says he was joking, I believe him." The NBA insisted that CBS show the press conference at halftime during the first game of the Finals. Such choreography fit into the NBA's overall marketing strategy of its black superstars, promoting those who smiled (Thomas, Jordan, and Magic) and performed without drawing attention to racial issues. Frank Dell'Apa wrote that Bird "acted the part of older brother" to Thomas, "the youngster in need of guidance." Such emasculating imagery of Thomas, "the man-child," was consistent with Mitch Albom's description of Rodman as "immature, excitable, and pliable, a guy who can be led to say almost anything if you ask the right way."[85] Once again, the prevalent language furthered the perception that only a Great White Hope could cleanse the image of the NBA. In this case, the white hero had saved the "Bad Negro" who could not control himself from acting out of his place.[86]

After the Thomas controversy cooled off, the Celtics lost to the Los Angeles Lakers in Bird's last appearance in the NBA Finals. Once again, the Bird-Magic, Celtics-Lakers rivalry drew great fan interest, registering the highest Nielson ratings in NBA Finals history. The Celtics were by far the most popular team on television. In 1987, their playoff games on WTBS averaged a 40 percent larger audience than the other games on the cable superstation. Thanks to these improved television ratings, CBS and WTBS commanded premium prices from companies wishing to advertise during Celtics games, including major sponsors such as McDonald's, American Airlines, General Motors, Coca-Cola, and Miller Brewing Co. Over the course of the 1980s, the marketing of superstars brought great financial rewards and drove league attendance up by 50 percent. In 1989, NBC signed a new television agreement that paid the NBA $150 million annually, a remarkable sum compared with the $43 million payout that CBS had made the previous year. The popularity of the NBA firmly placed the sport within the larger consumer culture. In 1989, the league earned more than $300 million in revenues from merchandise as diverse as basketballs, apparel, videos, backboards, and coffee mugs.[87] By the end of the 1980s, the NBA had become a full-scale entertainment brand.

On February 4, 1993, over fifteen thousand spectators made their way into the dingy and cramped Boston Garden to cheer one last time for a man they called Larry Legend. The Garden smelled of beer, cigarettes, and stale popcorn. Television trucks lined up along Causeway Street while scalpers offered overpriced tickets, some fetching as much as $400 apiece. Fans arrived early at the Fours, a sports bar across from the Garden, where patrons had to wait at least forty minutes just to get a seat. On this particular night, the Celtics were not playing a basketball game. No, the Boston faithful would not see him fire up any last shots, or dive across the parquet floor for loose balls. He was done playing. This night was about saying good-bye. And for two and a half hours Hub fans paid tribute to their hero whose jersey, bearing the almost mythic number 33, now hung from the rafters next to seventeen other retired numbers. The crowd rose to its feet when Magic Johnson, Larry Legend's greatest rival and close friend, said to him, "Larry, you told me one lie. You said there will be another Larry Bird. Larry, there will never, ever be another Larry Bird. You can take that to the bank."[88]

Magic was right. Since Larry Bird retired in 1992, no white player has achieved what he did on the court or in terms of national popularity. Without him, commentators and fans have continued to debate whether the NBA needs another White Hope, labeling nearly every white player with star potential "the next Larry Bird." In today's NBA, there is "a perception that white American players are a dying breed." In 2004, Bird, who had then become president of basketball operations for the Indiana Pacers, told ESPN reporter Jim Gray that he believed the NBA needs more white stars because "it's good for a fan base because as we all know the majority of the fans are white America. And if you just had a couple of white guys in there, you might get them a little excited." Adding the assertion that "it is a black man's game, and it will be forever," Bird revealed that he accepted the stereotype that black athletes were inherently better players. He admitted that he "really got irritated" when a white player guarded him "because it's disrespect to my game." Five years later, when he was asked why the Pacers seemed to have more white players than most NBA teams, he explained that the organization's personnel decisions were based on a player's talent, maintaining, "I don't see race at all."[89]

But race did matter. Bird understood that fans and players made certain assumptions about a player's ability based on race. His career demonstrated that the success of the NBA during the 1980s was built in large part on a racial rivalry between the Celtics and the Lakers, between Bird and Magic. The exploitation of these racial tensions generated great fan interest and ultimately increased attendance, television ratings, and revenues. Bird offered the NBA and its sponsors a marketable image of a white, blue-collar Middle American whose traditional values fit into the dominant conservative political climate. This image resonated with many basketball fans and commentators; it fed their desire to celebrate him because he rose above poverty, worked hard, and supposedly overcame the gifts that God didn't give.

The author thanks Nancy Gabin, Aram Goudsouzian, Eric Hall, Andrew Smith, the anonymous readers, and the editors and staff at the Massachusetts Historical Review.

Notes

1. Raymond Arsenault, "Beantown, 1986," in *The Rock, the Curse, and the Hub: A*

Random History of Boston Sports, ed. Randy Roberts (Cambridge, Mass., 2005), 316–350. For works by historians that deal with integration and basketball, see Randy Roberts, "The Battle of the Beards: Russell and Chamberlain," in *The Rock, the Curse, and the Hub*, 293–315; Aram Goudsouzian, *King of the Court: Bill Russell and the Basketball Revolution* (Berkeley, 2010) and "'My Impact Will Be Everlasting': Wilt Chamberlain in History and Memory," *Journal of Sport History* 32(2005):235–248. For works by journalists that deal with integration, see David Halberstam, *The Breaks of the Game* (New York, 1981) and *Playing for Keeps: Michael Jordan and the World He Made* (New York, 1999); John Taylor, *The Rivalry: Bill Russell, Wilt Chamberlain, and the Golden Age of Basketball* (New York, 2005); Terry Pluto, *Tall Tales: The Glory Years of the NBA, in the Words of the Men Who Played, Coached, and Built Pro Basketball* (New York, 1992); Ron Thomas, *They Cleared the Lane: The NBA's Black Pioneers* (Lincoln, Neb., 2002); and Nelson George, *Elevating the Game: Black Men and Basketball* (New York, 1992). On Bird and Magic, see Todd Boyd's *Young, Black, Rich and Famous: The Rise of the NBA, the Hip Hop Invasion, and the Transformation of American Culture* (New York, 2003). Journalist Michael Connelly argues that the 1981 Celtics championship team helped unify Boston in the aftermath of the city's racial divisions over busing during the 1970s. He claims that team was a "colorless entity." Unfortunately, he lacks evidence to support these statements. This essay shows that the Celtics, and Bird in particular, were not a colorless entity but rather viewed by the public through a racial lens in Boston and throughout the country. See Michael Connelly, *Rebound! Basketball, Busing, Larry Bird, and the Rebirth of Boston* (Minneapolis, 2008).

2. John Edgar Wideman, *Hoop Roots: Basketball, Race, and Love* (New York, 2001), 169.
3. Halberstam, *The Breaks of the Game*, 35.
4. A number of journalists have written about Bird and the Celtics. See Dan Shaughnessy, *Ever Green—The Boston Celtics: A History in the Words of Their Players, Coaches, Fans, and Foes, from 1946 to the Present* (New York, 1990); Peter May, *The Last Banner: The Story of the 1985–1986 Celtics, the NBA's Greatest Team of All Time* (Holbrook, Mass., 1996) and *The Big Three* (New York, 1994); Bob Schron and Kevin Stevens, *The Bird Era: A History of the Boston Celtics, 1978–1988* (Boston, 1988); Harvey Araton and Flip Bondy, *The Selling of the Green: The Financial Rise and Moral Decline of the Boston Celtics* (New York, 1992); Lee Daniel Levine, *Bird: The Making of an American Sports Legend* (New York, 1988); and Jeffrey Lane, *Under the Boards: The Cultural Revolution in Basketball* (Lincoln, Neb., 2007).
5. John Papanek, "Gifts That God Didn't Give," *Sports Illustrated* (hereafter *SI*), Nov. 9, 1981, pp. 82–96.
6. On the historical debate of black athletic superiority, see David K. Wiggins "'Great Speed but Little Stamina': The Historical Debate over Black Athletic Superiority," in his *Glory Bound: Black Athletes in a White America* (Syracuse, 1997), 177–199; Patrick B. Miller, "The Anatomy of Scientific Racism: Racialist Responses to Black Athletic Achievement," in *Sport and the Color Line: Black Athletes and Race Relations in Twentieth-Century America*, ed. Patrick B. Miller and David K. Wiggins

(New York, 2004); John Hoberman, *Darwin's Athletes: How Sport Has Damaged Black America and Preserved the Myth of Race* (Boston, 1997); and Gary A. Sailes, "The Myth of Black Sports Supremacy," *Journal of Black Studies* 21(1991):480–487.

7. J. Anthony Lukas, *Common Ground: A Turbulent Decade in the Lives of Three American Families* (New York, 1985), 323–326; Joseph Driscoll, quoted in "Youths Beat Black Lawyer at City Hall," *Boston Herald American*, Apr. 6, 1976. On the cultural significance of Stanley Forman's photograph of the attack on Ted Landsmark, see Louis P. Masur, *The Soiling of Old Glory: The Story of a Photograph That Shocked America* (New York, 2008).
8. Jeanne F. Theoharis, "'I'd Rather Go to School in the South': How Boston's School Desegregation Complicates the Civil Rights Paradigm," in *Freedom North: Black Freedom Struggles outside the South, 1940–1980*, ed. Jeanne F. Theoharis and Komozi Woodard (New York, 2003), 125–151; Ronald P. Formisano, *Boston against Busing: Race, Class, and Ethnicity in the 1960s and 1970s* (Chapel Hill, 1991), 1–21.
9. "The Ideal Celtic," *Time*, May 6, 1974; John Underwood, "The Green Running Machine," *SI* , Oct. 28, 1974, pp. 47–59 ; Herbert Warren Wind, "The Complete Basketball Player," *New Yorker*, Mar. 28, 1977, pp. 86–104; Curry Kirkpatrick, "It's the End of a Long, Long Run," *SI*, Apr. 10, 1978, p. 29.
10. Shaughnessy, *Ever Green*, 148.
11. "Runaway Redhead," *Time*, Feb. 5, 1973, pp. 45–46; "The Red and the Black," *Newsweek*, May 6, 1974, p. 48 ("lays back on defense "); Peter Carry, "Boston's Perpetual Motion Machine," *SI*, Apr. 2, 1973, p. 35.
12. John Powers, *The Short Season: A Boston Celtics Diary, 1977–78* (New York, 1979), 3–4.
13. Howard Bryant, *Shut Out: A Story of Race and Baseball in Boston* (Boston, 2002); Glenn Stout, "Tryout and Fallout: Race, Jackie Robinson, and the Red Sox," *Massachusetts Historical Review* 6(2004):11–37.
14. Thomas J. Whalen, *Dynasty's End: Bill Russell and the 1968–69 World Champion Boston Celtics* (Boston, 2004), 1–2.
15. B. J. Phillips, "What's Green and Goes 'Swish'?" *Time*, May 25, 1981, p. 79.
16. *Boston Globe* (hereafter *BG*), Feb. 25, 1980; Mark Ribowsky, "I Don't Really Care Who Likes Me," *Black Sports*, January 1978, pp. 17–23; Curtis Rowe, quoted in Kirkpatrick, "It's the End of a Long, Long Run," 29.
17. Jeffrey Cohen, quoted in Diane K. Shah, "The Bird and the B's," *Inside Sports*, October 1979, pp. 62–63.
18. Boyd, *Young, Black, Rich and Famous*, 25.
19. Roy Blount, Jr., "Let's Put Life into the N.B.A.," *New York Times*, Feb. 5, 1979.
20. Quotation in John Papanek, "There's an Ill Wind Blowing for the NBA," *SI*, Feb. 26, 1979, pp. 26–27.
21. "Is NBA Color Conscious?" *Sporting News* (hereafter *SN*), Jan. 12, 1980, p. 25; Bill Fleischman, "Sixers Poll-axed by Fans," *Philadelphia Daily News*, Dec. 3, 1980; "The Fan Flop," *Philadelphia Daily News,* Dec. 3, 1980; Julius Erving, quoted in Ray Didinger, "Lost in City of Winners," *Philadelphia Daily News*, Dec. 5, 1980;

Ted Stepien, quoted in George Vecsey, "White Heroes and Professional Basketball," *New York Times*, June 9, 1980. During the 1979–1980 season, Larry Bird's first season with the Celtics, Boston, New York, Seattle, and Portland were the only teams that averaged full attendance.

22. On the white backlash of the 1970s, see Dennis A. Deslippe, "'Do Whites Have Rights?': White Detroit Policemen and 'Reverse Discrimination' Protests in the 1970s," *Journal of American History* 91(2004):932–960; and Formisano, *Boston against Busing*, 3–4, 28–43, 108–202.
23. Bob Ryan, "Are NBA Games Losing Their Excitement?" *Basketball Digest*, February 1979, p. 62.
24. Chris Cobbs, "NBA and Cocaine: Nothing to Snort At," *Los Angeles Times* (hereafter *LAT*), Aug. 19, 1980; Paul Attner, "Fan Interest off Despite Poll Results," *Washington Post*, Feb. 13, 1979; Attner, "The NBA's Puzzle," *LAT*, Feb. 22, 1979; William Leggett, "Slam Dunked by the Ratings," *SI*, Oct. 16, 1978, p. 67.
25. Levine, *Bird*, 31–92; Larry Bird with Bob Ryan, *Drive: The Story of My Life* (New York, 1989), 7–18, 38–44.
26. Ray Compton, quoted in "Sycamores' Bird: A Program Builder," *Indianapolis News*, Feb. 2, 1977; Fred J. Nation, "1977 Is ISU's Year of the Bird," *Spectator* (Indiana State University, Terre Haute), Jan. 15, 1977.
27. Kent Hannon, "An Idea That's Gotten Way off the Ground," *SI*, Nov. 28, 1977, p. 46; Levine, *Bird*, 105, 122–124; Christopher Lasch, *The Culture of Narcissism: American Life in an Age of Diminishing Expectations* (New York, 1978).
28. Phillip M. Hoose, "Larry Bird—The Guy Down the Road," in *Hoosiers: The Fabulous Basketball Life of Indiana*, 2d ed. (Indianapolis, 1995), 246.
29. "Larry Bird," *Sport*, February 1979, p. 22; Bob Ingram, "Maybe Bird Is Too Good to Be White," *El Paso Herald Post*, ca. 1979, Larry Bird, University Archives Reference Collection, Indiana State University Archives, Terre Haute; Ted Green, "Is It Superman? No, It's a Bird, a Slow One at That," *LAT*, Feb. 15, 1979.
30. Pete Newell, quoted in Bruce Newman, "Flying to the Top," *SI*, Feb. 5, 1979, p. 16; Bill Jauss, "He's the Indiana State Bird!" *Chicago Tribune*, Jan. 20, 1978.
31. "Big Bird," *Newsweek*, Feb. 26, 1979, p. 99; Bill Jauss, "It's Magic vs. the Bird," *Chicago Tribune*, Mar. 26, 1979; "And Finally There Are Four," *SI*, Mar. 26, 1979, pp. 15–17; Steve Rushin, "That Magic Moment," *SI*, Mar. 15, 1999, p. 28; Jack Ebling and John Farina, *Magic Moments: A Century of Spartan Basketball* (Chelsea, Mich., 1998), 6–13, 18–21, 132–137. On the 1979 NCAA championship game between Indiana State and Michigan State, see Seth Davis, *When March Went Mad: The Game That Transformed Basketball* (New York, 2009).
32. Levine, *Bird*, 140–144, 205; Phil Berger, "The Sport Interview: Red Auerbach," *Sport*, June 1979, p. 29; Bob Ryan, "Latest 'New' Celtics Face Rough First Test," *BG*, Oct. 12, 1979.
33. Leigh Montville, "Bird Signs In—but Doesn't Dress for the Occasion," *BG*, June 9, 1979; Will McDonough, "No Savior, Says Bird," *BG*, June 9, 1979.
34. Red Auerbach, quoted in Berger, "The Sport Interview: Red Auerbach," 29 ("in certain areas of the country"); Levine, *Bird*, 204–205; Red Auerbach, quoted in

Shah, "The Bird and the B's," 63 ("My job"); Red Auerbach, quoted in *BG*, Feb. 25, 1980 ("a lot will be forgiven").

35. Martin Kane, "An Assessment of Black Is Best," *SI*, Jan. 18, 1971, p. 74.
36. Bill Rhoden, "Are Black Athletes Naturally Superior?" *Ebony*, Dec. 2, 1974, pp. 136–146; Legrand H. Clegg II, "Why Black Athletes Run Faster," *Sepia*, July 1980, pp. 18–22; "The Black Dominance," *Time*, May 9, 1977, pp. 57–60 (Jerry West, 58); Terry Bledsoe, "Black Dominance of Sports: Strictly from Hunger," *Progressive*, June 1973, pp. 16–19; Dominique Wilkins, quoted in John Cupouya, "The Art and Science of Jumping," *Sport*, June 1986, p. 62.
37. Jim Murray, "Here's a Rube Who's Master of City Game," *LAT*, Feb. 15, 1981.
38. Douglas S. Looney, "Two for the Show," *SI*, Oct. 15, 1979, p. 40 ("Designated Savior"); Boston official quoted in Richard O'Connor, "French Lick, You'll Just Have to Wait," *Sport*, March 1980, p. 20.
39. Frank T. Bannister, Jr., "Search for 'White Hopes' Threatens Black Athletes," *Ebony*, February 1980, pp. 133–134.
40. Jack Craig, "NBA Must Halt Ratings Dip or Bid Bye-Bye to TV Loot," *SN*, Jan. 12, 1980; Jack Craig, "Sportsview," *BG*, Feb. 3, 1980; Levine, *Bird*, 220.
41. Bob Ryan, "The Rare Larry Bird," *Saturday Evening Post*, March 1980, pp. 112–113; Araton and Bondy, *Selling of the Green*, 117; Shaughnessy, *Ever Green*, 184; Bob Logan, *Chicago Tribune*, Jan. 29, 1980; Bob Ryan, quoted in Ray Fitzgerald, "Boston Adores the Big Bird," *SN*, Feb. 9, 1980.
42. Halberstam, *Playing for Keeps*, 163.
43. Herbert Warren Wind, "Bird and Boston," *New Yorker*, Mar. 24, 1986, pp. 54, 61; Thomas Boswell, "Hyperbole in Birdland," *Washington Post*, Jan. 31, 1981; Papanek, "Gifts That God Didn't Give," 82–96.
44. John A. Fortunato, *The Ultimate Assist: The Relationship and Broadcast Strategies of the NBA and Television Networks* (Cresskill, N.J., 2001), 62–63; E. M. Swift, "From Corned Beef to Caviar," *SI*, June 3, 1991, p. 78; Alex Schare, "NBA Fans Stayed Away in Droves," *LAT*, Apr. 14, 1981; Johnette Howard, "Birds of a Feather Rescue Pro Basketball," *Detroit Free Press*, May 25, 1986.
45. Bruce Newman, "The NBA Goes Back to School," *SI*, Nov. 9, 1981, pp. 41–42; John Radosta, "Basketball Comeback," *New York Times*, Dec. 28, 1981; Jack Craig, "NBA May Land Network and Cable Pacts," *SN*, Nov. 7, 1981; "The NBA on TV: A Technical Foul?" *Sport*, November 1982, p. 50; Jack Craig, "A TV Bone in the NBA's Throat," *SN*, Jan. 24, 1983.
46. Paul D. Staudohar, *The Sports Industry and Collective Bargaining*, 2d ed. (Ithaca, 1989), 123–127; "The NBA's Ingenious Move to Cap Player's Salaries," *Business Week*, Oct. 31, 1983, p. 81; Halberstam, *Playing for Keeps*, 120.
47. Halberstam, *Playing for Keeps*, 118; Rick Welts, quoted in Matthew Grimm, "The Big Rebound at the NBA," *Adweek's Marketing Week*, Feb. 19, 1990, p. 19.
48. David Stern, quoted in Glyn Hughes, "Managing Black Guys: Representation, Corporate Culture, and the NBA," *Sociology of Sport Journal* 21(2004):171–172.
49. Fortunato, *The Ultimate Assist*, 68 ("began talking about the players"), 99 ("by focusing on the players").

50. Graham Thompson, *American Culture in the 1980s* (Edinburgh, 2007), 5. David Stern called the NBA's mission "the marketing of heroes" in Armen Keteyian et al., *Money Players: Days and Nights inside the New NBA* (New York, 1997), 61.
51. Mike Littwin, "Larry Bird," *LAT*, Feb. 14, 1982.
52. Robert M. Collins, *Transforming America: Politics and Culture in the Reagan Years* (New York, 2007), 27; William C. Berman, *America's Right Turn: From Nixon to Bush* (Baltimore, 1994), 78; Michael Kazin, *The Populist Persuasion: An American History* (Ithaca, 1998), 247–248; James T. Patterson, *Restless Giant: The United States from Watergate to Bush v. Gore* (New York, 2005), 131.
53. On greed and the 1980s, see Robert M. Collins's chapter "Greed Is Good? The American Business System in the Eighties" in his *Transforming America*, 93–100; and Mike Weber, "Bird TSN's NBA Player of the Year," *SN*, May 6, 1985.
54. Littwin, "Larry Bird"; Dan Shaughnessy, "Behind the Legend: An Up Close and Personal Look at Boston's Biggest Celebrity," *BG*, Apr. 19, 1985; Papanek, "Gifts That God Didn't Give," 86–87; Diane K. Shah with Ron LaBrecque and Martin Kasindorf, "Double Heaping of Magic," *Newsweek*, Mar. 17, 1980, p. 59; Bird and Ryan, *Drive*, 8.
55. Larry Bird, quoted in Ira Berkow, "Bird Does the Best He Can," *New York Times*, Apr. 25, 1982.
56. Larry Bird, quoted in Bob Schron, "Bird's Eye View: How the Best Rates the Rest," *Sport*, May 1986, p. 46.
57. Larry Bird, quoted in Jeff Lenihan, "Larry Bird Shows That the Best Can Get Better," *Basketball Digest*, April 1987, pp. 26, 30.
58. Jack McCallum, "'As Nearly Perfect As You Can Get,'" *SI*, Mar. 3, 1986, pp. 13–14; Tom Callahan, "Masters of Their Own Game," *Time*, Mar. 18, 1985, pp. 52–60; Levine, *Bird*, 308; Larry Bortstein, "Larry Bird: Player of the Year," *Basketball Digest*, June/July 1986, pp. 18–23; Paul Attner, "Man of the Year," *SN*, Jan. 5, 1987.
59. Christopher Colletti, "Bird Chooses to Be Selective," *Advertising Age*, Sept. 1, 1986, p. s-3; Kathleen Low, "Converse Makes Uses of Magic, Bird," *Footwear News*, Nov. 11, 1985, p. 33; Melinda Newman, "Celtics' Larry Bird Flies with Endorsements Worth $2 Mil," *Amusement Business*, Mar. 7, 1985, pp. 5, 8; Joanne Lipman, "Sports Marketers See Evidence of Racism," *Wall Street Journal*, Oct. 18, 1988 ("a white spokesman"). Although black athletes were extremely popular among all fans, in 1988 *Sports Marketing Newsletter* noted that of the twelve highest-paid athlete endorsers only one, Michael Jordan, was black.
60. David Stern, quoted in Mark Danner, "Sports: How Dirty a Game?" *Harper's*, September 1985, p. 49.
61. David Halberstam, "The Stuff Dreams Are Made Of," *SI*, June 29, 1987, p. 39. On the Celtics-Lakers rivalry, see Scott Ostler and Steve Springer, *Winnin' Times: The Magical Journey of the Los Angeles Lakers* (New York, 1986), 256–258; Scott Ostler, "Celtics-Lakers: More Than a Series, It's a Tradition," *LAT*, June 12, 1984; and Roy S. Johnson, "Two Great Rivalries Resume: Bird-Johnson, Celtics-Lakers," *New York Times*, May 28, 1984.

62. Dennis Johnson, quoted in Shaughnessy, *Ever Green*, 147. On "black" and "white" styles of basketball, see George, *Elevating the Game*, xiii–xvii, 62–63; Jeff Greenfield, "The Black and White Truth about Basketball," *Esquire*, October 1975, pp. 170–171, 248; and David DuPree, "It's a Stylish Game They Play," *LAT*, Feb. 24, 1978.
63. Pat Riley, quoted in Ostler and Springer, *Winnin' Times*, 245.
64. Throughout the 1980s, sportswriters referred to the Lakers as "thoroughbreds" and "greyhounds." See Mike Littwin, "On a Team of Greyhounds, Rambis Is the Rhino," *LAT*, May 30, 1982; Bryan Burwell, "Every Team Wants One of These," *Sport*, February 1983, p. 53; and "Lakers Run Like Thoroughbreds," *Chicago Sun Times*, June 3, 1987.
65. Cedric Maxwell, quoted in Ostler and Springer, *Winnin' Times*, 265.
66. Kareem Abdul-Jabbar, quoted in Tom Callahan, "Laker Talent, Celtic Team," *Time*, June 25, 1984, p. 60.
67. Bruce Newman, "Magic Faces the Music," *SI*, May 13, 1985, pp. 86–89.
68. Araton and Bondy, *Selling of the Green*, pp. 117, 122.
69. Jackie MacMullan, "Carlisle Survives—Again; Celtics Cut Clark and Thirdkill," *BG*, Oct. 23, 1985; Tom Callahan, "Impressions in Black and White," *Time*, Dec. 23, 1985, p. 60.
70. Bob Ryan, "Race Is No Issue," *BG*, Oct. 26, 1985; Dan Shaughnessy, "Issue Not Black-and-White: The Makeup of the Team Doesn't Mean the Celtics Are Racist," *BG*, Oct. 27, 1985.
71. Cedric Maxwell, quoted in Araton and Bondy, *Selling of the Green*, 178.
72. Victoria Everett, "Can Boston Be Saved?" *Black Enterprise*, February 1984, p. 99; Kenneth J. Cooper et al., "Boston: The Race Factor," *BG*, May 5, 1983 (also quoted in Everett, p. 101).
73. Callahan, "Laker Talent, Celtic Team," 60; Ryan, "Race Is No Issue."
74. Bob Ryan, quoted in Chuck Klosterman, "If You Root for the Celtics, You Probably Vote Republican," *GQ*, December 2002, p. 227.
75. Art Spander, "Bird's Flight to Top Earned through Effort," *SN*, Mar. 3, 1986.
76. Les Payne, "Has Bird Been Over-hyped?" undated newspaper clipping [ca. 1985], Larry Bird, University Archives Reference Collection, Indiana State University Archives, Terre Haute.
77. Spike Lee with Ralph Wiley, *Best Seat in the House: A Basketball Memoir* (New York, 1997), 127–134, 202; Spike Lee, quoted in Araton and Bondy, *Selling of the Green*, xi, 194–195. On Bird's image in Lee's films, see Kerr Houston, "Athletic Iconography in Spike Lee's Early Feature Films," *African American Review* 38(2004):637–649.
78. Gary Binford, "Bias Has His Foot in Boston's Door," *Newsday*, June 1, 1986; Andrew P. Jones, quoted in Gregory Witcher and Jonathan Kauffman, "Blacks Split on Backing the Celtics," *BG*, June 4, 1987; Jo Jo White, quoted in Araton and Bondy, *Selling of the Green*, 259; William Sampson, "Thomas Told Truth about Larry Bird," *Chicago Sun Times*, June 6, 1987.
79. Steve Bulpett, "Man of Steal!!!" *Boston Herald*, May 27, 1987.
80. Bulpett, "Man of Steal!!!"
81. Dennis Rodman and Isiah Thomas, quoted in Ira Berkow, "The Coloring of Bird,"

New York Times, June 2, 1987.

82. Michael Madden, "Reflections Keep Bouncing around His Head," *BG*, June 2, 1987; Melvin Durslag, "A Campanis Case in Reverse for NBA," *Los Angeles Herald Examiner*, June 3, 1987; Mitch Albom, "Don't Judge Isiah in Black and White Terms," *New Jersey Record*, June 7, 1987; Mark Vancil, "Thomas Claims Bird Remarks 'Misinterpreted,'" *Chicago Sun Times*, June 4, 1987; Mike Shalin, "Isiah's Mouth Masks His Poor Play," *Boston Herald*, June 3, 1987.
83. Isiah Thomas, quoted in Berkow, "The Coloring of Bird."
84. Papanek, "Gifts That God Didn't Give"; Scott Ostler, "It's Un-Natural the Way Some Athletes Can Play," *LAT*, July 2, 1984; Levine, *Bird*, 9, 230–231; Tom Callahan, "A 16th Flag in Sight," *Time*, June 9, 1986, p. 68; Halberstam, "The Stuff Dreams Are Made Of," 43.
85. Larry Bird, quoted in Rick Talley, "Bird Saves Thomas, At Least," *Daily News of Los Angeles*, June 5, 1987; Jim Baker, "NBA Steals the Thunder," *Boston Herald*, June 5, 1987; Frank Dell'Apa, "Happy Days Are Here Again for Isiah," *Boston Herald*, June 5, 1987; Albom, "Don't Judge Isiah in Black and White Terms."
86. Thomas credited Bird with "saving his career." Thomas said, "If he says nothing, I'm crucified. I die. The people who voted me the Walter Kennedy Trophy this year [*a Professional Basketball Writers Association of America award for citizenship and charitable contributions*] would have wanted to lynch me." See Phil Jasner, "There's No Way to Pigeonhole Bird," *Detroit Free Press*, June 10, 1987.
87. "Top Rate," *New York Times*, June 19, 1987; Jack Craig, "Celtics Pushed off CBS Stage but Network Is Rooting for Defending Champions as Lakers' Foes in Finals," *BG*, May 27, 1987; Brian Moran, "NBA Caps Big Year in Marketing Push," *Advertising Age*, June 8, 1987, p. 83; "Basketball Is Bouncing Back under Stern," *Adweek's Marketing Week*, Apr. 24, 1989, p. 6; Grimm, "The Big Rebound at the NBA," 18–19, 22; Tom Kertes, "'80s Basketball," *Sport*, October 1989, p. 64. The 1987 record for finals ratings stood until 1993, when the Chicago Bulls defeated the Phoenix Suns. See Fortunato, *The Ultimate Assist*, 87.
88. Steve Fainaru, "Lobbying for Larry," *BG*, Feb. 5, 1993; Bob Ryan, "Larry! Larry! Larry! Bird Bids Adieu amid Adulation," *BG*, Feb. 5, 1993; Jan Hubbard, "Boston Says Thanks, Larry," *Newsday*, Feb. 5, 1993.
89. Bruce Schoenfeld, "The Loneliness of Being White," *New York Times Magazine*, May 14, 1995, pp. 34–37; S. L. Price, "What Ever Happened to the White Athlete," *SI*, Dec. 8, 1997, pp. 30–34, 36, 38, 40, 42; Tim Crothers, "Worth Waiting For," *SI*, Jan. 19, 1998, pp. 40, 45; Larry Bird, quoted in Rudy Martzke, "Bird: NBA Needs More White Stars," *USA Today*, June 8, 2004; Ross Siler and Steve Luhm, "Dying Breed?" *Jazz Notes: The Utah Jazz and NBA* (blog), *Salt Lake Tribune*, Feb. 3, 2009, http://blogs.sltrib.com/jazz/2009/02/dying-breed.htm; Larry Bird, quoted in Bob Kravitz, "Are Pacers Too White? No, All Bird Cares about Are Finding Guys Who Can Play," *Indianapolis Star*, July 8, 2009, http://www.indy.com/articles/bob-kravitz/thread/are-pacers-too-white-no-all-bird-cares-about-are-finding-guys-who-can-play.

Corporate Funding of Public Schools in Antebellum Massachusetts

The Waltham Exception

JOHN W. COX & DENNIS SHIRLEY

The bell of the upper factory has for about forty-six years, twice a day, from its lofty position, proclaimed itself a friend to education. Twice a day with clamorous voice it reminds the youths of our town that the schoolhouses are open, the accomplished teachers in attendance to learn them that which it is necessary for them to know to become good citizens, and worthy of the republican form of government under which they live. Its brazen throat seems to utter—'Learn!—Learn!—Learn!—Learn!' In winter and summer, storm and sunshine, heat and cold, it proclaims schooltime. Unfortunate is the youth who gives no heed to it.[1]

AFTER THE REVOLUTIONARY WAR, increasing numbers of Americans believed that an educated citizenry was indispensable to the future success of the new republic. Education, these citizens argued, would help ensure social mobility by providing talented, hardworking individuals with the tools necessary to rise above the station of their birth. In addition, education would inculcate republican values in the hearts and minds of pupils. As Thomas Jefferson wrote, "No other sure foundation can be devised for the

---

JOHN W. COX teaches history at Waltham High School in Waltham, Massachusetts. He is a Ph.D. candidate at the Lynch School of Education at Boston College.

DENNIS SHIRLEY is professor of education at the Lynch School of Education at Boston College. He is the author of *The Fourth Way: The Inspiring Future for Educational Change* (Corwin Press, 2009) with Andy Hargreaves and *The Mindful Teacher* (Teachers College Press, 2009) with Elizabeth MacDonald.

preservation of freedom, and happiness" than the "diffusion of knowledge among the people."[2]

In their disparate writings on education, the nation's founders took for granted that they were discussing the subject in a largely agrarian society. At the time of the first federal census in 1790, approximately 95 percent of the American people lived in settlements of less than 2,500 people.[3] Ten years later, Jefferson, a confirmed agrarian, became president. Although his views on manufacturing would evolve over time, Jefferson exalted farmers as the backbone of the American republic, once referring to those who tilled the soil as "the chosen people of God . . . whose breasts he has made his peculiar deposit for substantial and genuine virtue."[4]

Yet even as Jefferson assumed the presidency, the first stirrings of industrialization were already taking place in the United States, challenging the new leader's belief in a self-governing nation of yeoman farmers and artisans. In 1789, Samuel Slater, an Englishman with a thorough knowledge of textile mills and machinery, emigrated to the new nation and soon partnered with Moses Brown to establish a cotton mill in Pawtucket, Rhode Island. During the first decade of the nineteenth century, others followed their example, establishing numerous spinning mills in southern New England that harnessed the abundant power of the streams and rivers found throughout the region. With the Embargo Act of 1807 closing off trade with England, the number of textile mills in the United States proliferated. By 1810, there were 238 textile mills in the nation, including 94 in Massachusetts, Rhode Island, and Connecticut.[5] For the most part, these "Rhode Island system" mills tended to be relatively small, family-owned businesses operating with minimal capitalization.[6]

In Waltham, Massachusetts, a close-knit group of wealthy merchants, often referred to as the "Boston Associates," established an entirely new system of manufacturing along the banks of the Charles River. Here they constructed the first large-scale textile mills to mass produce cotton cloth. The mill town of Waltham became the prototype for future textile centers such as Lowell and Lawrence in Massachusetts and Manchester in New Hampshire. In Waltham, as well as other factory towns, the manufacturers hired "mill girls" to attend power looms and other textile machinery. The girls lived in company-built boardinghouses, closely supervised by company-appointed matrons.[7] These factory towns overturned traditional New England agrarian societies and ushered in a new era of industrial capitalism that eventually served as a magnet for foreign (predominantly Irish) laborers and spawned the first forms of American trade unionism.

Although the manufacturing system established in Waltham became the model for other textile communities, the relationship between Waltham's newly established mills and the town's public schools appears to have been unique and to have reflected the rapidly changing era in which new systems of public schooling and social welfare were still fluid and variable from one town to another. Jefferson and his allies feared the rise of the new manufacturing sector, anticipating that it would demolish the landowning farmers' self-sufficiency, which he prized so greatly. And while the rise of industrialization may have led, in the long run, to a loss of personal independence, in the short run new corporate elites piloted a number of different projects that institutionalized support for social services intended to strengthen society, such as public education.

We contend that events in Waltham, where the new business elite actively promoted and generously funded education not only for factory employees but for local townspeople as well, illustrate this point. In the decades prior to the Civil War, the management of the Waltham factory constructed two public school buildings and covered many of the operational costs for them.[8] Did this corporate funding result in an abrogation of the local self-governance that many founders prized in the new republic? Not in the case of Waltham. Despite corporate funding, control of local education resided in the hands of town voters who approved the school budget and elected a school committee to set curriculum and ensure that state laws were followed. Also, each school district had a "prudential committee" responsible for hiring teachers (with the approval of the school committee) and overseeing day-to-day operations.[9] Waltham thus seems to have enjoyed for several decades a unique combination of corporate funding and democratic control. Finally, Waltham is also unique in the unanimity with which town residents and historians have, for almost two hundred years, praised the Boston Associates for their enlightened treatment of workers and generosity to the town, as exemplified by their interest in promoting education.

What led Waltham to take this distinctive path in the formation of its public school system? Why did the Boston Associates provide most of the financing for public schools in the factory districts while accepting public control of the schools? Why did Waltham citizens so universally praise the Boston Associates' motives in regard to education when residents of other towns in which they established textile mills often criticized *many of the very same men* for their lack of civic leadership and democratic participation? What circumstances led the unique arrangements in Waltham to draw to a close after decades of successful private and public collaboration? Finally, how should contemporary historians endeavor to understand this Waltham exception in light of other antebellum educational developments?

I

At the outset, it is perhaps important to recall the significance of education in the lives of the early New England settlers. Education was not simply a matter of learning the basics of math, reading, and writing; rather, education was considered indispensable for the salvation of souls. Direct access to the word of God, through literacy, was one means of protecting children from wayward interpretations of Christian gospel. Even after intense religious zeal fell into disfavor following the Salem witch trials (1692–1693) and eventually mutated into a less doctrinaire form of Christianity known as Congregationalism, the settlers continued to emphasize the importance of education in the lives of young children.

It should come as no surprise, then, that a controversy involving education led, at least in part, to the birth of the township of Waltham in the eighteenth century. Waltham was a section of Watertown when first settled, referred to in town records after 1713 as the West Precinct. A school had been built in 1649 to serve the children of the eastern section of Watertown, but the children of the western section were underserved for many years. In 1727, a long-running argument began between residents of the East and West Precincts over the location of the town school. In 1733, after "many years of strife," residents of the town finally appropriated sixty pounds to build a second school in the West Precinct and repair the old school in the East Precinct.[10] However, bickering over the location of the schoolhouses, along with other disagreements, divided the townspeople, causing the provincial House of Representatives to incorporate the West Precinct as the town of Waltham in 1738.[11]

The controversy over the location of schools did not end with Waltham's separation from Watertown. Residents of the newly incorporated town were widely dispersed, making it difficult for children to attend the one centrally located schoolhouse. Therefore, to accommodate inhabitants living in outlying areas, Waltham required its schoolmaster to teach in the schoolhouse part of the year and then in private houses known as "moving schools" at other times.[12] "Moving schools" were abandoned in 1756 when Waltham returned to using one central schoolhouse.

By the early nineteenth century, the town had established four small schools to meet the needs of its children.[13] Like other New England townships, Waltham paid its school expenses with local taxes. In this regard, it drew upon the earliest Massachusetts Bay Colony laws, including the famous "Old Deluder Act," requiring towns with more than fifty households to appoint a resident "to teach all such children as shall resort to him to write and reade."[14]

In 1810, the United States Census Bureau recorded 1,014 people residing in Waltham.[15] Most residents were farmers, trying to eke out a living from the rocky soil. Although the terrain proved difficult for farming, the geography was ideally suited for manufacturing. Two waterfalls along the Charles River provided power, and the Boston Post Road, which at the time was the main thoroughfare in Massachusetts, connected Waltham with the port of Boston, only nine miles away. Waltham became even more attractive as a potential manufacturing center when trade with England ground to a halt following Jefferson's Embargo Act of 1807 and throughout the War of 1812. With trade at a standstill, wealthy Boston merchants eagerly sought new opportunities for financial gain.

One such merchant was Francis Cabot Lowell. Born into a prominent Massachusetts family in 1775, Lowell attended Harvard College. In his senior year, Lowell was suspended for lighting a bonfire in Harvard Yard and was rusticated to the village of Bridgewater, where he lived with the Reverend Zedekiah Sanger. Sanger was impressed with his high-spirited student, writing that Lowell had "a happy genius for mathematics. I presume few, if any of his class, equal him in mathematical and astronomical attainments."[16] Despite his youthful transgressions, Lowell graduated from Harvard in 1793 with the highest honors in mathematics.

Upon graduation, Lowell embarked on a highly successful career as a Boston merchant. In 1810, exhausted by his relentless work pace and in poor health, he traveled to England for a two-year vacation.[17] While there, Lowell "had frequent conversations on the subject of the Cotton Manufacture" with his friend and fellow Boston merchant Nathan Appleton, and he decided to visit Manchester "for the purpose of obtaining all possible information on the subject, with a view to the introduction of the improved manufacture in the United States."[18] Lowell paid particularly close attention to the power loom, the most technologically advanced machine of its time.

Just prior to the outbreak of the War of 1812, Lowell returned to the United States. On the return journey, a British frigate seized his ship and took it to Halifax. Twice, British authorities searched Lowell's luggage but found nothing. He had outsmarted his captors. Realizing it was against the law to smuggle plans for textile machinery out of England, he used his aptitude in mathematics to commit the architecture and functioning of the complex machinery to memory. This daring example of industrial espionage was instrumental in launching America's Industrial Revolution.[19]

Safely back in the United States, Lowell was determined to establish his own textile factory. Brushing aside warnings from an uncle who had previously lost money in a textile venture in Beverly, Massachusetts, Lowell purchased the larger of Waltham's two waterpower sites on the Charles River and, with the help of master mechanic Paul Moody, began to replicate the power looms he had observed while touring English textile mills.[20] Lowell approached wealthy relatives and friends to raise $400,000 for his new corporation.[21] In 1814, Francis Lowell's Boston Manufacturing Company "earned distinction as the first fully *integrated* factory in which all processes from raw material to finished product were *powered* under one roof."[22]

The establishment of the Boston Manufacturing Company was a seminal event in American history. The forces of industrialization, immigration, and urbanization would soon sweep away the idyllic image of New England as a region populated by hardworking yeoman farmers of English stock. No longer would New Englanders depend primarily on the land, sea, and forest for their livelihoods. As Alexander Hamilton had prophesied, the future of the young republic now lay in manufacturing, with close reliance on England's technical expertise and markets an essential precondition for success.

Yet just as Hamilton's adversary Thomas Jefferson always feared, the rapid growth of industry eventually affected the social structure of the United States, creating both poor wage earners and enormously wealthy men. Lowell and his partners, however, were not blind to the potential pitfalls of industrialization. To entice young women to work in their mill and to contribute to their own version of a flourishing republic, the Boston Associates offered not only cash wages and company-supervised boardinghouses but also a church, a lyceum, and schools.[23] They designed these institutions not simply to replace the social fabric of the small villages that the mill girls had left but to provide a superior kind of manufacturing community that would improve on its English counterparts and reinforce widely disseminated and popularly held ideas about the proper role of girls and women in the American republic.[24]

II

During his two-year sojourn in England, Lowell saw for himself the dangers posed by rapid industrialization. He commented on the "very dirty" manufacturing towns and "the great corruption of the highest and lowest classes, and the great number of beggars and thieves."[25] According to Nathan Appleton, he and Lowell were deeply concerned with the impact of industrialization "on the character of our population."[26] They wondered whether the "degradation" of workers they observed in England was "the result of the peculiar occupation, or of other and distinct causes. We could not perceive why this peculiar description of labor should vary in its effects upon character from all other occupation [*sic*]."[27]

Historians have speculated on how large an impact Robert Owen's utopian textile mill in New Lanark, Scotland, may have had on the thinking of Lowell and Appleton. Unlike other textile manufacturers in the British Isles, Owen took special care to provide his workers with amenities that addressed their educational, health, and social needs.[28] We do not know whether Francis Lowell ever toured Owen's mill, but as he stayed just thirty miles from New Lanark, he was at the very least aware of it. We do know that Appleton visited New Lanark, where he most likely observed Owen's factory.[29] He later hinted at the positive impression that this factory made on him, claiming that "the introduction of the cotton manufacture has added greatly to the mass of human happiness" and that "the elevation of all labor above the right to a mere subsistence . . . is my ardent wish."[30] Owen's mill and the communitarian values he espoused inspired people on both sides of the Atlantic and seemed to prove that the harsher aspects of industrialization could be mitigated with careful planning and proper consideration for the needs of the new working class.

Returning to America in 1812, Lowell, his brother-in-law Patrick Tracy Jackson, and Appleton began planning their novel textile company in the United States, eager to prove that it was possible to create a factory system in America without the grinding poverty and degradation of labor so prevalent in English industrial centers. In 1813, Lowell and his partners officially incorporated the Boston Manufacturing Company, which began operations the following year. They constructed a massive, four-story, red brick mill building in Waltham, with a ten-foot waterfall on the Charles River providing power. For their labor force, Lowell and his associates tapped into the "well educated and virtuous" young women of New England, who would live in boardinghouses established "at the cost of the Company, under the charge of respectable women with every provision for religious worship."[31] Unlike their European counterparts, the mill girls in Waltham were never meant to be a permanent workforce. Rather, the young women arrived in the town, worked in the mills for a couple of years, and then returned home with a tidy sum of cash. Due to the water-powered machinery, working in the textile mills was not as strenuous as it was tedious. Employees of the Boston Manufacturing Company worked Monday through Saturday, from five in the morning until seven at night, averaging close to 80 hours per week.[32]

For their efforts, the mill girls earned, on average, about two dollars to three dollars and fifty cents a week.[33]

With its substantial cash reserves and technologically advanced machinery, the Boston Manufacturing Company was an immediate success. The Waltham mill manufactured a coarse, white cotton cloth that was suitable for just about any purpose. Those who invested in Lowell's company earned enormous profits. Between 1817 and 1821, dividends averaged 19.25 percent per year and actually reached 27.5 percent in 1822.[34]

In addition to constructing textile mills along the Charles River, Francis Lowell and his partners also established a vibrant community in the area around their factory. The early records of the Boston Manufacturing Company are replete with expenditures not directly connected to the business of manufacturing cloth. The company built houses, dug wells, laid out roads, purchased a fire engine, and planted trees, all at a considerable cost to the new corporation.[35] The firm even took an interest in religious affairs, spending $2,365 for twenty pews in a local church.[36]

The Boston Manufacturing Company made its strongest commitment to the local community through its expenditures for education. In 1817, the corporation began constructing its first school: a one-room schoolhouse on Elm Street, just a stone's throw from the factory itself. The company carefully recorded its building expenses, including $139.99 for carpentry work, $22.93 for plastering, $22 for 4,400 bricks, $6.60 to carry the bricks, and $8.80 to lay 3,200 bricks (undoubtedly the 1,200 unaccounted for bricks were put to good use by the corporation).[37] Even as small an expense as $1.25 for two pairs of fire irons was noted in company books.[38] All told, the Boston Manufacturing Company spent $584.24 to construct its first schoolhouse.[39]

In 1860, the local newspaper, the *Waltham Sentinel,* published the detailed reminiscences of James Moore, who attended the factory school as a young boy during the 1820s.[40] His remarkable (and lengthy) account provides a glimpse of education inside the factory school during the early years of the Industrial Revolution. This "unassuming temple of learning," as Moore describes it, was a modest, one-story building that faced a cornfield and potato patch (now the Waltham Common).[41] The outer vestibule, covered with students' names and accompanying graffiti, was lined with hooks on which students hung their hats and coats. A brown, dilapidated door led to the classroom itself. The teacher's capacious pine desk, large enough for six boys to fit underneath, sat at the front of the classroom. On the corner of the desk the teacher kept a stack of pupil writing books, many of which bore the quaint admonition, "Touch not this book for fear of shame, For don't you

"Cotton Mills in 1820," Proceedings at the Celebration of the Sesqui-Centennial of the Town of Waltham *(Waltham, Mass., 1893), p. 74.*

see the owner's name?"[42] The floor rose steeply from the front to the back of the classroom so that students sitting in the back could touch the ceiling. The boys sat on one side of the room; the girls, on the other. The worst punishment that the teacher could inflict on a misbehaving student, according to Moore, was to move a boy's seat to the girls' section, or vice versa. Those students who suffered this cruel fate "called upon themselves the sharp, tormenting ridicule of the whole school."[43]

Moore describes one of the factory school's unique possessions: a model of the solar system constructed in the machine shop of the Boston Manufacturing Company. The sun was approximately ten inches in diameter; the planet Mercury the size of an apple. The apparatus, which "created as much of a sensation in the minds of the pupils as the original in the mind of father Adam," was suspended from the ceiling above the master's desk.[44] The planets were designed to orbit around the sun. Unfortunately, the model never worked properly, and the celestial bodies that once hung majestically in the factory school were eventually "bowled most recklessly up and down the street in front of the schoolhouse by contending parties of boys."[45]

Moore recalls the school day itself as being exceptionally tedious and dull with little to captivate the interest of the students. The younger pupils would stare morosely at *Mrs. Barbauld's Easy Lessons*, while the older students would use such books as *Murray's Reader*, *Murray's Grammar*, *Scott's Lessons*, *Adams' Arithmetic*, *Cummings' Geography*, and *Pierpont's First Class Book*. During the writing hour, the teacher kept busy using a sharp penknife to reshape the students' spattering quill pens. There was no blackboard and no chalk. The factory school, according to Moore, instilled in students working-class virtues such as hard work, perseverance, and self-reliance. The students had little doubt as to where they would spend their lives: "The boys, when speculating on the future, were not apt to ask each other, 'Whose clerk shall you be?' 'What divinity school shall you enter?' 'Whose office for the law, and whose studio for the arts?' But the questions asked were, 'When do you enter the corporation's machine shop?' 'What winding staircase shall you trot up as a bobbin boy?'"[46]

In comments made at a school reunion, the most illustrious pupil to attend the factory school, Nathaniel P. Banks (who would go on to serve as governor of Massachusetts, Speaker of the U.S. House of Representatives, and a Civil War general), supported Moore's view that the school's primary focus was discipline. Banks commented on the rapid turnover of teachers in the factory school, comparing them to a flock of geese. However, one teacher, Harriet Lane, made a strong impression on him. Banks admitted that he did not "learn much of books, but her character made an impression upon me never to be forgotten. She knew perfectly well how to govern children and how to impress upon their minds good principles."[47]

At the conclusion of the winter term, members of the school committee visited the factory school to measure the academic achievement of the students. Moore's narrative conveys the excitement and anxiety that students, parents, and teachers felt on examination day, the high-stakes test day of the nineteenth century. A contingent of volunteer female students scrubbed the classroom clean the night before and trimmed the bare walls with evergreens. For the schoolmaster, examination day was a trial. Would the school committee judge him a success or a failure? Parents gathered expectantly in the front of the schoolroom, eager to see their sons and daughters demonstrate their knowledge. Students, dressed in their Sunday best, were also apprehensive, closely eyeing the members of the school committee, described by Moore as a "dignified, portly platoon of [the] most substantial citizens of the town."[48] Once the exercises commenced, the school committee quizzed the students in reading, spelling, parsing, history, natural philosophy, arithmetic, abbreviations, oratory, and writing. Upon conclusion of the examinations, the chairman of the school committee rose from his seat, "and in solemn tones expresses his satisfaction."[49]

When the factory school opened, the town of Waltham voted to create a new school district encompassing it.[50] At this time, there were three governing bodies that divided administrative control over Waltham's five school districts: the town meeting, which controlled the school budget; the school committee, which determined the curriculum and ensured that state laws were implemented; and a separate prudential committee for each school district, which oversaw the day-to-day operation of the schools.[51] In 1817, voters at the town meeting selected Patrick Tracy Jackson, a major investor in the Waltham factory and Francis Lowell's brother-in-law, to serve as a one-man prudential committee for the factory school district.[52] Undoubtedly, Jackson's responsibilities as treasurer and clerk of the Boston Manufacturing Company left little time for overseeing the factory school. Therefore, in 1819, the town meeting voters selected three men to replace Jackson on the prudential committee, including Paul Moody, the master mechanic of the Boston Manufacturing Company and the inventor of the American power loom.[53] The selection of prominent men, such as Jackson and Moody, and their willingness to serve on the prudential committee illustrate the importance placed on education by the fledgling Waltham corporation.

One of the more interesting entries in the records of the Boston Manufacturing Company is a single reference to a teacher being paid $9.75 for teaching Sunday school in 1818.[54] Who attended this school? Was the curriculum religious or secular? Why did the company stop funding the Sunday school shortly after its inception? Unfortunately, the company records are silent on these questions. Perhaps the Boston Associates were following the lead of fellow industrialist Samuel Slater, who offered young employees a Sunday school in which they were given basic instruction in reading and writing and taught such useful virtues as obedience, punctuality, and honesty.[55] For whatever reason, the Sunday school did not suit the purposes of the Boston Associates and was discontinued after only nine months of operation.

The Boston Manufacturing Company was not the only factory in Waltham to operate its own school during the 1810s. Another textile mill, the Waltham Cotton and Wool Factory, stood about a mile downstream from Francis Lowell's corporation. An 1815 article probably written by Unitarian minister Samuel Ripley describes the factory as a prosperous company of more than 200 employees, including 150 women and children. The Waltham Cotton and Wool Company was "free from the disorder and immorality" often found in other factories and managed by a superintendent who promoted "virtue, subordination, and industry among his people. The proprietors support a school for the instruction of the children and youth employed in the factory. A school is taught six months by a woman, and in the evenings by masters during the winter."[56] In 1815, the company was "an extensive and profitable establishment"[57] but soon found itself in dire financial straits and was purchased by the Boston Manufacturing Company in 1819. The following year, the Boston Manufacturing Company demolished the factory and erected a new mill, the Waltham Bleachery and Dye Works, to manufacture, bleach, and dye cotton cloth.[58] The Boston Associates demonstrated their commitment to education by continuing to operate the public school previously established by the Waltham Cotton and Wool Company.

In 1837, the Boston Manufacturing Company constructed a new building to replace its original schoolhouse on Elm Street. This modern stone building was the second public schoolhouse the Boston Associates built in Waltham. Reverend Ripley described it in a letter to Horace Mann as "a neat, handsome, modern, stone building two stories high, one room for an infant school, the other for the district school."[59] The stones used to construct it were "ledge stone for a schoolhouse with granite blocks with square ends suitable for the corners of the building."[60] Construction costs totaled $971.95, including $256.75 for stone, $259.61 for lumber, $356.69 for labor, $3 for two dead locks, $6.93 for nails, and $16.50 for glass.[61]

For many years, residents of Waltham considered this company-constructed and supported school building to be the town's best. In their annual report for 1845–1846, the members of the school committee praised the school, reporting that

> There is but one school house in town, which may be said to be *good*, and *suitable* for the purpose for which it was erected, and comfortable for the teacher and the children. This is in No. 5, built by the Man. Corporation. This is the only house in which the children seem to be comfortable in their seats. . . . [I]t is the only house, which on entering, your Committee find [*sic*] perfectly neat and well ventilated in summer, and warmed at a proper temperature in winter.[62]

Construction costs for school buildings were not the only educational expenses the Boston Manufacturing Company incurred. Maintenance bills, fuel costs, textbooks, and other incidental expenses had to be paid. Occasionally, the company records list specific school expenses: $39.62 for school books, $13.04 for cutting and trimming wood in the school yard, $1.50 for whitewashing the schoolhouse, $5.23 for fuel, $23.80 for paint, and $16.80 for glass for the schoolhouse.[63] More often, school expenses were grouped together under listings such as "schooling paid sundry bills,"[64] making it impossible to determine exactly what the expenditures were.

By far, the Boston Manufacturing Company's most significant educational expense was teachers' salaries. In a letter to Horace Mann, Rev. Samuel Ripley claimed that the company "always employed the best teachers & paid the highest wages."[65] In November 1817, the first entry for a teacher's salary appears in company records: "paid S. Burroughs for one month keeping school ending this day (November 15) [$]12."[66] For the next twenty-six years, the Boston Manufacturing Company paid the salaries of those teachers employed in the factory schools. The early records of the company listed both the teacher's name and salary for each month. For example, for almost three years, Burroughs's name appears at the end of each month, earning the same salary of $12. However, as the company expanded and its expenses multiplied, the records of educational expenses became somewhat muddled. The high turnover rate among teachers working in the factory schools further exacerbates the problem. By 1821, a neat line item for each month clearly listing the name and salary of the teacher no longer exists. Instead, several months of salaries are often bundled together in one line item, with no indication given as to who is being paid and for what months. This becomes especially problematic beginning in the 1820s when the Boston Manufacturing Company operated three schools in two school buildings and employed three teachers (two primary school teachers and one sub-primary school teacher). For instance, in February 1839, the Boston Manufacturing Company paid $70.39 to the schoolmaster and $84.50 to the schoolmistress.[67] The next entry for teachers' salaries, $222.25, is recorded on August 31, with no indication as to who received how much money or for what months.[68]

To defray a portion of the cost of operating its public schools, the corporation received a small annual subsidy from the town of Waltham. When its first school was opened for the 1817–1818 academic year, the Boston Manufacturing Company "rec'd of S. Clark (Town Treasurer) as our proportion of the money raised in Waltham for the support of schools [$]86.13."[69] For the next twenty-one years, the town partially reimbursed the company for expenses incurred in educating the children in the factory schools. The corporation received its last reimbursement, $225, from the town treasurer on February 28, 1839.[70] All told, from April 1818 through February 1838, the town paid the Boston Manufacturing Company $3,735.66 to help with educational expenses.[71]

The Waltham School Committee's annual reports provide further information on the state of education in the company-sponsored schools.[72] During the 1842–1843 school year, 168 children attended the three factory schools, with one teacher employed in each school. The school committee reported that the sub-primary school was in a "flourishing state," the primary school at the Boston Manufacturing Company "may now be said to rank as one of the first in discipline and attainment," and the bleachery school, "although it has ever been one of our poorest schools . . . is much better than formerly."[73]

Throughout the following year, however, controversy enveloped the factory schools. After noting that schools in Waltham "have all suffered from unusual interruptions," the school committee proceeded to criticize the students attending the stone schoolhouse for their "exceedingly disorderly and insolent" behavior and labeled the bleachery school "unusually backward, and its advancement is slow."[74] Town voters rejected the school committee report and appointed a committee to investigate the matter. The report of the investigating committee defended Waltham's schools, criticizing the school committee report for its "exhibitions of personal feeling, of private animosity, of party prejudice, of malicious denunciation."[75]

After the troubles of 1843–1844, the factory schools were once again in the good graces of the school committee and were often commended in its annual reports. In 1851–1852, the school committee credited the teacher employed in the stone schoolhouse with advancing the quality of instruction, stating that "the School has steadily improved and is now in very much better order than it was one year ago. The present Teacher is deserving a large share of the praise."[76] By 1855–1856, the committee reported that the sub-primary school at the Boston Manufacturing Company was prospering "under the care of [a] faithful and enthusiastic teacher," the primary school "has been improving, and we hope may attain a more satisfactory position," and the bleachery school "still maintains its high position."[77]

It is worth noting that although the annual reports generally present a positive account of education in Waltham, they are by no means Pollyanna-ish in their tone and message. When necessary, members of the school committee were not averse to criticizing students, teachers, and even parents for their perceived shortcomings. For example, in 1843, the school committee reported that the school in District One "ranks lowest in point of discipline and attainment."[78] In 1857, the committee criticized the teacher in the District Three schoolhouse for "lack[ing] the power . . . of bringing the unruly and disobedient into subjection," while noting that in the District Five factory school there was "a strong spirit of restlessness among the children, amounting almost to contempt of authority" that was encouraged by some parents who were "undermining the teacher's influence."[79]

In addition to its generosity towards public schools, the company also assumed a paternalistic attitude in regard to the social lives of its employees. When British writer Harriet Martineau visited Waltham during her tour of the United States, she noticed a sign in the Waltham factory "warning that no young lady who attended dancing-school that winter should be employed: and that the corporation had given directions to the overseer to dismiss any one who should be found to dance at the school."[80] When Martineau inquired about this company policy, the overseer told her that during the previous winter, some of the young employees had danced until two or three o'clock in the morning and were then "unfit for their work the next day."[81] To soften the blow of the ban on attending dancing school, the overseer promised the workers that once a new room in a local hotel was constructed, dances would be held every two weeks. However, the dances would break up early, and most likely to the chagrin of the young workers, the overseer and his wife would also be present. "We will all dance together," the overseer promised.[82]

In addition to constructing and funding public schools, the Boston Associates also supported the Rumford Institute for Mutual Instruction, a lyceum founded in 1826 by employees of the company. One of the first lyceums in the United States, the Rumford Institute sponsored lectures, discussions, debates, and concerts, and it soon became a "potent influence in social, moral, and educational affairs" in Waltham.[83] In 1827, the Boston Manufacturing Company constructed the Rumford Building at the corner of Main and Elm Streets. The manager of the company, Ebenezer Hobbs, forwarded a letter to the institute, offering to "let the Hall to said Society for all lectures and other meetings of said Rumford Institute for the sum of sixty dollars per year . . . which sum is to be expended by the Society in the purchase of books for said Society."[84] By January 1828, the institute had 108 members, 90 of whom were women. In 1850, the company dedicated a substantial sum (over $2,500) to remodeling the Rumford Building and enlarging and renovating Rumford Hall, where lectures were held.[85] Also in 1850, as a further act of generosity, the Boston Manufacturing Company contributed all of the rent derived from the hall above $50 to the Rumford Institute.[86] Four years later, the Boston Manufacturing Company sold the Rumford Building to the town.

Throughout its storied history, the Rumford Institute sponsored lectures by such prominent nineteenth-century luminaries as Daniel Webster, Charles Sumner, Edward Everett, Ralph Waldo Emerson, Horace Mann, George Bancroft, Louis Agassiz, Oliver Wendell Holmes, and Samuel Clemens.[87] For one of his early lectures in Waltham, Emerson was paid five dollars plus feed for his horse. By 1860, however, Emerson was able to command a fee of twenty dollars for his lecture "Manners" at the Rumford Institute. Apparently, the institute considered Massachusetts statesman Edward Everett a much better draw, for he was paid one hundred dollars to lecture in 1858 and again in 1860. Lectures were held on Saturday evenings at 7:00 P.M., and one year's membership to the institute could be purchased for fifty cents.[88]

At their annual meeting on October 2, 1821, the directors of the Boston Manufacturing Company appropriated five hundred dollars "towards establishing a Library, for the use of persons in their employ."[89] They entrusted the Reverend Sewell Harding with the task of selecting appropriate volumes for the new "manufactory library at Waltham."[90] In an era when public libraries in small towns were virtually unheard of and few people could afford their own books, the use of the corporation's library was a major benefit for the company's operatives. The availability of a library also made factory life more attractive to those considering working in the Waltham mills. Although most likely committing to print an apocryphal account, a biographer of Nathaniel P. Banks relates the story of young "Nat's" mother telling him that he had to leave school to go to work for the Boston Manufacturing Company. To make the prospect of working in the factory more palatable, Nat's mother told him, "There is one thing to be thought of for your advantage. You love to read, and the manufacturing company have [*sic*] a good library for the operatives. You can take out books, and read evenings."[91] Harriet Martineau also commented on the availability of books for the corporation's employees, praising the company for providing "a lyceum, which they have furnished with a good library, and where they have lectures every winter,—the best that money can procure. The girls have, in many instances, private libraries of some merit and value."[92]

In 1830, the Boston Manufacturing Company transferred its Manufacturers' Library to the Rumford Institute with the stipulation that all members of the institute would have the right to borrow the books. Over the years, the number of volumes in the library steadily increased: approximately 1,000 in 1837, 1,400 in 1848, and 3,700 in 1865.[93] The *Waltham Sentinel* considered the library "one of the best things that our town can boast."[94] Local historian Nathan Warren speculated that "many a boy who has risen to eminence in his profession can doubtless date back to the Saturday night when the well filled shelves of the Rumford Library were opened to him for his first inspection for knowledge beyond that of the school and the home."[95] This library would become the precursor to the Waltham Public Library. In 1854, the Boston Manufacturing Company sold the Rumford Building to the town and, "as a final instance of its fostering care, relinquished the control over the library" to the Rumford Institute.[96] In 1865, the Rumford Institute offered its library to the town under the proviso that Waltham establish a free public library. The town accepted the offer.

III

Following their success in Waltham, the Boston Associates proceeded to establish water-powered textile mills throughout Massachusetts, Maine, and New Hampshire. When establishing a new corporation, the associates employed the same organizational system used at the Boston Manufacturing Company. This system, often referred to as the Waltham system, featured large corporations, heavy capitalization, and an emphasis on mass production, with young female employees living in company boardinghouses. In contrast, textile mills using what was called the Rhode Island system were often family owned, minimally capitalized, and engaged in the manufacture of diverse products, with children and families employed and living in tenement houses.[97] Working conditions in textile mills and the quality of life in mill towns varied greatly, depending on such factors as the individual mill owner and the strength of the national economy. However, it is safe to say that no mill owners were as committed to public education over an extended period of time as were the Boston Associates in Waltham. Nonetheless, particularly in the decades before Irish immigration, there are instances of corporations, established by the Boston Associates as well as others, providing a more limited kind of support to public education in mill towns founded after the establishment of the Boston Manufacturing Company in 1814.

One such example is the town of Lowell. Seeking more waterpower than could be supplied by the Charles River, the Boston Associates purchased land in 1821 along the Merrimack River in East Chelmsford and constructed the Merrimack Manufacturing Company along with its attendant boarding houses, church, and school. The factory village grew rapidly and in 1826 was incorporated as the town of Lowell, in memory of Francis Lowell.[98] In this newly founded town, the Waltham system reached its apogee.

Although many of the investors in the Lowell mills were also involved in the Boston Manufacturing Company (with the notable exception of Francis Lowell, who died in 1817), their commitment to education was neither as strong nor as sustained as it was in Waltham. The first textile corporation in Lowell, the Merrimack Manufacturing Company, constructed a school on its own property in 1824 and defrayed all expenses for one year.[99] Two other mills founded by the Boston Associates, the Hamilton Manufacturing Company and the Appleton Manufacturing Company, also built a schoolhouse in 1829 and paid the teacher's salary.[100] Despite these examples of corporate

Lowell in 1825 *by John I. Coggeshall, 1906, based on a painting by Benjamin Mather.* The Record of a City *(New York, 1912), frontispiece.*

largesse, historian Hannah Josephson claims that the Lowell textile companies were "not interested in education *per se*, and were determined to transfer the expense and the responsibility to the town as soon as possible."[101] In fact, one year after the Merrimack Manufacturing Company opened its school, corporation agent Kirk Boott wrote to the town selectmen, asking "if the Inhabitants will appropriate the money paid by the Merrimack Manufacturing Company and persons in their employ for supporting the School established by them."[102] By 1832, Lowell needed new school buildings due to the town's rapid growth. The Lowell textile corporations strongly opposed a town meeting proposal to appropriate $20,000 to build two new schoolhouses. Speaking at the town meeting, Boott claimed that Lowell was already in debt, could not afford such a large expenditure of money, and had already done enough for its public schools. In spite of corporate opposition, the town meeting voted in favor of the school appropriation. At a subsequent meeting held to reconsider the original vote, company lawyers argued that the mill owners would be responsible for paying the lion's share of this "extravagant appropriation" because of the taxes levied on their large property holdings. The attorneys also claimed that the corporations would derive no benefit from the new schools and that it was unfair to "vote away the property of non-resident proprietors."[103] Town residents rejected the companies' arguments and once again voted in favor of the expenditure.

Following the "great school fight of 1832," the Lowell corporations did not accept their defeat with equanimity.[104] According to nineteenth-century Lowell historian Charles Cowley, when the town meeting voted in favor of the appropriation, company executives had nothing to do with "the schools thus erected contrary to their sovereign will and pleasure."[105] The Lowell corporations even went so far as to seek revenge against the Reverend Theodore Edson, rector of St. Anne's Church and member of the Lowell School Committee, who was a leading advocate of the school proposal. When the lease on St. Anne's Church expired, the Lowell Locks and Canals Company demanded payment for the church property, even though it had originally been billed as a corporate gift to the community. In a singularly vindictive move by the Merrimack Manufacturing Company, Edson was evicted from the church rectory until 1866, when his congregation finally raised the money required by the corporation to purchase the parsonage.[106]

It is also interesting to note the reactions of townspeople in Lowell toward the massive mills lining the Merrimack. A local newspaper, the *Mercury*, recognized that the town was completely dependent on the cotton mills and that to oppose their interests would be "suicidal."[107] Dr. Elisha Bartlett, the first mayor of Lowell, noted that the community was controlled by outside interests whose "proprietors do not reside among us" and whose "profits are not expended among us."[108] Prominent Massachusetts Democrat, Civil War general, and Lowell native Benjamin Butler struck a similar theme when he stated, "our city has been a hive of industry, and, as a rule, the honey has been gathered by others."[109] Cowley sarcastically wrote that it took a visit from Henry Clay for "their High Mightinesses [*corporation executives*] . . . to let the light of their countenances shine for a moment on the benighted little Hottentots that filled the North and South Grammar Schools."[110] Clearly, some Lowell residents harbored strong feelings of resentment towards the giant corporations in their midst, in part due to the manufacturers' meager support of local schools.

In other textile mill towns, the degree of company support for education varied greatly. In Rhode Island, young children employed in Samuel Slater's mills attended Sabbath schools on Sundays after working the previous six days.[111] In Lawrence, Massachusetts, the Essex Company donated land for the construction of eleven schools, and also rented a one-room schoolhouse to the town.[112] In 1855, a Fall River mill agent set a new standard for corporate arrogance when he stated, "I regard my work people just as I regard my machinery. So long as they can do my work for what I choose to pay them,

I keep them, getting out of them all I can. What they do or how they fare outside my walls, I don't know, nor do I consider it my business to know."[113] How strange such words seem when juxtaposed with the philanthropic sentiments expressed by the founders of the Waltham mills four decades earlier!

IV

When considering why the Boston Associates instituted such enlightened labor practices in Waltham, historians often emphasize Francis Lowell and Nathan Appleton's desire to avoid the sordid working conditions they had observed while touring English factory towns. We must also take into account the personal values and sense of public responsibility that animated the actions of the Boston Associates in Waltham. These were men who believed in philanthropy and public service. The charities they supported included schools, colleges, hospitals, and cultural institutions such as the Massachusetts Historical Society, the Boston Public Library, and the Boston Athenæum.[114] Therefore, it is not surprising that the directors of the Boston Manufacturing Company felt some degree of corporate responsibility for the factory village they created in Waltham. It is certainly true that the Rumford Institute bore little resemblance to the Boston Athenaeum, and the Manufacturers' Library was a far cry from the Boston Public Library. It is also true, however, that these institutions provided local citizens with cultural and social opportunities virtually unheard of in a small village such as Waltham. Had the Boston Associates been less civic minded, these opportunities would most certainly not have existed.

If the Boston Associates were, to some degree, motivated by a sense of public responsibility, then why were their educational policies in Lowell so different from their policies in Waltham? Part of the reason may be the untimely death in 1817 of Francis Lowell, a man "beloved and respected by all who knew him" and "especially devoted to arrangements for the moral character of the operatives."[115] While Francis Lowell was the "informing soul"[116] of the Waltham Company, the associates chose Kirk Boott to oversee their factory community in Lowell. Boott, a principal stockholder and agent and treasurer of the Merrimack Manufacturing Company, was an iron-willed, authoritarian man with a commanding manner. A contemporary described him as the "master spirit of the place."[117] According to his personal physician, Dr. John Green, Boott's role in the development of Lowell was all-encompassing: "engineer, architect, draughtsman, conveyancer or clerk, moderator of town meetings, representative in the legislature."[118] When Boott arrived in East Chelmsford, the town already had a district school system in place, which he augmented with two factory schools. In Boott's mind, this was more than adequate to meet the needs of his workers, most of whom were young, transient, single women who were expected to work in the mills for a temporary period and then return to their families or get married.[119] For these reasons, Boott showed little interest in promoting education, believing that the town "had done for public schools what was required; they [*the schools*] were proper and sufficient for the poor, but would never serve for the better sort of the community."[120]

Lowell's rapid growth may have also discouraged any sustained corporate support for public education. During the 1820s, the textile industry overwhelmed Lowell, sweeping away the past and creating an entirely new industrial community dominated by out-of-town businessmen. This was not the case in Waltham. As newcomers in a stable, long-established community, the Boston Associates may have felt an obligation to offer financial support to the town, many of whose residents lived on the same small farms that had been cultivated by their great-grandparents. In Lowell, however, the mill owners were in a dominant position, with little incentive to curry favor with longtime residents. As Mayor Elisha Bartlett glumly pointed out, "The graves of our fathers are not here. The haunts of our childhood are not here. . . . The large and gradually accumulated fortunes of nearly all our older towns are not to be found here. The great mass of wealth which is centered here, and which has made our city what it is, is owned abroad."[121]

V

When the Boston Manufacturing Company first opened, Francis Lowell and his associates recognized the novelty of the factory system that they had established in Waltham. Nathan Appleton wrote that the "contrast in the character of our manufacturing population compared with that of Europe, has been the admiration of the most intelligent strangers who have visited us."[122] And visit they did. Henry Clay, John C. Calhoun, Harriet Martineau, even Pres. James Monroe, all came to Waltham to see firsthand the industrial experiment taking place at the Boston Manufacturing Company. Henry Clay's reaction to what he observed in Waltham was typical: "The greatest order, neatness, and apparent comfort, reigned throughout the whole establishment."[123] Hearing such positive comments from their distinguished visitors affirmed for the Boston Associates their success in avoiding the pitfalls of English manufacturing towns and satisfied their desire to make "every possible provision for the moral character and respectability of the operatives."[124]

A number of historians and family biographers have also commended the Boston Associates for their civic leadership in Waltham. Francis Lowell in particular is often singled out for praise, perhaps partially due to his untimely death in 1817 at the age of forty-two. According to Patrick Tracy Jackson's brother James Jackson, Lowell's "moral character was most pure and most elevated. He was singularly devoid of selfishness. He had the greatest love of doing good."[125] Family biographer Ferris Greenslet claims that Lowell was "concerned about the character and health of his people from humanitarian as well as business motives."[126] Fellow associate Nathan Appleton wrote that Lowell was "beloved and respected by all who knew him."[127] Author Freeman Hunt described Lowell as an "extraordinary man" and the Boston Associates as "those wise and patriotic men, the founders of Waltham."[128]

It is also interesting to compare the opinions Waltham townspeople had of the mills with those of Lowell residents. The resentment often expressed by citizens of Lowell towards the wealthy businessmen who dominated their town is conspicuously absent among the citizens of Waltham. Without exception, local historians and other nineteenth-century residents of the town lavishly praised the Boston Associates for their efforts in support of education in Waltham. The *Waltham Sentinel* commended the Boston Manufacturing Company for providing "all the families in their employ an opportunity to send their children to free schools; beside, others, not employed by them, were not denied the privilege of attending school."[129] Local historian Charles Nelson claimed that company support for education could be attributed to the unwillingness of the associates to have their factory "surrounded by the vice and poverty that prevailed in the manufacturing towns in England."[130] In a publication of the Waltham Board of Trade, Ephraim Barry credited the Boston Manufacturing Company with establishing "schools for the benefit of the working people," which proved that "at least one corporation has a soul and that it was greatly interested in the welfare and improvement of those within its care."[131]

Even Horace Mann, secretary of the Massachusetts Board of Education, commended the Boston Manufacturing Company for its commitment to education. After criticizing factories that ignored the state's newly enacted child labor law, Mann singled out the Waltham company for having "gratuitously erected three schoolhouses,—the last one in 1837, a neat, handsome, modern, stone building, two stories in height,—and maintained schools therein at a charge, in the whole, upon corporate funds, of a *principal* sum of more than seven thousand dollars." He applauded the company for its "generous acts" and regretted that "the identity of the individual members, who have performed these praiseworthy deeds, should be lost in the generality of the corporate name."[132]

When descendants of Lowell, Jackson, and Appleton attended a celebration for the 150th anniversary of Waltham's founding in 1888, they were prominently seated on the platform with other dignitaries. The main speaker at the event, local historian Frederick Stone, praised the Boston Associates as

> great not only in their mechanical and executive abilities, but in a far nobler sense. . . . They determined that the moral and intellectual worth of the operatives should be a factor in the new enterprise. . . . For upwards of half a century, as regularly as the bell summoned the operatives to their work, its daily peal at a quarter to nine in the morning summoned the children to the school. . . . What a noble policy! . . . All honor to the men who thus ennobled labor and added to its dignity all the sweet influences of culture and refinement![133]

In a lecture before the Citizens' Club of Waltham, Nathan Warren acclaimed the "generous and commendable zeal of the Boston Manufacturing Company for the welfare of the community and the moral and educational improvement of its operatives. Too much credit cannot be given to those liberal and broad minded men who were at the head of this pioneer manufactory."[134]

Visiting dignitaries, nineteenth-century historians, family biographers, and local residents have been effusive in their praise of the Boston Associates' commitment to education in Waltham. But is this praise justified? Can their motives be interpreted differently? Could it be that the associates supported education in Waltham out of self-interest? When opened in 1814, the Boston Manufacturing Company was located in the extreme southern part of Waltham, an undeveloped section far removed from most townspeople. Did the associates build and subsidize schools solely to make their mill more attractive to potential workers? Did they calculate that by offering such amenities as schools, a lyceum, and a library, that their workers would be more productive?

Amidst the glowing testimonials bestowed on the Boston Associates by prominent visitors to their Waltham factory, there was another voice—that of labor reformer Seth Luther of Providence. Based on his visit to Waltham, Luther considered the idyllic image of the Boston Manufacturing Company a carefully crafted illusion, little more than a Potemkin village behind which lurked every imaginable evil. Sarcastically acknowledging the tributes of other visitors, Luther referred to the Waltham factory as "that pink of perfection" where there was a "great cry about the schools, and lyceums, and books."[135] Noting that the factory operatives worked "like slaves for 13 or 14 hours every day," Luther compared the Waltham workers to "Tantalus, up to the chin in water," with little spare time to indulge in the luxury of reading.[136] Even young Nathaniel Banks, when told by his mother that he could borrow books from the Manufacturers' Library and read after work, responded, "There will be scarcely any time for me to read after coming out of the factory at seven o'clock; and besides, after working from five o'clock in the morning until seven at night, I think I shall like the bed better than books."[137] Although highly unlikely that twelve-year-old Nathaniel ever uttered these exact words to his mother, the passage does illustrate the inherent contradiction between the factory's long hours and its efforts to provide educational benefits to employees.

Some historians further removed from the Waltham area commend the humanitarian policies of the Boston Associates, while at the same time acknowledging their desire to earn profits; other historians believe their benevolent actions were motivated by self-interest. One chronicler of the textile industry, Hannah Josephson, refers to the Boston Associates as "hard-headed businessmen" who "did not assume that because they were contributing to the economic development of the town they had license to defile it."[138] Based on an examination of company records, economic historian Howard Gitelman argues that the Boston Associates were motivated by a need to recruit and retain workers. He believes that

> company contributions to the Waltham community were prompted in the first instance by self-interest. . . . It is in this light that the Company's contributions to education and to intellectual and religious pursuits are to be understood. . . . The precise types of diversion provided—above and beyond relatively high monetized earnings—were those most likely to satisfy the work force: a school for workers who wanted their children to be literate; [*and*] a lyceum for mill girls and mechanics.[139]

Marxist economists Samuel Bowles and Herbert Gintis also question the benevolence of the Boston Associates, citing as evidence a statement from a Lowell mill agent who wrote that the company that "has the best educated and most moral help will give the greatest production at the least cost per pound."[140] In his comprehensive study of the Boston Associates, Robert F. Dalzell argues that recent scholarship has been "more skeptical" of the claim that their actions "represented a new and singularly benign kind of industrial order. . . . The tough-minded businessmen who built the great mills at places like Waltham, and later Lowell and Lawrence, meant to make a profit and did."[141] The French historian François Weil questions the validity of Nathan Appleton's account of the founding of Waltham and Lowell, calling it a "self-serving text written by Appleton forty-five years after the opening of the

Waltham textile factory, in defense of Francis Cabot Lowell and his friends, including Appleton himself."[142]

VI

How does one account for these contradictory views of the motives of the Boston Associates? Unquestionably, in their effusive praise of the owners of the Boston Manufacturing Company, some Waltham historians and local observers have engaged in typical hometown boosterism. Proud of their city's role in the Industrial Revolution, these historians romanticize its past and believe the Boston Associates were driven by only the purest of motives. What is striking, however, is the complete absence of any criticism of the Boston Associates by local townspeople *over the past two hundred years*! Without exception, all local historical accounts of the Boston Associates and their Waltham corporation are positive in nature.

In 1819, the Boston Associates provided approximately 33 percent of the school funding in Waltham (the company funded two of the six Waltham schools). However, this high percentage diminished over the years, a result owing less to corporate stinginess than to rapid population growth brought on by industrialization. As Waltham's population grew, the town continued to construct new schools. When the Boston Manufacturing Company built its first school in 1817, there were only five school districts in Waltham. By 1860, there were ten school districts containing seventeen schools housed in eleven buildings.[143]

The increasingly competitive market, accompanied by a decline in profits, probably best explains the decrease in the mill owners' school support. In its first ten years of operation, the Boston Manufacturing Company achieved a level of success unmatched by any subsequent New England textile corporation. In 1816, demand for Waltham-produced cloth was so great that it sold for thirty cents a yard.[144] During the early 1820s, the company earned a profit of nine cents on every yard of cloth sold.[145] With strong demand for its cloth resulting in soaring profits for investors, the Boston Manufacturing Company was financially able to make community improvements, building churches, constructing roads, planting trees, purchasing a fire engine, promoting a library, and supporting education.

The fabulous success of their Waltham factory encouraged the Boston Associates and others to construct additional textile mills throughout the northeast. By 1860, virtually all of New England's rivers provided power to spin and weave cotton cloth. As expected, the large-scale expansion of the textile industry resulted in dwindling revenue and smaller profits for investors. In

"The Old Factory School House," Proceedings at the Celebration of the Sesqui-Centennial of the Town of Waltham *(Waltham, Mass., 1893), p. 55.*

Waltham, cloth that sold for thirty cents a yard in 1816 brought only six and a half cents by 1845; the nine cents per yard profit of the 1820s dwindled to a half cent a yard by the 1850s.[146] In order to remain profitable in the highly competitive textile industry of the 1850s, mill owners had to watch every penny and look for the smallest of savings. Under such conditions, allocating scarce company funds to support education was a luxury they could no longer afford.

Corporate support for public school funding in Waltham ended in 1864, when the Boston Manufacturing Company's agent requested that the town vacate the old stone schoolhouse adjacent to the mill, thus bringing to a close the corporation's almost fifty-year history of involvement in education. The members of the Waltham School Committee recognized this as the end of an era and commended the company for its past generosity and support of public education. Their statement serves as a fitting epitaph for the educational efforts of the Boston Associates:

> We cannot close these remarks without adverting for a moment to the liberality practised by the Agents of the Boston Manufacturing Company, in furnishing accommodations so ample for educating the children

> of this section of our town. A house has been furnished by the Company for more than forty years, and for many of the first years of this time they furnished teachers, fuel, and all the paraphernalia of the schoolroom; —a munificence rarely met with in manufacturing villages. We hope our Town at no distant day will tender a vote of thanks to the *Boston Manufacturing Company* for thus extending their liberal hand for so noble a purpose.[147]

In 1893, Waltham recognized Francis Cabot Lowell's commitment to education by naming a school in his honor.

The Boston Manufacturing Company's arrival in 1814 and its rapid growth throughout the antebellum period hit Waltham with the force of a tidal wave. Between 1810 and 1860, the town's population increased more than six-fold from 1,014 to 6,397. Much of the population growth was due to the arrival of Irish immigrants who found employment in the Boston Manufacturing Company, the Waltham Bleachery and Dye Works, and the Newton Chymical Company (which manufactured chemicals for use in the bleaching process). Virtually all of the Irish immigrants lived in row houses and tenements clustered around the town's factories. By 1860, the southern part of Waltham along the Charles River had become a bustling center of manufacturing and commerce, while the northern section of town remained decidedly agrarian.[148]

By the mid nineteenth century, the Boston Manufacturing Company was no longer on the cutting edge of the Industrial Revolution. Even in Waltham, the firm was eclipsed by a new corporate presence—the American Waltham Watch Company, the first company in the world to mass produce machine-made watches. During the latter half of the nineteenth century, the watch company was enormously profitable. The factory also became the largest employer in Waltham, providing residents with high-paying jobs and numerous fringe benefits. Despite its profitability, the American Waltham Watch Company made no attempt to follow the example set by the Boston Associates in supporting public education. Such a move would have seemed strangely at odds with the increasing bureaucracy and administrative centralization found in Waltham's post–Civil War school system.

The Boston Manufacturing Company began the transformation of Waltham from a quiet farming community to a busy industrial center. Today, tract housing and hundreds of businesses, large and small, have replaced the farms. These businesses have made Waltham a prosperous city, creating jobs for residents and filling the treasury with tax revenue. However, with a handful of exceptions, today's business owners have no interest in the local school system. Unlike the Boston Associates, they offer no financial support, and they certainly do not construct public school buildings. In this regard, it is worth noting a suggestion made by the Waltham School Committee in its annual report of 1864–1865. After commending the Boston Manufacturing Company for its generous support of education, the school committee remarked, "We trust that this example may induce others to go and do likewise."[149]

Unfortunately, the hoped-for corporate contributions never materialized. The shift from a certain public spiritedness to a more insular model falls in line with the larger social shift from the preoccupation with republican virtue and social propriety in the early republic and antebellum era to the more competitive and self-interested strategies pursued by industrialists during the Gilded Age. Historian Michael Katz argues that the sweeping societal changes brought about by the Industrial Revolution led to this shift.[150] He claims that educational reformers in Massachusetts were cognizant of the "frightening kinds of social and moral decay"[151] found in industrial communities and believed that schools could mitigate the problems created by industrialization by emphasizing the virtues of regular attendance, punctuality, obedience, and discipline. According to Katz, education became a means of social control,[152] a way to "supply individuals with a set of inner restraints"[153] that would make them efficient factory workers in the future. Educational reformers "were not answering the demands of a clamorous working class: they were imposing the demands; they were telling the majority, your children shall be educated, and as we see fit."[154]

In their study of educational change in nineteenth-century Massachusetts, Carl Kaestle and Maris Vinovskis also acknowledge the connection between industrialization and the emphasis on discipline and personal responsibility in schools during the 1840s and 1850s.[155] They believe, however, there is little evidence that the intention of policy makers was for schools to teach students the work habits needed in the manufacturing sector of the economy. Rather, the authors argue that the emphasis on discipline can be attributed to a number of factors, including "urban disorder, Jacksonian malaise, immigration, pedagogical theories, and the bureaucratic nature of schools."[156] Also, manufacturers certainly did not need schools to inculcate good work habits in future employees since "the best place to learn productive behavior for a factory is in a factory."[157]

In line with the findings of Katz and Kaestle and Vinovskis, the annual reports of the Waltham School Committee from the 1840s and 1850s often emphasized the importance of regular attendance, punctuality, discipline, and good behavior. There is little to suggest that school committee members stressed these traits in order to prepare Waltham's children for employment in the town's mills. An analysis of the composition of the school committee may help explain the rationale behind its thinking.[158] From 1842 to 1860, virtually all members of the school committee (fewer than forty men) were drawn from the town's professional class, including twelve Protestant ministers. No Irish Catholics and only one industrial worker were elected. The substantial citizens who served on the school committee were heavily vested in the community and more concerned with the rapid pace of change in Waltham than they were with emphasizing social control in the schools to benefit manufacturing. In language reminiscent of Thomas Jefferson, the Reverend Samuel Ripley, a member of the school committee in 1845, even stated that Waltham's rural schools "should take higher rank" because they are "composed of children of the same rank and class in society—they are remote from the noise and temptation of the village."[159]

Also, Waltham's prior history may help explain the lack of conflict between the town and its most prominent antebellum industry. Waltham was never a classic mill town, created by a corporation to serve corporate interests. Rather, the history of Waltham reaches back to the earliest days of the Massachusetts Bay Colony when Gov. John Winthrop led an expedition near the banks of the Charles River in 1631. By the time the associates built the Boston Manufacturing Company in 1814, Waltham's history stretched back almost two hundred years, first as a precinct of Watertown and later as an independent town. It is also important to keep in mind that the sluggish current of the Charles River restricted the growth of the Boston Manufacturing Company. Due to these factors, Waltham's economy was never completely dependent on the textile industry, thereby lessening the potential for conflict between the townspeople and industrialists.

In retrospect, we might view the Boston Associates as practical businessmen intent on making a profit who nonetheless had a large and generous civic vision of what they wanted to achieve in Waltham. They were under no obligation to support public schools, a library, and a lyceum but chose to do so to make their factory more attractive to potential employees and to fulfill their vision of a harmonious and well-educated American society. They opened the public schools they funded to all, including those who did not work in the mills but simply resided in the community. Governance of the schools was democratic from beginning to end, thereby conveying the Boston Associates' conviction that corporate philanthropy was entirely compatible with self-governance of the citizenry in regard to education.

Notes

1. *Waltham Sentinel*, Oct. 19, 1860, p. 2.
2. Thomas Jefferson to George Wythe, Aug. 13, 1786, in *The Papers of Thomas Jefferson*, ed. Julian Bond et al. (Princeton, 1950), 10:243–245.
3. U.S. Census Bureau, Selected Historical Decennial Census Population and Housing Counts, Urban and Rural Populations, www.census.gov/population/www/censusdata/files/table-4.pdf.
4. Thomas Jefferson, *Notes on the State of Virginia*, ed. William Peden (Chapel Hill, 1955), 165.
5. Steve Dunwell, *The Run of the Mill* (Boston, 1978), 21.
6. Dunwell, *Run of the Mill*, 52.
7. Nathan Appleton, *Introduction of the Power Loom and Origin of Lowell* (Lowell, Mass., 1858), 16.
8. Kenneth F. Mailloux, "The Boston Manufacturing Company of Waltham, Massachusetts, 1813–1848: The First Modern Factory in America" (Ph.D. diss., Boston University, 1957), 157. Mailloux claims that the Boston Manufacturing Company constructed three schoolhouses, including one "near their lower mills, for $350" (157). However, we were unable to locate this expenditure in company records.
9. George M. Woytanowitz, "Educating 'Watch City': The Transformation of Education in Waltham, Massachusetts, 1840–1880," *Journal of the Midwest History of Education Society* 6(1978):17–38.
10. Edmund L. Sanderson, *Waltham as a Precinct of Watertown and as a Town, 1630–1884* (Waltham, Mass., 1936), 48.
11. Sanderson, *Waltham as a Precinct*, 48–52.
12. Sanderson, *Waltham as a Precinct*, 53.
13. Alexander Starbuck, "Waltham: Schools and Newspapers," in *History of Middlesex County, Massachusetts*, ed. D. Hamilton Hurd (Philadelphia, 1890), 3:735.
14. "Massachusetts School Law of 1647," in *Education in the United States: A Documentary History*, vol. 1, ed. Sol Cohen (New York, 1974).
15. *Vital Records of Waltham, Massachusetts, to the Year 1850* (Boston, 1904), 3.
16. Zedekiah Sanger to John Lowell, Apr. 29, 1793, Francis Cabot Lowell (1775–1817) Papers, Massachusetts Historical Society.
17. Ferris Greenslet, *The Lowells and Their Seven Worlds* (Boston, 1946), 124–126.
18. Appleton, *Introduction of the Power Loom*, 7.
19. Greenslet, *Lowells and Their Seven Worlds*, 130.
20. Dunwell, *Run of the Mill*, 30–31.
21. In his willingness to jettison a lucrative career as a merchant and take his chances in manufacturing, Lowell fits the entrepreneurial profile Joyce Appleby discusses in her essay "New Cultural Heroes in the Early National Period," in *The Culture of the Market*, ed. Thomas L. Haskell and Richard F. Teichgraeber III (Cambridge, Eng., 1993). Appleby examines the personal qualities of several entrepreneurs who helped develop a free-market economy in the United States during the first three decades of the nineteenth century. She argues that the growth of a national mar-

ket depended on the willingness of many young men to leave the security of their hometowns and seek new opportunities in business. Although not the subjects of her essay, Samuel Slater and Francis Lowell certainly fit Appleby's description of the type of men who helped develop America's free-market economy. As Appleby notes, the "willingness to be uprooted, to embark on an uncharted course of action, to take risks with one's resources. . . . This receptivity to change cannot be taken for granted" (166).

22. Dunwell, *Run of the Mill*, 32.
23. Mailloux, "The Boston Manufacturing Company of Waltham," 154–165.
24. Appleton, *Introduction of the Power Loom*, 15–16.
25. Lowell to William Cabot, May 29, 1811, and Jan. 2, 1812, quoted in Robert F. Dalzell, *Enterprising Elite: The Boston Associates and the World They Made* (Cambridge, Mass., 1987), 12.
26. Appleton, *Introduction of the Power Loom*, 15.
27. Appleton, *Introduction of the Power Loom*, 15.
28. Robert Owen, *A New View of Society and Other Writings*, ed. Gregory Claeys (New York, 1991).
29. Frances W. Gregory, *Nathan Appleton: Merchant and Entrepreneur* (Charlottesville, 1975), 145.
30. Nathan Appleton to Middlesex Mechanics Association, Dec. 30, 1846, quoted in Joseph W. Lipchitz, "The Golden Age," in *Cotton Was King: A History of Lowell, Massachusetts*, ed. Arthur L. Eno, Jr. (Somersworth, N.H., 1976), 101.
31. Appleton, *Introduction of the Power Loom*, 15–16.
32. Mailloux, "The Boston Manufacturing Company of Waltham," 197.
33. Edith Abbott, *Women in Industry: A Study in American Economic History* (New York, 1910), 273–279.
34. Dalzell, *Enterprising Elite*, 38.
35. Administrative Records, vol. 2; journal vols. 10, 13, Boston Manufacturing Company, Baker Library Historical Collections, Harvard Business School (hereafter Boston Manufacturing Company records)
36. Journal 14:523, Boston Manufacturing Company records.
37. Journal 13:127, 136, 149, Boston Manufacturing Company records.
38. Journal 13:147, Boston Manufacturing Company records.
39. Journal 10:164, Boston Manufacturing Company records.
40. James G. Moore, "High School Re-union," *Waltham Sentinel*, Aug. 17, 1860, pp. 1–2.
41. Moore, "High School Re-union," 1.
42. Moore, "High School Re-union," 1.
43. Moore, "High School Re-union," 1.
44. Moore, "High School Re-union," 1.
45. Moore, "High School Re-union," 1.
46. Moore, "High School Re-union," 2.
47. Moore, "High School Re-union," 2.
48. Moore, "High School Re-union," 1.

49. Moore, "High School Re-union," 1.
50. City of Waltham Records 1812–1828, Apr. 7, 1817, p. 104, no. 1679–5, reel 5 (microfilm), Waltham Public Library.
51. Woytanowitz, "Educating 'Watch City,'" 19.
52. City of Waltham Records 1812–1828, Apr. 7, 1817, p. 104, no. 1679–5, reel 5 (microfilm), Waltham Public Library.
53. City of Waltham Records 1812–1828, Apr. 5, 1819, p. 145, no. 1679–5, reel 5 (microfilm), Waltham Public Library.
54. Journal 13:218, Boston Manufacturing Company records.
55. Barbara M. Tucker, *Samuel Slater and the Origins of the American Textile Industry, 1790–1860* (Ithaca, N.Y., 1984), 166–171.
56. M. U. [Samuel Ripley], "A Topographical and Historical Description of Waltham, in the County of Middlesex, Jan. 1, 1815," *Collections of the Massachusetts Historical Society*, 2d ser., vol. 3 (Boston, 1815), 264. Charles A. Nelson attributes authorship of this piece to Ripley in *Waltham Past and Present* (Cambridge, Mass., 1882), 128.
57. M. U. [Samuel Ripley], "A Topographical and Historical Description of Waltham," 263.
58. Edmund L. Sanderson, *Waltham Industries: A Collection of Sketches of Early Firms and Founders* (Waltham, Mass., 1957), 125–126.
59. Samuel Ripley to Horace Mann, Dec. 6, 1839, in Mailloux, "The Boston Manufacturing Company of Waltham," 158.
60. Administrative Records 6:92, Boston Manufacturing Company records.
61. Journals 11:181, 183, 187, 16:1476, 1486, Boston Manufacturing Company records.
62. *Annual Report of the General School Committee of Waltham, for the year 1845 & 1846* (Waltham, Mass., 1846), 9.
63. Journals 11:152, 158, 14:670, 15:961, Boston Manufacturing Company records.
64. Journal 14:521, Boston Manufacturing Company records.
65. Mailloux, "The Boston Manufacturing Company of Waltham," 157.
66. Journal 13:154, Boston Manufacturing Company records.
67. Journal, 16:1541–1542, Boston Manufacturing Company records.
68. Journal 16:1556, Boston Manufacturing Company records. In 1856–1857, primary school teachers in Waltham were paid $200 per year. The school committee recognized the difficulty in hiring teachers with "the highest intellectual activity and power, joined with the highest moral and religious character, with an enthusiastic love of children and of teaching, and with the greatest aptness to teach and to govern a school, all for $200 a year." *Report of the School Committee of the Town of Waltham for the Year 1856–7* (Waltham, Mass., 1857), 4.
69. Journal 13:185, Boston Manufacturing Company records.
70. Journal 16:1540, Boston Manufacturing Company records.
71. Journal vols. 11, 13, 14, 15, 16, Boston Manufacturing Company records.
72. The Waltham School Committee did not begin to issue annual printed reports until 1842.

73. *The Annual Report of the General School Committee of the Town of Waltham, for the Year Ending April 3d, 1843* (Waltham, Mass., n.d.), 5.
74. *The Annual Report of the General School Committee, of the Town of Waltham, for the Year 1843 and 4* (Waltham, Mass., n.d.), 4.
75. *The Annual Report of the General School Committee, of the Town of Waltham, for the Year 1843 and 4* (Waltham, Mass., n.d.), 4.
76. *Report of the School Committee of the Town of Waltham: For the Years 1851 and 1852* (Waltham, Mass., 1852), 5.
77. *Report of the School Committee of Waltham, Mass., Prepared to Be Read in Town Meeting, March 3d, 1856, Adopted by Vote of Gen. School Committee, Feb. 27th, 1856* (Waltham, Mass., 1856), 4.
78. *The Annual Report of the General School Committee of the Town of Waltham, for the Year Ending April 3d, 1843* (Waltham, Mass., n.d.), 4.
79. *Report of the School Committee of the Town of Waltham, for the Year 1856–7* (Waltham, Mass., 1857), 5.
80. Harriet Martineau, *Society in America* (1837; New York, 1966), 2:356.
81. Martineau, *Society in America*, 2:356.
82. Martineau, *Society in America*, 2:357.
83. Nathan Warren, "Historical Sketch of Rumford Institute," in *Papers Read Before the Citizens Club of Waltham, 1892–1893* (Waltham, Mass., 1893), 4.
84. "Rumford Institute," *Waltham Sentinel*, Feb. 12, 1857, p. 1.
85. Journal 12:482–509, Boston Manufacturing Company records.
86. Warren, "Historical Sketch of the Rumford Institute," 15.
87. Walter F. Starbuck, *Picturesque Features of the History of Waltham* (Waltham, Mass., 1917), 30–35.
88. Starbuck, *Picturesque Features of the History of Waltham*, 30–35.
89. Administrative Records 1:63, Boston Manufacturing Company records.
90. Journal 14:534, Boston Manufacturing Company records.
91. William Makepeace Thayer, *The Bobbin Boy; or, How Nat Got His Learning* (Boston, 1860), 97–98.
92. Martineau, *Society in America*, 2:248.
93. Warren, "Historical Sketch of the Rumford Institute," 15.
94. "Rumford Institute," *Waltham Sentinel*, Feb. 15, 1856, p. 2.
95. Warren, "Historical Sketch of the Rumford Institute," 15.
96. Warren, "Historical Sketch of the Rumford Institute," 15.
97. Dunwell, *Run of the Mill*, 52.
98. Before the arrival of the Boston Associates, East Chelmsford is often portrayed as a sleepy village populated by a handful of farmers. However, in 1821, the community contained at least fifty homes, several small mills, a power canal, two inns, two schools, and three stores. See Robert Weible, "'More of a place than represented to have been': East Chelmsford, 1775–1821," in his *The Continuing Revolution: A History of Lowell, Massachusetts* (Lowell, Mass., 1991), 1–37.
99. Hannah Josephson, *The Golden Threads: New England's Mill Girls and Magnates* (New York, 1949), 45.

100. Joshua Merrill, "School District No. 5 and My Connection with It," *Contributions of the Old Residents' Historical Association, Lowell, Mass.* 1(1874):25–41.
101. Josephson, *Golden Threads*, 45.
102. Josephson, *Golden Threads*, 46.
103. For a detailed account of the school building controversy, see Alfred Gilman, "History of the Lowell Grammar Schools," *Contributions of the Old Residents' Historical Association, Lowell, Mass.* 4(1888):91–96. For a more analytical account, see Brian C. Mitchell, "Good Citizens at the Least Cost per Pound: The History of the Development of Public Education in Antebellum Lowell, 1825–1855," in *Continuing Revolution*, 118–123.
104. Josephson, *Golden Threads*, 55.
105. Charles Cowley, *Illustrated History of Lowell* (Boston, 1868), p. 105.
106. Josephson, *Golden Threads*, 53.
107. Josephson, *Golden Threads*, 53.
108. Elisha Bartlett, mayoral inauguration speech, 1837, quoted in Josephson, *Golden Threads*, 53.
109. Benjamin Butler, "Address at the Semi-Centennial of Lowell," 1876, quoted in Fidelia O. Brown, "Decline and Fall: The End of the Dream," in *Cotton Was King*, 145.
110. Charles Cowley, *Illustrated History of Lowell* (Boston, 1868), p. 105.
111. Tucker, *Samuel Slater*, 166–171.
112. Donald B. Cole, *Immigrant City: Lawrence, Massachusetts, 1845–1921* (Chapel Hill, 1963), 23.
113. General Oliver quoting a mill agent in Norman Ware's *The Industrial Worker 1840–1860: The Reaction of American Industrial Society to the Advance of the Industrial Revolution* (Gloucester, Mass., 1959), 77.
114. Dalzell, *Enterprising Elite*, 113–163.
115. Appleton, *Introduction of the Power Loom*, 15.
116. Appleton, *Introduction of the Power Loom*, 15.
117. Henry A. Miles, *Lowell as It Was and as It Is* (ca. 1845; New York, 1972), 228.
118. Dr. John O. Green, "Kirk Boott. A Letter from Dr. John O. Green to Rev. Theodore Edson, D.D.," *Contributions of the Old Residents' Historical Association, Lowell, Mass.* 4(1888):110–112.
119. Mitchell, "Good Citizens at the Least Cost per Pound," 115–135.
120. Gilman, "History of the Lowell Grammar Schools," 93.
121. Elisha Bartlett, mayoral inauguration speech, 1837, quoted in Lipchitz, "Golden Age," 100.
122. Appleton, *Introduction of the Power Loom*, 16.
123. Henry Clay, "Speech on the Tariff, 1820," in *The Papers of Henry Clay*, ed. James F. Hopkins and Mary M. W. Hargreaves (Lexington, Ky., 1961), 2:830.
124. Appleton, *Introduction of the Power Loom*, p. v.
125. James J. Putnam, *A Memoir of Dr. James Jackson* (Boston, 1905), 139.
126. Greenslet, *Lowells and Their Seven Worlds*, 159.
127. Appleton, *Introduction of the Power Loom*, 15.

128. Freeman Hunt, *Lives of American Merchants* (New York, 1858), 1:560, 564.
129. "Waltham As It Was," *Waltham Sentinel*, May 30, 1862, p. 1.
130. Nelson, *Waltham Past and Present*, 131.
131. Ephraim L. Barry, *The City of Waltham, Massachusetts: Its Advantages to Manufacturers and as a Place of Residence* (Waltham, Mass., 1887), 70–71.
132. *Third Annual Report of the Board of Education Together with the Third Annual Report of the Secretary of the Board of Education* (Boston, 1840), 42.
133. Charles F. Stone, Nathan Warren, and Thomas H. Armstrong, *Proceedings at the Celebration of the Sesqui-centennial of the Town of Waltham, 1888* (Waltham, Mass., 1893), 55–57.
134. Warren, "Historical Sketch of Rumford Institute," 12.
135. Seth Luther, *An Address to the Workingmen of New England* (Boston, 1832), 18, 28.
136. Luther, *Address to the Workingmen of New England*, 18, 29.
137. Thayer, *Bobbin Boy*, 98.
138. Josephson, *Golden Threads*, 33.
139. Howard M. Gitelman, *Workingmen of Waltham: Mobility in American Urban Industrial Development, 1850–1890* (Baltimore, 1974), 4–5.
140. Samuel Bowles and Herbert Gintis, *Schooling in Capitalist America: Educational Reform and the Contradictions of Economic Life* (New York, 1976), 162.
141. Dalzell, *Enterprising Elite*, 4.
142. François Weil, "Capitalism and Industrialization in New England, 1814–1845," *Journal of American History* 84(1998):1337.
143. *Annual Report of the General School Committee of the Town of Waltham, for the Year 1859–60* (Waltham, Mass., 1860), 3.
144. Josephson, *Golden Threads*, 207.
145. Dalzell, *Enterprising Elite*, 162.
146. Josephson, *Golden Threads*, 207; Dalzell, *Enterprising Elite*, 162.
147. *Annual Report of the School Committee of Waltham, for the Year 1864–5* (Waltham, Mass., 1865), 11–12.
148. RG 029 population schedules for the 1810 and 1860 United States censuses, National Archives and Records Administration.
149. *Annual Report of the School Committee of Waltham, for the Year 1864–5* (Waltham, Mass., 1865),12.
150. Michael B. Katz, *The Irony of Early School Reform: Educational Innovation in Mid-Nineteenth Century Massachusetts* (Cambridge, Mass., 1968).
151. Katz, *Irony of Early School Reform*, 40.
152. See John R. Bodo, *The Protestant Clergy and Public Issues, 1812–1848* (Princeton, 1954); Charles C. Cole, Jr., *The Social Ideas of the Northern Evangelists, 1820–1860* (New York, 1954); and Clifford S. Griffin, *Their Brothers' Keepers: Moral Stewardship in the United States, 1800–1865* (New Brunswick, N.J., 1960) on the desire for "social control" by religious humanitarians.
153. Katz, *Irony of Early School Reform*, 124.
154. Katz, *Irony of Early School Reform*, 47.
155. Carl F. Kaestle and Maris A. Vinovskis, *Education and Social Change in Nineteenth-*

Century Massachusetts (Cambridge, Eng., 1980).

156. Kaestle and Vinovskis, *Education and Social Change*, 44.

157. Kaestle and Vinovskis, *Education and Social Change*, 44.

158. Woytanowitz, "Educating 'Watch City,'" 23–24.

159. *Annual Report of the General School Committee of Waltham, 1845* (Waltham, Mass., 1845), 28.

Leadership Class

College-Educated New Englanders in the Civil War

KANISORN WONGSRICHANALAI

At the turn of the twentieth century, Civil War hero Joshua Lawrence Chamberlain penned the introductions to a two-volume series entitled *Universities and Their Sons*. The former Maine governor and retired college president began broadly by discussing "the desire of the human mind for knowledge." He noted that the quest to preserve humanity's "acquisitions and communicate them to other minds" had "been manifest in the institutions which have marked the flourishing epochs of nations and the ascendancy of great minds." The enlightened founders of the American republic had seen the "blessings of education" as "prominent objects," and in return, America's earliest institutions of higher learning had reciprocated by training her political leaders, preachers, ministers, teachers, writers, journalists, and orators "for the country's need and honor!"[1]

Chamberlain praised "the old classical colleges" for being "well fitted to bring out the best powers of mind and character,—to build up a well-rounded manhood." He insisted that more important than an emphasis on "the multitude of studies" was the development of a good and strong "character." "No student," Chamberlain explained, "could fairly enter into fields then laid open without wakening in the mind a sense of its possibilities, and enforcing a certain discipline which gives the self-reliance and strength characteristic of manliness." Students who had "profited as they were able by years of per-

Kanisorn Wongsrichanalai is an assistant professor of history at Angelo State University. He graduated from Bowdoin College and received his Ph.D. from the University of Virginia. This article is based on a manuscript he currently has in progress on the development of nationalism and the birth of a young leadership class in the Civil War–era North.

sonal, intimate relations with the chosen masters of knowledge," in turn, became "not only producers of their specialty, but new centres of influence radiating their light and strength into the great common life to which they belong."[2]

Chamberlain's vision of the noble sons of a college, fortified by a strong sense of character, going out to help the world was, more or less, a reflection of his own career. In 1862, as federal armies struggled to save the Union, Chamberlain, a graduate of Bowdoin College, heard his nation's call and left his professor's chair to fight in the American Civil War. During the conflict, he served with distinction on battlefields from Fredericksburg to Five Forks. The two actions for which he is most remembered were his defense of the Union army's left flank at the Battle of Gettysburg in July 1863 and his participation in the surrender ceremonies of the Army of Northern Virginia at Appomattox Courthouse in April 1865.

Joshua Lawrence Chamberlain is only one example of the thousands of college-educated Northerners who fought to preserve the Union. Their common academic experiences bound them together as a self-identified group, and their choice to attend college connected them as members of the North's middle and upper classes. In a period when higher education was a privilege enjoyed by the most fortunate and determined, choosing to attend college also meant starting a professional career path. People with undergraduate degrees entered society as lawyers, doctors, ministers, and merchants. These privileged young men, as a class set apart, attempted to live by a code of behavior that distinguished them from the rest of society. Colleges taught their students how to behave like gentlemen, emphasizing the importance of attaining and maintaining "character." Educated young men believed that they had a responsibility to maintain a gentlemanly bearing and do what was "right" even if that course was unpopular. The Civil War provided a chance for these elite young men to serve their nation on the battlefield. Here they could act as leaders of society by serving as officers in the armed forces. While not everyone took advantage of this new opportunity—some believed that their professional responsibilities on the home front were more important—those who volunteered saw their actions as a display of gentlemanly behavior consistent with their role as society's leaders. Class position was an important factor in determining how one served. The college men who joined the armed forces demanded that their status as professionals be honored with military commissions. They would volunteer to fight, but as a historian of the famed Twentieth Massachusetts Regiment—also known as the "Harvard Regiment"—observed, they wanted to serve as "gentlemen."[3]

Antebellum colleges helped many young Americans become "gentlemen" by elevating their social and economic status. Although schools such as Harvard and Yale were, for the most part, the bastions of the wealthy and privileged, other institutions catered to ambitious young men of diverse economic backgrounds. Because they appealed to students who often had to work to pay their tuition, New England's smaller, rural colleges attracted a somewhat different set of youths. These students were poorer on the whole than those at Harvard and Yale, and they needed both to hold jobs and to secure scholarships to support their ambitions of entering the world of the middle-class professional. One indicator of a growing population of less privileged students was the age of the undergraduate body itself. In wealthy families, fathers paid their sons' tuition. Students with less affluent parents often needed to delay matriculation until they had earned their own way. According to one researcher's tally, approximately one in four of all New England college men was over twenty-five years old at graduation between 1830 and 1860. At the newly created rural colleges, about one-third was twenty-five or older. In order to accommodate and attract farm boys and working-class students, rural colleges designed their calendars around work and harvest seasons. Young men also took winter breaks as an opportunity to teach in local schools (an activity that may have helped their leadership skills). Colleges attempted to accommodate such students by offering cheap tuition and inexpensive lodging. These new schools may have also been the only hope for parents who wished their children to do well "in a declining rural social order that could not absorb them."[4]

Most men, no matter what their social and economic position at matriculation, completed college with a chance to become middle-class professionals. By and large, college graduates entered five occupations: law, education, medicine, business, and the clergy. Of the 1,538 men who graduated from Amherst, Bowdoin, and Waterville (later Colby) Colleges between 1850 and 1865, approximately one-quarter practiced law, one-quarter became clergymen, one-sixth entered the educational field, one-tenth were involved with medicine, and one-tenth pursued business opportunities.[5] In all these instances, a very small fraction of college graduates returned home to become farmers or planters. Eventually, some of these professional men also became society's leaders in local, state, and national politics.

Many college graduates maintained a close connection to their alma maters even after they had left the halls of learning. Schools instilled an institutional pride in their students. In June 1850, Harvard student Wilder Dwight wrote his brother William about a rousing address that the college's president,

Lt. Col. Wilder Dwight, carte de visite by John Adams Whipple ca. 1860–1862. Photo 70.19 from the Wolcott Family Civil War Carte de Visite Album, collections of the MHS.

Jared Sparks, had given after prayers one morning. Sparks urged Harvard men to attend a ceremony marking the anniversary of the Battle of Bunker Hill. He "made us an enthusiastic patriotic speech and told us that he hoped to see such numbers as should make him proud of the name of *Harvard*." Sparks's final comment had come "well near resulting in a desecration of the college chapel . . . by a universal class." Dwight continued, "You must know that if there is any one word or appeal to which a Cambridge student is susceptible that word is 'Harvard.'" The very name brought "more enthusiasm than any other word," Dwight explained to his brother. It was a "watchword in a fight," "the open sesame to the pocket," and "a perfect talisman for all emergencies." College events often attracted alumni back for visits. During the war, graduates who were fighting pined for the comfort of their old campuses. Yale graduate William Wheeler, while campaigning in Virginia, lamented that he was not at home, "especially just this week, Commencement, when the old college friends are coming together at New Haven, and another class goes away from its classic home."[6]

Young men had other reasons to continue to identify with their alma maters. College graduates, as historian Peter D. Hall has noted, maintained communications in "extensive networks of graduates." This benefited school fundraising and the graduates themselves because they "came to regard collegiate affiliation and society membership as important indicators of character and trustworthiness and, hence, credit-worthiness and employability."[7]

A college degree signified that a young man had been taught proper and moral behavior, an important reason for society to place its trust in him. Colleges fostered in the young men both national and class identities. Themes of history, Americanism, and proper behavior were common in undergraduate writings. Most important, the college environment allowed young men to learn the leadership skills that they would need in the professional world. Americans in the mid nineteenth century expected a leader to embody the best qualities of gentlemanly behavior. Historians who study Southern honor have elaborated on these traits, but few have considered their Northern counterparts. "Character," a term the men in this study used frequently, is defined here as an *idealized internal standard of behavior that emphasizes independent thought and selfless action*. Although character was an ingrained trait, it was one that might be expressed publicly, especially during times of crisis. Invariably, gentlemen judged each other by how they behaved. Northern character was different from Southern honor because it emphasized the importance of an individual's internal beliefs. Where Southern honor was primarily concerned with public reputation, Northern men of character were supposed to behave in the manner that they thought just no matter what society's opinion dictated.[8]

After college, young graduates entered the professional world believing that they were society's natural leaders. They served in higher stations than their neighbors and bore themselves in a manner befitting their status. They tried to live as men of character. When the war broke out, however, the issue of their class and proper station became a topic of conflict. Did their responsibilities lie on the home front or in the military? Although many of them never volunteered, college men were well represented in the Union's armed forces.

Most college-educated New Englanders could have arranged for substitutes and avoided service in the war. Instead, many served and fought. The North mobilized about one half of its military-age population over the course of the war. College-educated men volunteered in higher rates than the Northern average during the first two years of the conflict when 24 percent of military-age men served, suggesting that they were more motivated than fellow Northerners. Historian Phillip Shaw Paludan observed that just under a quarter of Harvard's and Yale's graduates from the classes of 1841 to 1861 served in the war. Of the 4,254 living Yale graduates at the end of the conflict, 22 percent (932) had served: 18 percent in the Union armed forces (775) and 4 percent (157) in Confederate service. College men from classes graduating close to the outbreak or during the war enlisted at an even higher rate. For example, 35 percent of Yale graduates from the classes of 1851 through 1863 saw service (in both the Union and Confederate armies). The numbers are even more impressive for the most recent graduates. Fifty-six percent of Harvard's class of 1861 served, as did 42 percent of the same class from Yale.[9]

Small colleges also contributed to the Union armed forces. Of the 1,770 Bowdoin alumni who were alive at the start of the war, 443 (25 percent) fought, while 669 of Dartmouth's 2,800 living alumni (24 percent) served. Three hundred seventeen Williams men from thirty-eight classes (1825–1870) worked in various capacities for the Union cause (249 graduates, 68 non-graduates). According to Amherst College historian William S. Tyler, the class of 1862 was "the banner class, thirty of its members having gone to the war," or just under half of the total number of graduates. Twenty-three men from each of the classes of 1861 and 1863 as well as 15 from the class of 1864 and 21 from the class of 1865 served. Ultimately, 247 Amherst men contributed to the war effort in some manner. As at the larger colleges, those classes graduating closest to the outbreak of the war participated in even larger proportion. For example, 51 percent of the Bowdoin College class of 1860 and 57 percent of the class of 1862 served in the war.[10]

The butcher's bill for these institutions was gruesome. Ninety-two Harvard graduates, forty-four men from Bowdoin, and twenty-two from Williams perished in the war.[11] The large number of war dead reflects the leadership roles of these young men. College men served as field officers, leading companies and regiments into combat. Their exposed positions made them easy targets. Even those volunteers who served in non-combat roles, such as chaplains, surgeons, or paymasters, were exposed to the hazards of camp and campaign life.

What Makes a Good Leader?

In his 1895 history of Amherst College, William S. Tyler declared, "No class of men, as statistics prove, contributed to the grand army which saved the Union and the nation in the Civil War in so large proportion to their numbers, and none contributed an element of such military value and moral power, as the graduates and under-graduates of our colleges." Amherst had not fallen "behind her sisters in devotion to the cause," and it was "her pride and glory to have borne her full share in the burdens and sacrifices, if not in the honors and rewards, of this patriotic and heroic service." Boasting of his college's record, Tyler claimed, "Never before nor since, not even in the Prussian army in the late Franco-German war, were there so many bayonets that could read, and so many shoulder-straps that could think, as there were in the army of the United States that put down the great rebellion."[12]

More important than the numbers in which they served, college-educated men contributed their moral outlook, demonstrated their commitment to duty, and exemplified gentlemanly leadership. These qualities, which they had tried to cultivate as civilians, were important to their approach to wartime affairs and influenced their attitudes towards their men. Taught to be moral exemplars and society's leaders, college men believed that they exemplified good character. Dartmouth's Ozias Pitkin defined "character" as "the result of all the artificial & accidental circumstances of life." Character "comprehends all the habits[,] tendencies, principles, everything connected with our present state of existence & our powers for attaining to a better state in the future." Wesleyan University student Robert Pitman told a commencement assembly that character "is above success." He said all knew "that it is of more consequence what a man *is* than what he *has*."[13] Although the ideals of proper character were taught to all segments of society, colleges hammered home their importance, and the students fully embraced sound character as a sign of their social class.

College did more than instill knowledge of Latin, Greek, and other lessons of a classical curriculum. New England's colleges also taught their students to act as leaders, preparing them for their professional roles. As men who would have important positions in society, college men needed to set good examples for less fortunate citizens. The mandatory "moral philosophy" class, usually taught as a capstone course during the senior year by the school's president, touched on various disciplines such as political science, history, legal philosophy, and economics. Moral philosophers served as "society's moral navigators" and attempted to "bring all knowledge into a proper moral focus, instilling in the nation's educated class an enlightened respect for basic Christian beliefs and virtues." In addition, these classes taught that the moral man exhibited certain qualities. He practiced good habits, such as keeping clean, and displayed good character by controlling his emotions. In theory, such men inspired others in society at large. Courses in moral philosophy were the colleges' attempts to give their students some direction for living as society's most enlightened leaders.[14]

College students, for their part, accepted that they had to behave in a gentlemanly fashion as appropriate for their class and as an example to others. During Harvard's Class Day exercises in 1850, James C. Carter implored his fellow students to uphold virtue and behave as good citizens. Whatever "else we may be," he said, "let us at least be men." The graduates needed to develop a "character that will secure respect" and bear themselves so "as not to dishonor the cause of learning and the place in which we have been bred."[15]

One of the key components of that "character that will secure respect" was informed independent thought. College graduates believed that they, above all others, had been trained to see all situations with clarity. They felt that they needed to maintain intellectual and moral independence in the face of pressure to conform to fashionable and popular views. Only by sustaining their independence as thinkers could college men hope to be successful leaders. Levi Little, a student at Dartmouth, noted the "prevalent idolatry of Fashion, that most *fickle* goddess," as a clear sign that there were few upright individuals in society. "What one *is*," he wrote, "matters less than what he *wears*." Little complained that the "cut of a coat, the style of a hat, or pin or a ribbon, seem more essential to manhood than a sound judgment or an honest heart." "The world," Little declared, "wants men of character: men whose minds are their own—who think for themselves & call no man master." In contrast to men of character, "Common men receive their opinions at second hand; derive their theology & politics from the commentary & newspaper under whose (too often baleful) influence they happen to have been born."[16]

Such anxiety about individualism and emphasis on independent thought was hardly surprising given that many antebellum Americans were wary of "confidence men and painted women." Concerned with authenticity and honesty, members of the North's professional class worried about the rise of mob rule. One Wesleyan student warned that "Society is becoming too much like a puppet show, its members all moving upon the platform of life as the leader turns the crowd." It was important, therefore, for the man with a sense of individualism to have and to be stubbornly attached to moral positions. According to Dartmouth student Charles Cutter, morality was critical for all who were concerned with "the assertion of duties." Moral power, "the little rudder which directs the mighty vessel," was "the result of the practice of duties," for it forced the soul to "act in unison with all that is pure and noble." What was important to the scholar, wrote Harvard student Henry Spaulding, was "the question of individual action as opposed to social inertia,—of manly self-assertion as opposed to compliance and routine,—of original thinking and feeling as opposed to thinking by rule and feeling by pattern."[17] Even before they entered the professional world, college-trained men were echoing the belief that they needed to maintain their individualism and morals in order to serve as society's leaders. Without men of character to see clearly, speak truthfully, and act consistently with their morals, American society might be in jeopardy.

A man of character acted for the benefit of society and, even when his decisions were unpopular, stood firm, fully committed to what he thought was morally correct. Charles Russell Lowell, a member of the Harvard class of 1854, warned that a man's character could be threatened or challenged by too keen a desire for personal accolades and laurels. Lowell explained that first among the dangers to individuality was the "affectation which arises from a love of distinction." "Experience," he continued, "shows that neither the great nor the small are exempt from it," for it was "the badge of the court fool and it shines through the holes in the coat of the philosopher." Such warnings against the "love of distinction" were aimed primarily at politicians. College men constantly blamed the era's sectional tensions and political instability on weak-willed lawmakers who catered to crowds and compromised their principles. If the world's problems were to be solved, these young college men argued, men of true character and principle—men such as themselves—ought to be in charge.[18]

But what sort of nation did these young men propose to lead? Another important theme that college men considered was national identity. This may have resulted from the academic emphasis on classical education. The students thought and wrote about connections between the United States and civilizations of old and praised their young republic's accomplishments. Indeed, college students' and graduates' wartime belief that the Union was worth preserving stemmed from their prewar ideas about the exceptionalism of the United States. For the most part, these students saw America as the culmination of human progress and argued that their country was the most important nation on earth. Harvard student James Chase asked, "*Where* then, and by whom, is the destiny of man on earth to be accomplished?" "Reason and analogy, the laws of nature and the laws of history," he answered, "point to the American continent, and the American people. Here, on our own soil, is growing up the great people of the future."[19]

College students found in the nation's past, particularly in the Revolutionary period, examples of good character to emulate. The Revolution, with its dashing heroes and self-sacrificing patriots who fought for liberty and the greater good, was seen as a defining moment when Americans had displayed their best character traits. "The spirit of unobtrusive self-sacrifice," Harvard student Francis Balch claimed, "pervaded the whole country, the women gave up their tea, and left party and gossip to work for those who fought, the boys did the work of their absent fathers and wished that they were men, the men obtained a nobler victory over discomforts and vexations and delay than over the enemy." "'Give me Liberty or Give me Death' was the spirit of all and was echoed by many of the most popular songs of the American Revolution," Leander Collamore from Dartmouth proclaimed. The success of the Revolutionary War, wrote Harvard student David Kimball, "taught monarchs that there was a limit beyond which even the mightiest despots may not pass, that weakness becomes strength when its cause is just." The Americans had given "the oppressed of the world an example by which they can obtain a release from their sufferings" and had taught that a man must be free "to think, to speak, to act for himself." "Every struggle of the persecuted against the persecutor," wrote Kimball, "every privilege, social, political, or religious that has been wrested from tyrants and from oligarchy, every step forward in human progress was heralded by the American Revolution."[20]

Colleges taught that American civilization had emerged from ideas about freedom and individual rights and that its distinguishing mark was its republican form of government, which was, in turn, "a new phase in political history." According to Harvard student Hermann Warner, a republican government was "the grand realization of the dream of by-gone ages—the perfect rule of the people." Warner bragged that a "state of society has arisen without its parallel in the world's history, in which public opinion has become the expression of the moral sentiment of communities." The origin of American republicanism, Warner explained, could be traced to "our Puritan fathers" who "sowed those seeds of political equality, and watered them with their tears, from which our civil liberty sprang—that liberty which could thrive through oppression and mature through outrage and civil war."[21]

The generation of young leaders inherited something that was more important than America itself. The success of the republic, they realized, was critical for the cause of liberty all around the world. Frederick Dodge, a student at Dartmouth, explained that oppressive regimes had to be careful if they were to survive in an age of democratic awakenings. Oppress a people, he warned, and "Boston Harbor is black with unexpected tea; the oldest thrones in Europe are toppled down; kings surrender their dearest prerogatives to the people." Dodge argued that men had a "*moral* duty to reassert" lost rights. The true progression of history, therefore, was that "*every* government must be Democratic." Wesleyan student Edwin Rushmore declared that "Civil Liberty" from its beginnings in "the British Magna Charta to the present day has . . . been gradually rising in the estimation of the world and in its influence upon the character and destiny of nations." The result was that "the condition of the subject is everywhere improved and . . . men are much better informed with respect to their rights & duties, than at any former period with which we are acquainted." Rushmore concluded that the only system of government "better than all others" in its ability to "give effect to its laws, and secure their obedience" was one that proceeded "from the people."[22]

Like other Americans of the era, these college men believed that their nation was blessed by a kind Providence. Undergraduates praised the richness of the natural resources of the nation's interior. They regarded Americans as "the pioneers of progress" and "the vanguard of the restless Caucasian family." According to one Dartmouth student, America had risen "from the retiring deluge of British oppression, like the sacred mountain from a subsiding flood, to bear upon her summit the emb[r]io of a purer, nobler civilization." The fact that these young men espoused such views suggests the importance of a progressive—if racially based—ideology about the American nation.[23]

Antebellum college students, perhaps dreaming of their own futures, were extremely optimistic about America's prospects. "What will be the condition of this country in power and territory two or three centuries hence," wrote William Burrage of Harvard, "is a question which we often ask of our imagination." The question was posed "for the simple purpose of enjoying the complacent satisfaction afforded by the answer which our imagination is accustomed to give, trained as it is to look through one peculiar vista of the future that is bright with anticipated national glories." This glorious vision was one of "a mighty republic extending over the whole North American, if not over the whole Western continent, and holding moral sway over the whole world." This "fond dream of almost universal empire," he noted, was also "not peculiar, as some may think, to the more ardent class of our countrymen—to that class called for distinction's sake Young America." Indeed, Burrage claimed that there was "scarcely one who does not cherish in some degree the idea of a future American empire immense in territory, as well as in political and moral influence." There were those who were so certain of this future that they referred to it as "our manifest destiny." Such a term was "flattering to our national vanity" and was "considered heresy to challenge, but which are nevertheless almost meaningless words." The idea of "manifest destiny," Burrage wrote, was based on "the general idea that this country as the first representative of true republican principles is to serve as a nucleus around which other republics on this continent will cluster as they may be successively formed."[24]

As the nation's young leaders, these men were also responsible for standing guard against any threats to the Union. One among these dangers was the institution of slavery. Harvard student Charles Gregory calculated that "at the beginning of the next century we shall number a hundred millions of people." This was an exciting prospect, and the world had "never seen the splendid spectacle of a hundred millions of free people united into a democratic republic." But "if we do not steer carefully," he warned, "the world will never see it." Gregory urged caution because there "exists one cause of alarm; one institution yet remains which renders us obnoxious to keen reproach and the charge of inconsistency." Gregory trusted, however, that "the moral conflict which has commenced, and the gentle but powerful influence of Christianity will render the institutions of Slavery obsolete before the opening of the twentieth century." Harvard student Robert Babson worried about the fate of the Union in the present age, seeing in mid-nineteenth-century America the same pitfalls that led to Rome's demise. Aside from America's love of expansion and desire for even more land, he thought the system of slavery was "unparalleled in the History of the race." "To enumerate" the "evils" of slavery, he wrote, "would be to count the sands on the sea shore."[25] Slavery's ability to create factions and expand in step with territorial gains was troubling for young men who believed that the institution ought to be on the decline as the nation looked westward towards the future.

The issue of slavery was, for these young men, fully connected to the threats of secession. While most students refused to believe that Southerners would actually sunder the Union, they understood what secession would represent. As they praised the United States, its expansive reach, and its importance for human civilization, these men argued implicitly against any danger to the Union as a whole. Some men openly discussed the threat of secession. Dartmouth student David Quigg, for example, contended in 1855 that it would be "most base & shameful if we prove incapable to discharge the duties necessary to fulfill this trust" of safeguarding the Union forged by the founding fathers. Speaking to his audience about contemporary issues—perhaps the violence in the Kansas Territory—Quigg noted, "in these times of our country, there must inevitably spring up in every American soul a thousand emotions—mingled of joy, hope & fear." "Anarchy & civil war, that destroyed the ancient republics & which is the destruction of all nations without God & conscience," might yet reach American shores. "Indeed," Quigg continued, "there has been going for the past few years in this land so boastful of peace & happiness[,] a civil warfare, more odious & more to deprecated than any other history has yet recorded." This state of affairs threatened "to destroy, the fairest structure of government, that human prudence & human foresight ever reared." "The consequences of disunion," Quigg concluded, "we will not attempt to describe," for "no human pen could enumerate them."[26]

Given their attachment to the Union and their belief in its importance for the spread of democratic principles around the world, Northern college-educated men naturally responded to secession by volunteering to protect the government. If the progressive image of the United States, which they praised, was to be sustained, then the country's young leaders needed to step forward and do their duty. These young men had often spoken of the greatness of the

American nation, and when given the chance to defend it, they did not shy away from displaying their character as Northern gentlemen.

When War Came

The outbreak of the Civil War led to a variety of reactions by college men. All of them, however, viewed their options through the lens of class. The young men debated how best to perform their duty as society's leaders in a time of conflict. Some rallied to the cause immediately; others stayed behind, often at the urging of loved ones, to work on the home front and keep the economic, political, and intellectual foundations of the North strong. A decision about whether to serve came down to a matter of interpretation. Were these men, as society's leaders, supposed to fight, or was it their responsibility to stay home and serve the nation through other means? Often, the parties involved came to differing conclusions. Harvard graduate Benjamin W. Crowninshield had to turn down a captaincy in a new regiment, explaining "My own wishes about active military life and those of my family do not agree. All my efforts to get away have proved vain." Possessive employers sometimes stood in the way of wartime service. When Bowdoin College officials learned that Prof. Joshua L. Chamberlain was planning to volunteer, they did everything they could to prevent his departure. "I find I have to encounter an unexpected degree of opposition in the Faculty of the College," Chamberlain wrote to Maine governor Israel Washburn. He was, however, still determined to go, noting "I trust that the representations that they propose to make to induce you to withhold my commission, will have no more weight with you than with me. I feel it to be my duty to serve my Country." Although he regretted that he had to "act against the wishes of my colleagues," the professor thought that he had no other choice.[27] This conflict over how best to fulfill one's duty to the country is played out in the letters of former Maine governor John Hubbard, Sr., to his sons. Upon hearing that his son John was thinking about volunteering in the war, Hubbard, Sr., admitted his fear that such a step would "not prove an advantageous step for your future prospects in life." Despite his belief that the contest was "now a question of life or death to our institutions of government, or no government, of order or anarchy," the elder Hubbard only reluctantly acquiesced to his son's desire to serve. Unfortunately for the former governor, his troubles did not end with John's enlistment. His other son, Thomas, also expressed interest in going. Afraid of losing two sons, John, Sr., wrote again. He conceded that, in theory, military service was "the duty . . . every man owes to his country." However, he reminded Thomas that

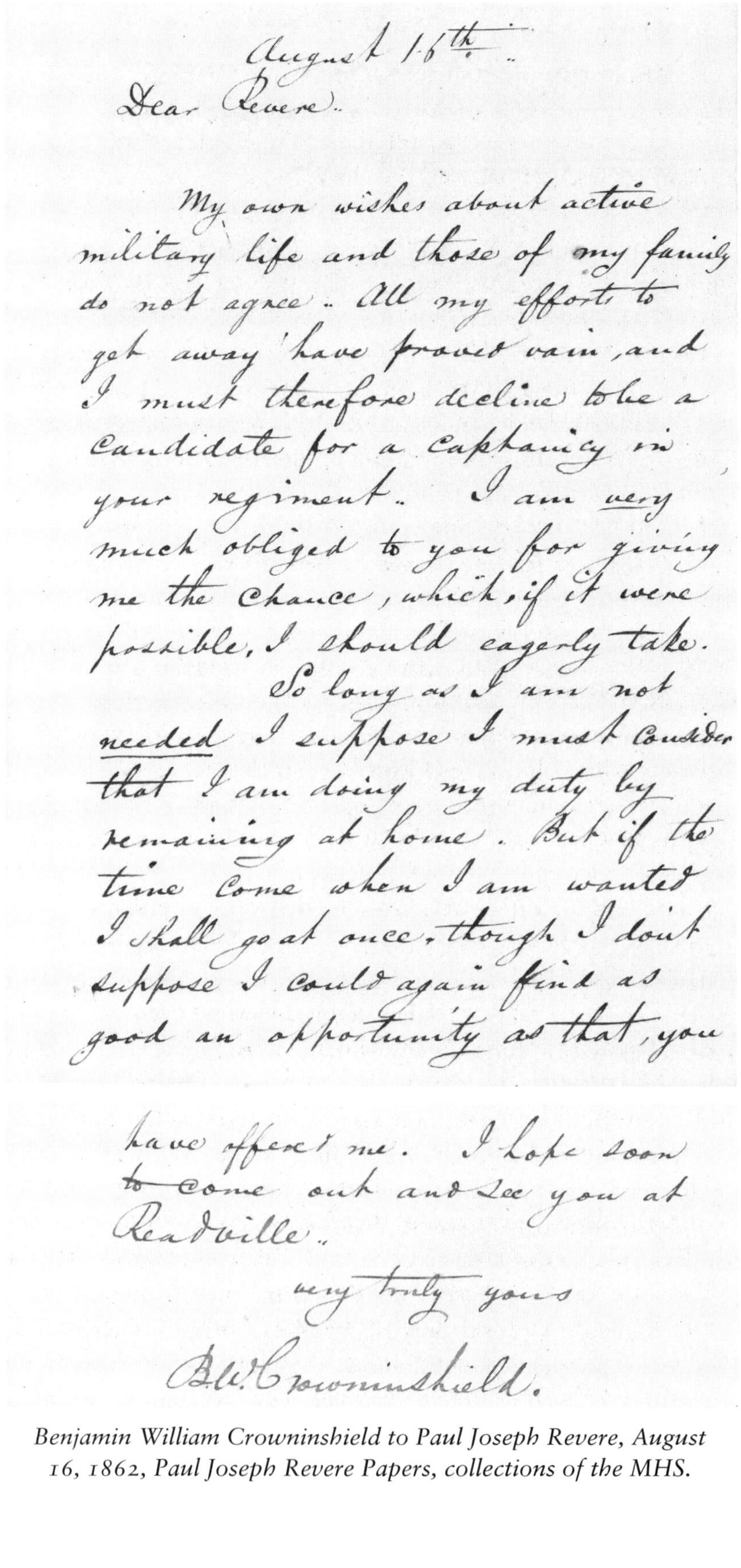

August 16th.
Dear Revere.

My own wishes about active military life and those of my family do not agree. All my efforts to get away have proved vain, and I must therefore decline to be a candidate for a captaincy in your regiment. I am very much obliged to you for giving me the chance, which, if it were possible, I should eagerly take.

So long as I am not needed I suppose I must consider that I am doing my duty by remaining at home. But if the time come when I am wanted I shall go at once, though I don't suppose I could again find as good an opportunity as that, you have offered me. I hope soon to come out and see you at Readville.

very truly yours

B.W. Crowninshield.

Benjamin William Crowninshield to Paul Joseph Revere, August 16, 1862, Paul Joseph Revere Papers, collections of the MHS.

"there are other ways than that of bearing arms, other means than going to the field of battle and of slaughtering and death, in which a man may quite as efficiently and usefully render his aid in discharge of his whole duty." "Civic duties" were "no less important," the elder Hubbard declared. He reminded his son that during the Revolutionary War the "Franklins and Jeffersons, and Wythes" provided "aid and council in her . . . struggles," while the "Madisons and Jays" laid "the foundations of our constitution." All these men served as civilians, and their memories were no less cherished for their contributions. Every man, Hubbard continued, was "fitted for usefulness in his proper sphere of action." Referring to his son's personal qualities, he noted, "in my judgment, you have capabilities and qualifications, which, in the ordinary course of Providence, will, with such efforts as you will make, insure to you a *high* position of usefulness and distinction in civil life."[28] Nearly a year later, when Thomas again tried to enlist, his father argued that he could "be a more useful man, useful to yourself[,] useful to society and to the country in some other sphere than as a soldier." In the army, he warned his son, "you put yourself upon a footing with every one, the low[,] the vulgar, those who have no adaptedness, no talent for usefulness, elsewhere or to be shot at and mangled or perhaps fall victim to disease without the power of . . . remedying." "For you," he concluded, "a different sphere is fitted and allotted."[29]

College men who volunteered rejected what they saw as their parents' attempts to turn the conflict into a "rich man's war but a poor man's fight." Lewis Pennell, whose son Christopher was an Amherst student at the outbreak of the war, contended that there were plenty of men whose lives were less important who could volunteer and fight. Christopher rejected this argument. He did not like the "sentiment" that the volunteers "can be had in plenty from among a class which will not be missed, whose lives are not worth so much as yours or mine." Christopher maintained that even the "poor boys" of the Sixth Massachusetts Regiment who had been "murdered at Baltimore" as they marched through the streets on their way to Washington, D.C., "left families. Do not say they are not missed." "When our soldiers, be they Irish, Dutch or Yankee, shall be mown before the enemies' cannon in ranks, even though they come from the very humblest classes," he continued, "shall not the wail of the widow the orphan & the *childless* go up for them as piteously as for the dead of the proud & petted Seventh Regiment? Do not say they will not be missed, that their lives are worth nothing." Christopher Pennell eventually joined the army and was killed at the Battle of the Crater in 1864.[30]

A large number of college-educated men volunteered to serve in the war, but many others decided against enlistment. The fact that the college classes closest to the outbreak of the war saw the highest proportions of volunteers suggests that age and life circumstances played a role in these men's choices. Younger men who were in the prime of their health and had not yet established themselves in their careers were more likely to serve. Charles Eliot Norton, a Harvard graduate, was thirty-three at the start of the war but had health problems that prevented his volunteering. Joshua L. Chamberlain, Norton's junior by one year, had an established professional life and was almost prevented from volunteering by his employer. Familial obligations and opposition by parents also kept some men on the home front. Charles Francis Adams, Jr., an officer in the Union army, urged his brother Henry not to volunteer, citing their parents' age; someone had to look after them. Charles P. Bowditch balked when his father continually refused to allow him to enlist. "Those who have families to support or whose absence would bring distress to many others have some reason for staying at home," Bowditch acknowledged, "[b]ut all others ought to go." Bowditch, whose brother Henry had been allowed to enlist, viewed volunteering as a man's duty and wondered "why is it not mine as much as other people's? I have nobody to depend upon me and am not in a position to bring misery on any one by going. What can be more clearly my duty than to go?" "If you are not willing to send your sons," he poignantly asked, "why should others be willing to send theirs?"[31] The dialogue between Charles Bowditch and his father illustrates the difference in their perspectives. A member of the older generation thought that the sacrifice of one son was sufficient, but one young man, who did not have a family to care for or responsibilities to tend to, felt compelled to do his part. Whatever prevented college men from volunteering, they still served the cause of the Union on the home front, while many of their cohort marched in the armies of the United States.

Charles P. Bowditch, photo 100.11 from "Boys of Harvard 1863," collections of the MHS.

The heart-wrenching debates about whether a college-educated man should serve in the war highlight a critical distinction between the generations. Older Northern professionals had sent their sons to college to prepare them for life in the middle and upper classes. This, in turn, was supposed to save them from having to toil as laborers or risk their lives in wartime. The young men, who had deep attachment to their nation and took their social responsibilities very seriously, heartily disagreed with their parents. In a sense, the debate stemmed from differing interpretations of civic roles and duties. In times of peace, young men had no problem serving as professionals and letting the common workers labor in the factories and fields. In wartime, however, they reasoned that by virtue of their status their role was to lead their fellow citizens in battle. The older generation balked when they thought that their own sons, who had been given the opportunity to escape the fate of the lower classes, would also be put at risk. Ultimately, these arguments and other considerations kept many college-educated men on the home front. But despite their privileges, their plentiful excuses for not volunteering, and opposition from their parents, many other college men felt compelled to serve.

Some student bodies were especially excited for war, and many men from these schools volunteered. The Sunday after they heard the news about the fall of Fort Sumter, Amherst students gathered in the college's chapel. Dozens of young men, including the president's son, offered their services to the governor of Massachusetts. They deemed "it a Christian duty not unbecoming the Lord's day to enlist in such a war." The governor declined their services, but many of them joined other units anyway. On campus, a general military drill began. Meanwhile, classes during the war "were . . . so reduced that some of them seemed almost like the thinned ranks of an army after a battle."[32]

College men who volunteered accepted the fact that their duty required personal sacrifice. They also drew upon their antebellum beliefs about the importance of the Union and all it represented to justify their actions. Almost immediately, some men saw the war as an opportunity to eradicate the institution of slavery and redeem as well as restore the Union. Luther Clark Howell, a student at Amherst College, told his brother Sidney, "I ought to hold my life cheap in comparison with my country—it will be well sold if I shall aid in purchasing freedom for shackled humanity or in saving my country." A few months later, he reaffirmed his determination to enlist, writing "I am willing to go willing to sacrifice my prospects[,] my life to my country." Frazar Augustus Stearns, an Amherst graduate and the son of the college's president, told his father, "We are on the eve of great events." Winning the war, he argued, would lead to "new things" that would "astound the world." Out of the ashes of the war, he predicted "A great nation, *free and independent*, literally so, will be born, and the world shall rejoice." "The institutions of the country, indeed free institutions throughout the world, hang on this moment," Paul Joseph Revere, Harvard graduate and grandson of the Revolutionary War patriot, told his mother. Claiming that he would "be ashamed" if he "were to sit down in happy indulgence, and leave such a great matter as this to take its course," Revere hoped to serve in the "struggle for the freedom and for the principles that have built up this nation."[33]

On the eve of the First Battle of Bull Run, Sullivan Ballou, a former Brown student, told his wife, "I know how strongly American Civilization now leans on the triumph of the Government." Having always advocated a "pure love of country and of the principles," Ballou had no choice but to obey once he was "called upon" to serve his nation. Thinking about the risks he faced, Ballou wrote, "If I fall, I know it can never be in a better cause." He was "too thoroughly convinced of the justice of this war" and knew "too well the peril of our free institutions and the value to the world of our American civilization, even to hesitate to cast in my life if it is called for." Ballou admitted that he would be willing to "give up my children and take the battle-field in defence of the great principles of American civilization," for the republic offered something "the world has never yet seen." Men, he declared, "were never yet called upon to die in a nobler cause."[34]

College men believed that their education provided them with the broad perspective that one needed to understand fully the political stakes of the war. They also recognized that many politicians were unprepared for the level of sacrifice and commitment necessary to win. Williams graduate and future president James A. Garfield told his wife, Crete, that he could "see nothing before us but a long and sanguinary war." The state of national politics suggested to Garfield that politicians were unfit for handling such a conflict. "When I see the outrageous meanness of the democrats," he wrote, "and the timid and cowardly course of many of the republicans, it makes me long to be in the strife and help fight it out." In the present crisis, even more so than during the Revolution, there was a great "need of men to stand by the country and sustain its authority." The more he thought about the situation, the more he believed he could not "stand aloof from this conflict." Garfield offered his services to the governor of Ohio and was willing to serve "in any capacity he may see fit to appoint me." He explained his decision to enlist by noting that "men of military experience" were all serving and "still more were needed for the new regiments."[35]

College-educated men believed that they had an obligation to fight in the war because they felt they could inspire other men to follow their example. Amherst student Frazar Stearns argued that the sight of the nation's "educated

Maj. Paul Joseph Revere, carte de visite by John Adams Whipple, 1862. Photo 67.7 from the Twentieth Massachusetts Infantry Regiment Carte de Visite Album, collections of the MHS.

men going to fight the battles of the Lord" would "rouse the country quicker to a sense of its danger." Charles P. Bowditch lamented the fact that Northern citizens (including his father) seemed to be stuck "in a torpor." Because the regiments were not filling up as swiftly as needed, Bowditch proposed "that every gentleman and gentleman's son ought to go into the field. Such a proceeding would exercise a good influence on everybody. If a company or a regiment of gentlemen should be raised, those in the lower classes would be brought to understand that they too should be willing to sacrifice their lives for the good of the country." Joshua Chamberlain assured the governor of Maine that he could "get together a thousand men in a very short time, and shall hold myself entirely at your Excellency's command in so doing." Already, he reported, "Several young graduates of the College have come to me of their own accord, and say they will go with me as privates or any way." Paul Joseph Revere told his mother that he could "carry other men with me" as he set out to "struggle for freedom & the principles that have built up this country."[36]

Members of the professional class believed that they could have a good influence on the character of the men serving in the armed forces. Theodore Winthrop wrote to a friend, "I do not see that I can put myself,—experience and character—to any more useful use." Winthrop considered his "character" one of his key attributes. The Yale graduate was referring to the commonly held belief that the army was lacking in gentlemanliness. Exposure to men of sound character might aid the troops. "The regular army is to be enlarged as you will see," Winthrop explained. Referring to the men likely to seek commissions, he speculated that "Not many" of these "will be of the best tone" and many would "have less knowledge on the special subject than I. Few will have seen so much of the practical work of campaigning as my life has given me." Even fewer of those men, Winthrop declared, would "be such thorough Democrats by principle as to feel that their men are still citizens to be educated and elevated professionally and socially by the example of their superiors." Fellow Yale man Joseph Hopkins Twichell explained that he had chosen to volunteer as a chaplain in a regiment "composed as it is of rough, wicked men" because he saw "the companies of the better class of citizens were all attended by Chaplains, but nothing was said about these." Referring to a unit consisting mostly of Irish Catholics, Twichell claimed to have been "fitted by nature to influence this class of men." When he applied for a commission, Harvard graduate John B. Noyes offered his "liberal education," his experience as a private, and his "sobriety and gentlemanly traits (qualities how infrequent, or rather how not over and above common in the officers of our volunteer army)." With these strengths, he claimed that he was "far more qualified to sustain the position of an officer than many who are now in the service and are constantly being added to it."[37]

Rank in the armed forces was a surrogate for class, and many young professionals demanded that their status in civilian life be honored with military commissions. John Hubbard finally acquiesced to his son Thomas's desire to volunteer but despaired at the idea that his child would be a private, "subject to the order of any *upstart* officer, set up as a mark to be shot at, and to die unheeded[,] unknown without the chance even of distinction." He preferred to have his son "go into this war, in some position suited to his capacity and merits, from which should he survive the contest, there would be a probability of his reaping some advantages in his future course of life." Hubbard added that "the idea of his going into the crowd to be mixed up with rabble, without identification" was "absolutely intolerable." Writing to his other son, John, he noted, "if you are to continue in it [*the army*] I want you both at least to be in such positions as shall enable you to bring into requisition all the capacities you have arising from natural talent, education, and energy." He wanted his sons to have rank so that "your efforts may stand a chance of being useful to the country beyond that of being merely one of the crowd to fill a space for a mark to aim at."[38]

College men made it clear that they were volunteering as gentlemen and not as regular soldiers. They demanded, therefore, an officer's rank comparable to their antebellum class standing. To serve in a lesser capacity would have been unacceptable. Thomas Hubbard, surely to the delight of his father, declared that he did not have "the remotest design of Enlisting as a private." Such a step, he commented, "is asking too much of patriotism." He reiterated this sentiment a few months later, telling his father "I intend to play 'sojer' by the fall if possible, though I shall not in any Event *volunteer* in the ranks." "It would be the height of Egotism and cowardice for me to say to these 'go I am fitted for better things,'" he wrote. Observing that "many of my juniors and inferiors have commissions," he saw "no reason why I should give up everything for nothing." College-educated men maintained that marching in the ranks was no place for a gentleman. "I do think a man must be very patriotic or a very great fool to enlist in the army," Harvard graduate John C. Gray wrote. He referred to "a private's life" as "a dog's life," surmising that the men who marched in the ranks probably led "a dog's life at home."[39]

The war was an opportunity to test men's character. For young men who had been taught to control their passions, and thus maintain a restrained character in peacetime, the chance to demonstrate their personal qualities in war proved an exciting prospect. William Thompson Lusk, a former Yale student, wrote to his cousin on the day of his enlistment, "You must feel with me in my happiness! At length I am judged worthy to expose my life for my country's sake." Lusk explained that he was "going to see real danger, real privation, real work—not as a mere Carpet-Knight, talking valorously to girls, but going forth in all humility to help to conquer in the name of God and my Country." Samuel Nichols of Amherst College, responding to Union defeats on the battlefield, argued, "it was our imperative duty to take the places of our fallen soldiers, to meet the expectations of those whom we have bidden Godspeed, and who now are in extreme peril, and also to increase the original strength of the army." Where were the reinforcements to come from, "unless such men as you and I signify our willingness to go?"[40]

The high casualty rates that this cohort sustained speak to its members' exposed position on the field as officers and underscore their commitment to the Union war effort. Many schools built monuments to commemorate their fallen sons after the conflict. Harvard's massive Memorial Hall, for example, stood out in Cambridge as both a testament to the sacrifice of the men and a badge of honor for the institution that had sent so many of its sons to the war. Coinciding with the erection of monuments and memorials was the publication of a plethora of wartime correspondences and histories. Perhaps the most famous of these was the *Harvard Memorial Biographies*, which told the life stories of the college's alumni who died in the war. One of the lessons of the conflict, according to Thomas Wentworth Higginson, the editor of the two-volume memorial, was that there existed "no class of men in this republic from whom the response of patriotism comes more promptly and

Memorial Hall, Harvard University, Views Collection, collections of the MHS.

surely than from its most highly educated class." Their actions and sacrifices, Higginson argued, should refute "[all] those delusions which pass current in Europe . . . in regard to some supposed torpor or alienation prevailing among cultivated Americans." Such deeds spoke well of the nation's system of college education, which "must be on the whole healthy and sound, when it sends forth a race of young men who are prepared, at the most sudden summons, to transfer their energies to a new and alien sphere, and to prove the worth of their training in wholly unexpected applications."[41] The *Harvard Memorial Biographies* and similar publications influenced how the Civil War would be commemorated and remembered. These works also highlighted the principles and idealism of the young men who fought to save the Union. Future generations of students, who were raised on such stories or perhaps strolled past monuments to the honored dead, learned how gentlemen should behave and what sacrifices had once been required to keep the Union perpetual.

Notes

1. Joshua Lawrence Chamberlain, ed., *Universities and Their Sons: History, Influence and Characteristics of American Universities, with Biographical Sketches and Portraits of Alumni and Recipients of Honorary Degrees* (Boston, 1898–1900), 1:25, 34, 36.
2. Chamberlain, *Universities and Their Sons*, 1:37, 2:vii–ix.

3. Richard F. Miller, "Brahmins under Fire: Peer Courage and the Harvard Regiment," *Historical Journal of Massachusetts* 30(2002):76. Historian Lorien Foote has argued that serving as officers allowed members of the elite—in her case Harvard-educated men, mostly affiliated with the Second Massachusetts Volunteers—to maintain their class status and ideas of proper behavior. These men, Foote observed, applied "ideals of courage, self-discipline, and duty to other officers" and also employed organizational and institutional skills that they had acquired to help manage the men in their unit. Furthermore, they kept their own counsel, had stereotypical views of African Americans, and distrusted foreign-born troops. Their prewar worldview, therefore, influenced how they served in the war. Lorien Foote, "Rich Man's War, Rich Man's Fight: Class, Ideology, and Discipline in the Union Army," *Civil War History* 51(2005):269–287. Studies of the famed Twentieth Massachusetts (the so-called "Harvard Regiment") and the sons of Virginian planters (the "last generation" of slaveholders) have only recently suggested the importance of young, educated men during the Civil War era. The present essay considers the antebellum intellectual world and wartime contributions of young men who attended New England colleges in the late 1840s and 1850s. See Richard F. Miller, *Harvard's Civil War: A History of the Twentieth Massachusetts Volunteer Regiment* (Hanover, N.H., 2005); and Peter S. Carmichael, *The Last Generation: Young Virginians in Peace, War, and Reunion* (Chapel Hill, 2005). For examples of biographies and collections of letters, see Carol Bundy, *The Nature of Sacrifice: A Biography of Charles Russell Lowell, Jr., 1835–64* (New York, 2005); Robert Garth Scott, ed., *Fallen Leaves: The Civil War Letters of Major Henry Livermore Abbott* (Kent, Ohio, 1991); Russell Duncan, ed., *Blue-Eyed Child of Fortune* (Athens, Ga., 1992); Frederick D. Williams, ed., *The Wild Life of the Army: Civil War Letters of James A. Garfield* (East Lansing, Mich., 1964); Christian Samito, ed., *"Fear Was Not in Him": The Civil War Letters of General Francis C. Barlow, U.S.A.* (New York, 2006).
4. David F. Allmendinger, Jr., *Paupers and Scholars: The Transformation of Student Life in Nineteenth-Century New England* (New York, 1975), 9, 11–12.
5. Of the 748 men who graduated from Amherst College between 1850 and 1865, 253 (34 percent) were clergymen or missionaries, 121 (16 percent) were attorneys, 121 entered the educational field (teachers, professors, principals), 139 (19 percent) went into business, and 60 (8 percent) pursued medicine-related professions. At Bowdoin College, 589 men graduated between 1850 and 1865. Of those, 81 (14 percent) went into the clergy, 181 (31 percent) practiced law, 99 (17 percent) became educators, 33 (6 percent) went into business, and 52 (9 percent) became physicians. Waterville (later Colby) College, Bowdoin's Maine neighbor, boasted a smaller group of graduates: only 201 between the classes of 1850 and 1865. Of those, however, 43 (20 percent) entered a religious profession, 48 (24 percent) went on to practice law, 43 (21 percent) became involved with education, 17 (8 percent) entered into some form of business, and 12 (6 percent) became physicians. Note that many of these young men had more than one profession in their lifetimes. Many of them taught school at some point in their careers before pursuing other occupations. Calculated from Robert S. Fletcher and Malcolm O. Young, eds., *Am-*

herst College: Biographical Record of the Graduates and Non-Graduates, Centennial Edition 1821–1921 (Amherst, 1927); *General Catalog of Bowdoin College and the Medical School of Maine: A Biographical Record of Alumni and Officers, 1794–1950* (Brunswick, Maine, 1950); Edward Winslow Hall, *Third General Catalogue of Colby College, Waterville, Maine, 1820–1906* (Waterville, Maine, 1909).

6. Wilder Dwight to William Dwight, June 15, 1850, Dwight Family Papers, Massachusetts Historical Society; William Wheeler to his aunt, July 23, 1862, in *Letters of William Wheeler of the Class of 1855, Y.C.* (Cambridge, Mass., 1875), 340.
7. Peter Dobkin Hall, *The Organization of American Culture, 1700–1900: Private Institutions, Elites, and the Origins of American Nationality* (New York, 1984), 174.
8. In his landmark work, *Southern Honor*, Bertram Wyatt-Brown has defined honor as "the cluster of ethical rules . . . by which judgments of behavior are ratified by community consensus." At its most basic, honor was "the evaluation of the public" or "reputation." More recently, Kenneth S. Greenberg has studied what he terms the "language of honor," observing that "southern men of honor were 'superficial'" and were concerned with "the surface of things—with the world of appearances." Certain attributes signified honor as a Southern cultural phenomenon. For instance, it could be distinguished from simple "manliness" and "masculinity" because it "embraced hierarchy—especially about race." Slavery was "sustained by notions of honor." Because Southern honor entailed the sometimes violent defense of one's reputation through the ritual of dueling, scholars have been reluctant to ascribe the same code of conduct to Northerners. The omission of the North has led to the impression that Northerners themselves lacked any socially mandated moral code in their lives.

   Contrary to what the volumes of literature on Southern honor and lack of corresponding works on a Northern variant may unintentionally imply, Northerners did have a value system that governed their social interactions. Some scholars have proposed varying terms to describe such a system. Edward L. Ayers uses the term "dignity" and defines it as "the conviction that each individual at birth possessed an intrinsic value at least theoretically equal to that of every other person." Dignity also contrasts with honor because it entails self-restraint over retribution for offences. Another term that Northerners employed was "respectability," which Patrick Rael explains "served as a master value, encompassing a host of traits—not all of them compatible—that came to define an ideal for human character in an expanding market society." Because of its diverse use, it had "no simple or single definition" and was perhaps "an ideal in itself," and "attempts to ascribe to it a narrow and static" definition might "misrepresent its role in antebellum northern thought." Joseph F. Kett has argued that character was "not a set of doctrines or even a code of behavior." But the manner in which "character" was deployed by young men at the heart of this study suggests that, under certain circumstances, the term encompassed a variety of idealized behavioral traits. Amy S. Greenberg's study of antebellum American masculinity discusses the distinction between the codes of conduct that Northern and Southern men idealized. Greenberg distinguishes two types of manhood—restrained (successful and religious men who abhorred violence and supported temperance) and martial (men who took pride in physical feats and dominance)—and argues that "when antebellum Americans talked about character among men, they also were talking about masculinity." The men in her study "agreed . . . that a true man of character could, in theory, be dressed in rags." Those adhering to the martial idea of manhood, however, "depended on the public display of their masculinity to a much greater degree than did restrained men, the increasing focus on appearance as the sole marker of character in public proved far more devastating to the martial man, whatever his financial status, than it did to the restrained man." Bertram Wyatt-Brown, *Southern Honor: Ethics and Behavior in the Old South* (New York, 1983), xv, 14; Kenneth S. Greenberg, "The Nose, the Lie, and the Duel in the Antebellum South," *American Historical Review* 95(1990):58; Bertram Wyatt-Brown, *The Shaping of Southern Culture: Honor, Grace, and War, 1760s–1890s* (Chapel Hill, 2001), xii; Edward L. Ayers, *Vengeance and Justice: Crime and Punishment in the Nineteenth-Century American South* (New York, 1984), 19–20, 22–24; Patrick Rael, *Black Identity and Black Protest in the Antebellum North* (Chapel Hill, 2002), 130; Joseph F. Kett, *Rites of Passage: Adolescence in America, 1790 to the Present* (New York, 1977), 107; Amy S. Greenberg, *Manifest Manhood and the Antebellum American Empire* (New York, 2005), 11–12, 139–141.

9. Gary W. Gallagher, *The Confederate War* (Cambridge, Mass., 1997), 29; percentages calculated from "Historical Census Browser," retrieved Oct. 9, 2009, from the University of Virginia, Geospatial and Statistical Data Center: http://fisher.lib.virginia.edu/collections/stats/histcensus/index.html; and Frederick Phisterer, *Statistical Record of the Armies of the United States*, vol. 13, *The Army in the Civil War* (New York, 1885), 3–5; Phillip Shaw Paludan, *A People's Contest: The Union and Civil War, 1861–1865* (Lawrence, Kan., 1996), 132–133; Brooks Mather Kelley, *Yale, A History* (New Haven, 1974), 197–198.

10. Robert Poirier has presented these figures in order to compare Bowdoin, Dartmouth, and Norwich's contributions to the war effort. Robert G. Poirier, *"By the Blood of Our Alumni": Norwich University Citizen Soldiers in the Army of the Potomac* (Mason City, Iowa, 1999), 17. Poirier bases his numbers on the work of Charles C. Calhoun, author of the most recent history of Bowdoin College. Calhoun, in turn, has cited a *Boston Transcript* article by Bowdoin alumnus Edgar O. Achorn (class of 1881), which noted that "Bowdoin had outperformed Dartmouth by 25.02 percent to 22.82 percent (based on counting living graduates in 1867 who had seen Civil War service)." Calhoun cautions that these numbers "are not entirely reliable, for war records were not complete (at least for Bowdoin) and it is difficult to know whether to count various non-combatant jobs, such as Civil War government clerkships, or students who transferred to other colleges." Charles C. Calhoun, *A Small College in Maine: Two Hundred Years of Bowdoin* (Brunswick, Maine, 1993), 171–172. Leverett Wilson Spring, *A History of Williams College* (Boston, 1917), 188; William S. Tyler, *A History of Amherst College, during the Administrations of Its First Five Presidents from 1821 to 1891* (New York, 1895), 185–187. Data for Bowdoin College calculated from Horace Harmon Burbank, *Class of 1860. Bowdoin College* (Portland, Maine, 1882), 27; *General Catalogue of Bowdoin College and the Medical*

School of Maine.

11. Paludan, *A People's Contest*, 132–133.
12. Tyler, *A History of Amherst College*, 181, 186–187.
13. Ozias Cornwall Pitkin, essay, July 29, 1847, "Influence of Early Studies upon the Future of Character," Commencement Parts, Rauner Special Collections Library (henceforth Rauner), courtesy of Dartmouth College Library, Hanover, New Hampshire; Robert Carter Pitman, essay, Aug. 4, 1845, "Portrature of Character—Cardinal Wolsey—Character, not Success, the Object of Life," Commencement Orations, 1833–55, Special Collections & Archives, Wesleyan University, Middletown, Connecticut (henceforth SCAWU).
14. Wilson Smith, *Professors and Public Ethics: Studies of Northern Moral Philosophers before the Civil War* (Ithaca, N.Y., 1956), 8–9; D. H. Meyer, *The Instructed Conscience: The Shaping of the American National Ethic* (Philadelphia, 1972), vii, 4–5, 12, 63–69.
15. James Coolidge Carter, essay and Class Day oration, June 21, 1850, "Class Day Oration," Records of the Class of 1850, courtesy of the Harvard University Archives (henceforth HUA).
16. Levi Little, essay, July 27, 1854, "Men of the Right Sort," Commencement Parts, Rauner, courtesy of Dartmouth College Library.
17. J. S. Barrows, essay, July 31, 1854, "Individuality," Commencement Orations, 1833–55, SCAWU; Charles Cutler, essay, July 29, 1852, "The Advantages of Asserting the Duties Rather Than the Rights of Man," Commencement Parts, Rauner, courtesy of Dartmouth College Library; Henry George Spaulding, essay and exhibition oration, Oct. 18, 1859, "Individualism," Records of the Class of 1860, HUA. For a discussion about social anxiety in antebellum America, see Karen Halttunen, *Confidence Men and Painted Women: A Study of Middle-Class Culture in America, 1830–1870* (New Haven, 1982).
18. Charles Russell Lowell, essay and exhibition performance, "Affectation," Records of the Class of 1854, HUA. This belief in the importance of the educated classes may be seen as the culmination of an intellectual process that began in the period after the War of 1812. According to Harlow W. Sheidley, conservative Massachusetts elites attempted to reclaim their national prominence in the wake of the failed Hartford Convention by attempting to dominate the nation in political and cultural ways. Failing on the political front after the rise of Jacksonian democracy, they turned their efforts towards education. These New England elites argued that their region truly represented the young republic and that their upper-class values ought to qualify them to leadership roles. Ultimately, their arguments were not persuasive for the majority of Americans. Despite this, the sons of these early New England elites fully accepted this reading of history and social ordering. See Harlow W. Sheidley, *Sectional Nationalism: Massachusetts Conservative Leaders and the Transformation of America, 1815–1836* (Boston, 1998).
19. James Morss Chase, essay and Commencement Day oration, July 17, 1850, "A New People," Records of the Class of 1850, HUA.
20. Francis Balch, essay and exhibition oration, Oct. 19, 1858, "A Citizen of a Free

Country Who Feels No Interest in Politics," Records of the Class of 1859, HUA; Leander Collamore, essay, July 31, 1856, "The Ballads of the American Revolution," Commencement Parts, Rauner, courtesy of Dartmouth College Library; David Pulsifer Kimball, essay and Commencement Day oration, July 16, 1856, "The Influence of the New World upon the Old," Records of the Class of 1856, HUA.

21. Hermann Jackson Warner, essay and commencement oration, July 17, 1850, "Political Life," Records of the Class of 1850, HUA. Harlow W. Sheidly has noted that this particular narrative of American history in the 1820s, which focused on the triumph of liberty over English tyranny, was an attempt at establishing New England's claims to originating the ideals of the young republic. It focused on the Puritans and their search for religious freedom. In addition, this narrative necessarily ignored less savory details about the past and emphasized a triumphal story with New England leading the way to independence. See Sheidley, *Sectional Nationalism*, esp. chap. 5.
22. Frederick B. Dodge, essay, July 28, 1860, "The Moral Element in Political Revolutions," Commencement Parts, Rauner, courtesy of Dartmouth College Library; Edwin Clowes Rushmore, essay, Aug. 5, 1846, "Political Morality," Commencement Orations, 1833–55, SCAWU.
23. George Miller Hobbs, essay and Commencement Day oration, July 17, 1850, "Civilization in the Pacific," Records of the Class of 1850, HUA; Willard Heath, essay, July 29, 1858, "Necessity of a Liberal Spirit in American Statesmen," Commencement Parts, Rauner, courtesy of Dartmouth College Library. For a discussion of nineteenth-century Americans' notions of race and national expansion, see Reginald Horsman, *Race and Manifest Destiny: The Origins of American Racial Anglo-Saxonism* (Cambridge, Mass., 1981).
24. William Wirt Burrage, essay and commencement oration, July 16, 1856, "Our 'Manifest Destiny,'" Records of the Class of 1856, HUA.
25. Charles Augustus Gregory, essay and Commencement Day oration, Oct. 17, 1854, "The Last Census," Records of the Class of 1855, HUA; Robert Edward Babson, essay and commencement oration, "Ancient History as Applied to Modern Politics," Records of the Class of 1856, HUA.
26. David Quigg, essay, July 26, 1855, "The Relation of the New States to the Old," Commencement Parts, Rauner, courtesy of Dartmouth College Library.
27. Benjamin William Crowninshield to Paul Joseph Revere, Aug. 16, 1862, Paul Joseph Revere Papers, Massachusetts Historical Society; Joshua Lawrence Chamberlain to Israel Washburn, Aug. 8, 1862, in *Through Blood and Fire: Selected Civil War Papers of Major General Joshua Chamberlain*, ed. Mark Nesbitt (Mechanicsburg, Pa., 1996), 14.
28. John Hubbard, Sr., to John Hubbard, Jr., Oct. 23, 1861; and John Hubbard, Sr., to Thomas Hamlin Hubbard, Nov. 4, 1861, Hubbard Family Papers, George J. Mitchell Department of Special Collections & Archives, Bowdoin College Library, Brunswick, Maine (henceforth Hubbard Family Papers).
29. John Hubbard to Thomas H. Hubbard, Aug. 4, 1862, Hubbard Family Papers.

30. Christopher Pennell to Lewis Pennell, Apr. 29, 1861, Alumni Biographical Files, Archives and Special Collections, Amherst College Library, Amherst, Massachusetts.
31. Sara Norton and Mark A. DeWolfe Howe, eds., *Letters of Charles Eliot Norton with Biographical Comment* (Boston, 1913), 221; Charles Francis Adams, Jr., to Henry Adams, Aug. 23, 1861, in *A Cycle of Adams Letters, 1861–1865*, ed. Worthington Chauncey Ford (Boston, 1920), 1:30; Charles Pickering Bowditch to Jonathan Ingersoll Bowditch, Aug. 5, 1862, in "War Letters of Charles P. Bowditch," *Proceedings of the Massachusetts Historical Society* 57(1924):416–418.
32. Tyler, *A History of Amherst College*, 182–183.
33. Luther Clark Howell to Sidney Howell, Apr. 21, 1861, and Luther Clark Howell to "brother," Aug. 2, 1861, Luther Clark Howell Papers, Archives and Special Collections, Amherst College Library; Frazar Augustus Stearns to William Augustus Stearns, Dec. 29, 1861, in William Augustus Stearns, *Adjutant Stearns* (1862; Charlestown, Mass., 2004), 82; *A Memorial of Paul Joseph Revere and Edward H. R. Revere* (1874; Clinton, Mass., 1913), 50–52.
34. Sullivan Ballou to Sarah Ballou, July 19, 1861; Sullivan Ballou to Latimer W. Ballou, June 11, 1861; and Sullivan Ballou to "Charlie" (perhaps Charles Parkhurst), unspecified date, in Robin Young, *For Love and Liberty: The Untold Civil War Story of Major Sullivan Ballou and His Famous Love Letter* (New York, 2006), 624–626, 251–252, 359–360.
35. James Abram Garfield to Lucretia Garfield, Apr. 14, 1861; James Abram Garfield to Lucretia Garfield, Apr. 28, 1861; James Abram Garfield to J. Harrison Rhodes, Apr. 17, 1861; and James Abram Garfield to Eliza Ballou Garfield, Aug. 30, 1861, in *Crete and James: Personal Letters of Lucretia and James Garfield*, ed. John Shaw (East Lansing, Mich., 1994), 113, 114, 9, 33.
36. Frazar Augustus Stearns to his stepmother, Oct. 6, 1861, *Adjutant Stearns*, 78; Charles Pickering Bowditch to Jonathan Ingersoll Bowditch, July 28, 1861, in "War Letters of Charles P. Bowditch," 415; Joshua Lawrence Chamberlain to Israel Washburn, July 17, 1862, in *Through Blood and Fire*, 12; Mary Robbins Revere to unknown recipient, undated [1863], Paul Joseph Revere Papers, Massachusetts Historical Society.
37. Theodore Winthrop to George W. Curtis, May 5, 1861, in Ellsworth Eliot, Jr., *Theodore Winthrop* (New Haven, 1938), 24; Joseph Hopkins Twichell to Edward Twichell, Apr. 22, 1861, in *The Civil War Letters of Joseph Hopkins Twichell: A Chaplain's Story*, ed. Peter Messent and Steve Courtney (Athens, Ga., 2006), 16, 18; John B. Noyes to George Rapall Noyes, July 11, 1862, John Buttrick Noyes Civil War Letters (MS Am 2332), Houghton Library, Harvard University.
38. John Hubbard to John Barrett Hubbard, Sept. 14, 1862, Hubbard Family Papers. Historians have used soldiers' rank to address questions about class representation. See James M. McPherson, *What They Fought For, 1861–1865* (New York, 1995), 35. Richard F. Miller has noted in "Brahmins under Fire" that, with regard to the Twentieth Massachusetts Volunteers (the "Harvard Regiment"), "Military rank dovetailed nicely with the civilian social hierarchy already familiar to the gentlemen officers. In fact, rank provided a means of enforcing class distinctions that were

unavailable in civilian life" (85).

39. Thomas H. Hubbard to John B. Hubbard, Nov. 18, 1861; Thomas H. Hubbard to Sarah H. B. Hubbard, Aug. 10, 1862, Hubbard Family Papers; John C. Gray, Jr., to his mother, May 17, 1863, in *War Letters, 1862–1865, of John Chipman Gray and John Codman Ropes* (Boston, 1927), 111.
40. William Thompson Lusk to Cousin Lou (Mrs. Henry G. Thompson), June 27, 1861, in *War Letters of William Thompson Lusk, Captain, Assistant Adjutant-General, United States Volunteers 1861–1863, Afterward M.D., LL.D.*, ed. William Chittenden Lusk (New York, 1911), 47; Samuel Nichols to Alpheus Nichols, July 4, 1862, in *"Your Soldier Boy Samuel": Civil War Letters of Lieut. Samuel Edmund Nichols, Amherst, '65 of the 37th Regiment Massachusetts Volunteers*, ed. Charles Sterling Underhill (n.p., 1929), 15–16.
41. Thomas Wentworth Higginson, ed., *Harvard Memorial Biographies* (Cambridge, Mass., 1867), 1:v–vi.

Mary Endicott Chamberlain Carnegie. Photograph by Lafayette, London, 1921. Photo 53.1, Colonial Society Photograph Collection, MHS.

From New England to Old England

The Anglo-American Life of Mary Endicott Chamberlain Carnegie, 1864–1957

DANA COOPER

BETWEEN 1865 AND 1945, a number of prominent marriages united American heiresses with members of the British political and social elite. Some of the more notable Anglo-American marriages include those of Jennie Jerome to Lord Randolph Churchill in 1874; Mary Leiter to George Nathaniel Curzon in 1895; Consuelo Vanderbilt to Charles Spencer-Churchill, 9th Duke of Marlborough, also in 1895; and Nancy Langhorne Shaw to Waldorf Astor in 1906. Thus, when a young and beautiful American woman married a leading British statesman in 1888, it seemed that she had simply joined the ranks of the so-called "dollar princesses." But to dismiss the marriage of Mary Endicott to Joseph Chamberlain as just another transatlantic union so common during this period would be to reject a significant opportunity to examine the crossroads of cultural, diplomatic, transatlantic, and women's history.[1]

As the wife of Joseph Chamberlain, an outspoken Anglo-American advocate, Mary assumed a high-profile position in England. Following her marriage to Chamberlain in 1888, she accompanied him to a public meeting in his hometown of Birmingham, where the crowd welcomed her with shouts of "Three cheers for our American cousin!"[2] Although she was met warmly on this occasion, Mary soon discovered that her American identity proved to be both an asset and a liability in her interactions with members of leading po-

DANA COOPER is assistant professor of history at Stephen F. Austin State University where she teaches diplomatic and women's history. She would like to express a special thanks to the Massachusetts Historical Society for a Ruth R. and Alyson R. Miller Fellowship, which provided the time and material that made this article possible.

litical and social circles in England, a realization that many Anglo-American brides came to through their public and private lives in England. Endicott's marriage, however, differed slightly from other Anglo-American marriages as her husband was neither a member of the British aristocracy nor a member of the Conservative Party.[3]

As the wife of the British colonial secretary and the stepmother of Prime Minister Neville Chamberlain and Foreign Secretary Austen Chamberlain, Endicott exerted her own style of authority regarding Anglo-American diplomacy and influenced British perceptions of Americans until her death in London in 1957. Through an extensive transatlantic correspondence that spanned decades, as well as an ever-expanding circle of familial relations that stretched across the Atlantic, Mary succeeded in creating an Anglo-American network on both a personal and a professional level. Furthermore, she established a role for herself as a quiet and informal ambassador by facilitating cordial relations among leaders from both of her beloved countries at critical times in the history of their diplomatic relations.[4] Compared with other high-profile transatlantic brides of this period, Mary has received very little attention from scholars; only one biography, published in 1965, has chronicled her life. Considering the recent resurgence of interest in and a growing corpus of work concerning transatlantic history, an examination of Mary's Anglo-American life seems quite timely.

The Endicott family traced its roots back to the colonial period, an auspicious genealogy that served Mary particularly well following her marriage and permanent relocation to England. Her father, William Crowninshield Endicott, Sr. (1826–1900), descended from John Endecott (1588–1665), a soldier, surgeon, and company agent for the Massachusetts Bay Company, which brought him to the colony in 1629. The family founder held a variety of positions in the settlement—colonial assistant, deputy governor, governor, chief military official—until his death in 1665. Mary's father graduated from Harvard College in 1847, continued his legal studies at the same institution, and joined the Massachusetts Bar Association in 1850.[5] In 1859, he married his cousin Ellen Peabody (1833–1927), daughter of renowned philanthropist George Peabody (1803–1892); thus, Mary came from "Puritan stock that . . . [*could not*] be excelled."[6] Mary's parents hailed from two of the oldest and wealthiest families in Salem, Massachusetts, and they enjoyed great political and social successes both individually and as a couple. They began their own family in 1860 with a son, William Crowninshield Endicott, Jr.; Mary Crowninshield, so named for her paternal grandmother, was born in 1864.

Mary's early years shaped her political, social, and religious perspectives in a distinctly affluent New England manner. Her family's desire to abide by tradition and religious customs, significantly dictated by Salem's collective wish to remain somewhat aloof from contemporary developments, took root in Mary at an early age. Her parents and grandparents imprinted upon her what it meant to be "a lady."[7] They saw to it that she attended a select girls' school in the area, though she never excelled in the classroom. She spent much happier days during the summers with various family members at the farm in New Hampshire or at ancestral property in Nahant. Though somewhat unusual for American women of this period, she enjoyed a great deal of exposure to the discussion of current events. Conversations at the Endicott dinner table easily shifted from local affairs to the Franco-Prussian War, which prepared Mary to contribute to later discussions with political leaders on both sides of the Atlantic.[8]

Determined to impress upon their daughter the value of her English ancestry, Mary's family promoted a strong Anglo-American awareness early on. In 1876, Mary received a scrapbook that her mother had started for her some years before. Instead of photographs, the scrapbook contained a variety of poems, prayers, song lyrics, Bible verses, and newspaper articles from the United States and England. Some of the selected materials, initially chosen by her mother and to which Mary eventually added, included "The Star-Spangled Banner"; selections from *A Child's History of England*; several poems by Alfred, Lord Tennyson; "The Battle-Hymn of the Republic"; and an article promoting "Boston's Centennial" preceded by a prayer poem entitled "The Marriage at Windsor Chapel." Words from a sermon given at Westminster and a memorial poem concerning the death of Benjamin Disraeli were carefully arranged next to "God Save the President," printed by *Harper's Weekly*. From an 1880 sermon given by Dr. Phillips Brooks, the rector of Trinity Church in Boston, in Westminster Abbey, Mary learned that a Christian definition of Anglo-Americanism defied the expanse of the ocean that separated the two countries. Numerous articles and poems from the United States and England concerning the death of Pres. James Garfield in 1881 also appeared in the scrapbook. The magazine *Punch* published a poem titled "England to America," which included the line "Columbia's sorrow; 'tis our own."[9] Given to Mary at the tender age of twelve, the scrapbook clearly reveals that Mary was raised by a religious mother who was also an American patriot. Before Mary reached her teenage years, the Endicott family imparted to their young daughter a serious degree of religious devotion, American nationalism, and Anglo-Saxon consciousness.

In addition to the informal education that shaped Mary's identity, discussions at home concerning current events in Massachusetts and beyond also influenced her development. Though her brother attended Harvard College between 1879 and 1883, Mary had not yet made her debut on the Boston social stage and thus could not enjoy the expanding circle of eligible bachelors made possible through William, Jr.'s contacts.[10] Instead, she spent most evenings reading in her father's vast library and listening to the passionate legal and political debates in which his colleagues engaged. Such activities served Mary well in later years when she proved herself a "delightful and informed companion" on both sides of the Atlantic.[11] Such exposure to fervent political discussions was due largely to her father's frequent and mostly unsuccessful campaigns at the state and national levels. He eventually became a judge on the Massachusetts Supreme Judicial Court, where he served from 1873 until 1882, but his dedication to the bench took a toll on his health. Upon the advice of his doctors, and further pressing from his wife, Mr. Endicott agreed to embark on a tour of Europe, a common prescription for the affluent and overworked professional of this period.

Her parents decided that Mary would accompany them on this extended journey, and she was, at first, devastated by this news. Their desire to guard their daughter's place in society, and the unfortunate timing of her father's retirement, meant that she would not enjoy her formal entrance into Boston society with her friends. Instead, she spent her time as her parents' "courier"—an official coordinator and errand runner. She was visibly unhappy upon their departure from New York, and her uncle teasingly encouraged her to "Keep a stiff upper lip, Miserable!"[12]

Initially dismayed to "miss all the parties, pretty dresses, and new excursions to Boston and Cambridge," Mary nonetheless found the world beyond the shores of Massachusetts distracting and consuming.[13] Following a ten-day journey aboard the R.M.S. *Republic*, the Endicotts stopped over in Liverpool for a mere six hours before moving on to London, where they remained for most of June. They visited Piccadilly, Hyde Park, Buckingham Palace, the Houses of Parliament, and other city sights. Overwhelmed by the experience, Mary wrote in her diary that she "could hardly believe my eyes that I was really seeing the places I had always heard & read of. As to talking that was impossible. I had all *I could* to look with my eyes [*which*] felt twice their size."[14] Other visits throughout England and Europe all paled in comparison to London. Ventures to Berlin, Paris, Monte Carlo, Milan, and San Remo failed to impress Mary as much as London had. Even a brief stint in Manchester, which Mary referred to as "such a dingy place," did not compare to subsequent weeks in London.[15] Upon returning to London in the spring of 1883, she wrote that "our long journey has gone off well & here we are comfortably established in our old quarters. . . . It seemed quite like a home coming."[16] Her Anglo-American heart had found its home in London.

Twelve months into their European vacation, Mary recorded in her diary, "A year ago to-day we left our native land. How little we then thought so long a time would pass before our return!"[17] The Endicotts enjoyed another summer abroad, spending most of their remaining time in London. After they attended the opera there, Mary recorded her enjoyment of the evening and "wondered if I shall ever hear it again in Covent Garden."[18] As the family prepared to return home in the fall, Mary took a last walk through Piccadilly and sorrowfully mused, "This is the last night I shall pass in this beloved London, and for how long? That is the question."[19] They returned to Nahant, Massachusetts, in September 1883 in the same vessel that had brought them across the Atlantic more than a year before. Though happy to see Salem again, she expressed great sadness at leaving Europe and London in particular. Unbeknownst to her, this would not be the last time she saw the sights of this city she had grown to love.

Following their extensive tour of Europe, the Endicotts returned to business as usual. Mary resumed the activities expected of a young lady of her class and upbringing, which included French lessons, dancing lessons, and taking tea at Delmonico's. Meanwhile, her father returned to his public and political life in Massachusetts, including an unsuccessful run for governor in 1884. Nevertheless, the following year he was appointed secretary of war in Pres. Grover Cleveland's first cabinet, a position "Judge" Endicott held until 1889. His acceptance of the offer had consequences for the entire family. Mrs. Endicott made arrangements to set up house in Washington, D.C., and for the social migration from Massachusetts to the nation's capital. This was no small feat for the wife of a new cabinet official who also had to navigate her daughter's reception by Washington society, given the fact that the young lady's coming out would now take place there. After an initial trip to Washington, the family leased a Gothic mansion near another cabinet official, Secretary of the Navy William C. Whitney.[20] Together, Mary and her mother adjusted to the demands of Washington and were received well by the city's elite. Upon her first formal appearance at a presidential reception, the press reported that "Miss Endicott . . . was quite the belle of the Blue Parlor. . . . [M]en of distinction seek her side and are fascinated by her conversations."[21]

Though the Washington press frequently commented on her beauty and charms, Mary possessed an intellectual strength that she reserved for her most intimate circle. While the rest of the family attended Cleveland's inauguration, she chose to stay "behind and [*have*] time to think over what it meant to have Papa the Secretary of War."[22] She recognized that the initial excitement of the appointment was most exhilarating and that she "did not know whether I was on my head or on my heels."[23] But even for someone who spent the majority of her time "being brushed, combed, unhooked, and laced in and out of one tiny-waisted dress after another," Mary candidly acknowledged "an occasional sigh at [*this*] being the last of the old life."[24] She clearly recognized that her father's new political position signified the end of one life, but she realized that it marked the beginning of a new life as well.

In the fall of 1887, one year into Endicott's tenure as secretary of war, a British-American Fisheries Conference began its proceedings in Washington. The conference arose from larger, long-standing tensions between the United States and Newfoundland that threatened to wreck the already unstable relationship between the United States and Great Britain. The hope on both sides of the Atlantic was that the conference would strengthen Anglo-American relations. Invited by prime minister Lord Salisbury to serve as the head of the British delegation to the conference, Joseph Chamberlain came to the United States as chief plenipotentiary, but that choice struck many observers as an odd one. Then a member of Parliament for more than a decade, Chamberlain had a reputation for an array of conflicting personality traits, as implied by his many nicknames—Good Old Joe, Brummagem Lion, Pushful Joe, Orchid Joe, Old Man Eloquent.[25] Originally a strong proponent of Radicalism within the Liberal Party, Chamberlain ended up splitting his own party in the mid 1880s when he came out against the Irish Home Rule Bill, after which he returned to Parliament as a Liberal Unionist—the ad hoc entity that combined Radicalism with a traditionally conservative rejection of Irish nationalism. According to many fellow politicians and constituents, Chamberlain had betrayed Irish nationalism and wrecked the hopes of the Liberals with a single vote. It was at this moment in time that Lord Salisbury, recognizing Chamberlain's talent for business and his own desire for an alliance between the Liberal Unionists and the Conservative Party, sent Chamberlain overseas.[26]

The British delegation arrived in New York on November 7, and the Canadians followed ten days later. Chamberlain first met Secretary Endicott on November 20, at a dinner that preceded the first official meeting the next day. A reception was held at the British Legation a week later. Although the Endicotts had traveled home to Salem for Thanksgiving, Mary's brother returned to Washington to accompany her to the party where she met her future husband for the first time. Clearly, the new acquaintances shared something special; as one witness observed, "he froze to her an hour ago, and hasn't left her yet."[27] Shortly after this initial meeting, the Endicotts made Chamberlain the guest of honor at a dinner in their home. Following this event, Chamberlain wrote that the secretary of war was "of the bluest New England blood. . . . Mrs. Endicott is a very pleasant woman and their daughter one of the brightest and most intelligent girls I have yet met."[28] The Fisheries Conference ended its winter session on December 10, and Chamberlain organized a dinner that took place that night. He sent a basket of roses and a poem to Mary three days later—a day she described as "glorious"—and sent her a book on Christmas day.[29] To make his intentions entirely clear, he called on Mary at her home several days later.

When Chamberlain left for New York after the holidays, he spoke to the press about his reactions to the United States in general rather than saying anything specific about the Fisheries Conference. He declared that he had "been made to feel at home, quite as much so as in England. I brought with me strong feelings of sympathy and goodwill for the American people. They have been made stronger by personal acquaintance with them. But what has struck me most . . . is the resemblance between us and the Americans. I don't feel like a stranger here; I feel at home."[30]

Given Chamberlain's personal history, his pursuit of Mary may seem questionable. At fifty-one, he was twenty-eight years older than Mary, an age gap greater even than that between President Cleveland and his young bride, Francis Folsom. Chamberlain had already lost two wives to the hazards of childbirth.[31] After a failed courtship of children's author Beatrix Potter, it would not have surprised observers if Chamberlain had given up on finding love at this relatively late period in his life. Many of his children were grown, so he did not need a wife to raise his family.[32] His eldest daughter, Beatrice, now in her mid twenties, managed his house and numerous servants, which allowed Chamberlain to focus on his political career. It seemed that Chamberlain's relentless pursuit of Mary was, indeed, motivated by love and admiration for this remarkable woman who was regarded as both an American belle and an English beauty.[33]

Chamberlain increased the rate of his letters to and calls upon Mary and accepted all invitations that Washington presented in order to see more of her. Chamberlain's visible anxiety and melancholy since the death of his second wife apparently lifted during his weeks in the United States. Having refused to dance since Florence's death, he amended this decision in order to be closer to Mary.[34] Unfamiliar with the American custom of "cutting in," he was infuriated when a competitive suitor stole Mary away; thus, in the future, he

Joseph Chamberlain
Photograph by Gilliams Press Syndicate, 1907. Digital ID: cph 3b43817. Reproduction number: LC-USZ62–97724 DLC. Courtesy of the Library of Congress Prints and Photographs Division.

made it a practice to ask for "another turn" whenever he saw another man approach her.[35] He candidly wrote to Mary that he "knew that you were the only girl for me."[36] At a dinner, he held Mary's plate while she ate from it, declaring that neither his "dignity nor anything else [*would*] stand in the way of my determined purpose to make the Puritan maiden my wife if that were humanly possible."[37]

The twenty-three-year-old Mary responded kindly but coolly to Chamberlain's advances at first. At this point in history, Mary's age hardly helped her marital prospects, but she was determined to marry well *and* determined to marry someone in public life. Shortly before Chamberlain's arrival in the United States, as she later admitted, she had come "to the conclusion that my chances were against rather than for my marrying."[38] She did not reveal these sentiments immediately to Chamberlain but rather charmed him with her reserved hospitality and intelligent conversation. For her suitor, Mary was neither "superior" nor "silly." In his mind, Chamberlain had "lighted on the exact medium . . . [*of*] perfection" in Mary.[39] Even a month before their engagement, she nonchalantly described Chamberlain as a friend. Yet she wrote to a friend that she felt "like a safety match warranted not to go off—till struck on the right box. . . . I am in a very cool frame of mind."[40]

When diplomatic talks resumed, Chamberlain intensified his concentration on domestic pursuits. At the same time that he focused on the Fisheries Conference, his attention to Mary demonstrated that "the negotiation of a treaty of love was a matter of a good deal more importance and interest than the discussion of dry details relating to bait and seines."[41] On February 11, he wrote to Mary that "the time has come . . . when . . . I . . . pray you to end all uncertainty. . . . My work here is rapidly drawing to a close & my public duty will constrain me to return to England." He also offered his love and promised to assure her happiness as his wife. Finally, he wrote, "Now therefore decide. If you are not afraid & will trust me with your happiness, believe me, I will know how to guard it against the world."[42]

Mary had decided to accept Chamberlain and received his formal proposal at breakfast the next morning. But she kept her "great man" waiting until their meeting later that day when she finally informed him that "my Conqueror has won the victory."[43] Her acceptance of his proposal gave him incredible happiness, as he attested in a note describing how he suddenly found "all women were beautiful—all the men were witty—and I was in the seventh heaven because I had all the while a vision of a little bit of old English looking through a doorway with her lips parted in pleasant expectation."[44]

Her family reacted to the news of Mary's engagement with anything but pleasure. Her brother balked at the idea of his sister marrying someone with a working-class background despite his present position in British politics. Concerned with the political ramifications of the engagement, Mary's father worried about the risks that the pairing would pose, and he feared that his daughter could be lost amid Chamberlain's vast ambitions.[45] Mary's mother, while sympathetic to her daughter's emotions, was hardly pleased at the notion of her child establishing her home across the Atlantic. In an effort to challenge or perhaps discourage the match, the Endicotts delayed announcing the engagement. Their justifications were twofold. First, they argued, a potential union between the secretary of war's daughter and the chief British commissioner could endanger the outcome of the months of work regarding the fisheries. Furthermore, and infinitely more critical to Secretary Endicott's cabinet position, such an announcement might jeopardize Cleveland's re-election campaign later that year, since an Anglo-American union would likely cost him the Irish-American vote. Thus, at the insistence of Mary's family, the engagement was kept secret for nine months.[46] Chamberlain saw very little of Mary until their wedding. At her parents' urging, the two rarely corresponded until after the 1888 presidential election.[47]

While transatlantic marriages were hardly uncommon during this period,

Mary's nuptials with Chamberlain set something of a precedent. Typically, the American brides hailed from rich and aspiring families while the English husbands were poor but noble. In this case, however, the American Endicotts were the old and established family, and Chamberlain was the nouveau riche upstart who had risen from a modest background in manufacturing-based Manchester to make a name for himself in British politics. The Endicotts vehemently protected their public name and private life and worried that their daughter would find the abrupt transition from Boston to Birmingham more than she could handle. But her father's reluctance may have had more to do with his personal feelings than any practical or political concerns he expressed. During a visit to his daughter in England, he candidly told a journalist that "nobody knows a thing about these marriages except the parents. It's the fathers that have to suffer! Yet, after all, our daughters leave us. . . . They [*say*] good-bye . . . for life. . . . [*We*] never expected to see them again this side of the grave."[48]

Nevertheless, the announcement was set for the fall of 1888, after the election. Before that milestone could come, all parties involved had important work to address. The Fisheries Conference settled on a treaty in mid February, shortly after Mary and Joseph agreed privately on their engagement, and the requisite dinners and talk of Anglo-American amity followed. The success of the treaty allowed Chamberlain to return home with new political verve. Defying Mary's father's wishes, he wrote to her that—with his "feet on my native heath"—he felt revived, "the fighting spirit . . . coming out."[49] This refreshed spirit was due to more than just the treaty. In a letter to Mary later that summer, he recalled his disposition a year before as "much harder . . . striving to steel myself & to play the game of life till . . . the cards [*fall*] from my hands, & caring little how soon that time comes." But with Mary as his fiancée, he felt all the "artificial insensibility is broken down. My youth has come back to me & I am as eager & as sensitive as ever I was."[50]

Though he pledged to keep their engagement secret and severely restrict any communication with Mary, Chamberlain gave his fellow Englishmen frequent indications of his new enthusiasm for closer Anglo-American relations. Upon his return to England, he gave a speech to the Devonshire Club in which he discussed relations with the United States and the colonies. He spoke to and for his countrymen when he declared that "every good Englishman who is worthy of the name sympathises with the objects of my recent mission . . . [*and desires to*] remove all causes of difference between the United States and ourselves." He attempted to assuage his colleagues' fears concerning "the introduction of American institutions into this country," which, given the increasing number of Anglo-American marriages, was a carefully crafted sentence with multiple meanings. He went on to affirm England's "appreciation of American institutions, and of the American people, which, perhaps, did not exist a generation ago." He further discussed the "universal feeling of goodwill and admiration . . . and a cordial desire for a hearty and for a durable friendship" with the United States. Focusing on the relationship with Americans, Chamberlain highlighted the "common blood, and common origin, and common traditions of the Anglo-Saxon race." He candidly announced his identity as a "sentimentalist" who would "never willingly admit . . . any policy that [*would*] weaken the ties between the different branches of the Anglo-Saxon race." He concluded his speech by emphasizing the mutual affection between England and her "fellow-kinsmen who are proud of the glorious tradition of our country, who share with us our history, our origin."[51]

Chamberlain's desire to remain in politics was well known, and such words hinted at his ambition to become colonial secretary. For the reader who knows that he was at this moment secretly engaged to an American woman, his rhetoric takes on another meaning. In his political life, Chamberlain boasted publicly of his success regarding the fisheries treaty, but he also used his political language to prepare his colleagues and constituents for the eventual announcement of his marriage to a woman from across the Atlantic. Such an aggressive and open push for a renewal of harmonious observance of a shared Anglo-Saxon identity cannot be separated from his private decision to enter into a transatlantic marriage. As Chamberlain remarked, some twenty-five years later, upon the celebration of his and Mary's wedding anniversary, "I have done all that is in my power to promote a union between this country and America."[52]

The remaining months until the presidential election passed slowly for Chamberlain and Mary. Rumors of "a real treaty" swelled on both sides of the Atlantic, speculating that "Mr. Chamberlain had concluded a separate and private treaty—one which, happily, requires no ratification by a political body—a treaty of marriage." As the *Boston Daily Globe* surmised, "While the treaty was rejected, the suitor was accepted."[53] The engagement was announced in the United States the day after the November election and Cleveland's defeat. Having endured a long separation from her future husband, Mary soon would be permanently separated from her family and entire way of life. Chamberlain traveled to the United States to claim his bride, and the frequently referred to "treaty [*was*] concluded" when the "charming bride [*and*] happy groom" were married on November 15, 1888, at St. John's Episcopal Church in the capital.[54] The president, the Supreme Court justices, and members of the cabinet attended the wedding for the "fair Puritan and English commoner," as the American press continued to refer to Chamberlain. Cleveland offered a toast at the reception. Despite their initial reluctance at the union, Mary's family eventually accepted Chamberlain into the fold largely based on Mary's apparent happiness.

Despite her impressively family-centric upbringing, Mary was entirely unprepared to become a mother. But her stepchildren quickly put her anxieties to rest. The first letter to arrive was from twenty-five-year-old Austen, Chamberlain's eldest son. Dispensing with any opening pleasantries, Austen joyfully greeted his new American stepmother by exclaiming, "You will be to him all that we could not be and make him far happier than we have been able to do." Chamberlain had shown Austen a picture of his soon-to-be bride, and Austen wrote that "I began to feel as if we knew each other. I hope it won't be long before we have you here. . . . [T]his letter won't tell you how glad I am for I can't write what I feel."[55] A letter from Beatrice, Austen's older sister, followed soon after with an even greater message of delight at Mary's imminent arrival. Beatrice began her missive by wishing "many times . . . that there was no Atlantic between us. . . . I find it very difficult to express on paper the warm welcome that I am longing to give you." Noting that some women would regard Chamberlain's children as "a heavy drawback," Beatrice beseeched Mary to "soon think of your family on this side of the water as belonging no less nearly to you than your family on that."[56] Letters from the other children followed in short order. Neville, then not quite twenty years old and Chamberlain's oldest son from his second marriage, wrote that he "look[*ed*] forward to this great change not only for father's sake but also for our own. With such good feelings on both sides beforehand how can we help being friends?"[57] With such a warm reception by so many eager family members, Mary had every reason to look forward to her marriage and relocation to England. Though Mary "never forgot the land of her birth," she "thoroughly identified herself with the land of her adoption."[58]

As Mary prepared to embark upon her new life, she received countless cards and letters of congratulation and encouragement before leaving for her honeymoon and new home in England. One letter from a cousin wished her "much love and many good wishes for the future. Your health and happiness. I shall be ready with a joyful greeting when you come to town." This cousin went on to express the caution, however, that many of Mary's friends and family likely harbored based on her transatlantic marriage: "Being an American . . . so long living here . . . my thoughts recount to New England as my home and country. But Englishmen will welcome you in their land and be proud of you. Believe me."[59]

When "the little Puritan maid" and "flower of American aristocracy" landed in England, she and her new husband were met with the melodies of "Hail, Columbia" and "Yankee Doodle."[60] Chamberlain's constituents in Birmingham showered Mary with jewelry, including pearls, diamonds, and brooches made in the city. Her husband, for his part, had a rose-house built as a wedding present. Upon her arrival as the new mistress of Highbury, the Chamberlain estate, she found three roses in bloom, which pleased her greatly. Her proud brother, who never fully accepted Mary's life in England, inquired often as to "how the roses have turned out. I hope well, for I should like to have you show those Britishers how much finer our roses are than theirs."[61] Even in matters of flora, William never lost his fiercely competitive Anglo-American streak.

Such competitiveness existed on the English side as well. During her formal presentation to the people of Birmingham, unprompted cries from the crowd boasted that "[*our*] Joe can make love even more successfully than he makes laws!" which was followed by the proud claim that "Our Joey's a match for any Yankee!" When Chamberlain addressed the people, he described his wife's transatlantic journey to her new home in biblical terms. He declared that his "little maid from Massachusetts" was fully "prepared to take up her life amongst us, in the country to which she has come, in all its fullness and that she will say, with Ruth of old, 'Thy people shall be my people,'" which was met with thunderous applause. He concluded his speech by mentioning that he was most thankful that the "American Senate had nothing to say about his private negotiations, which his hearers had just ratified by their presence." Her introduction to Birmingham was a success according to the spectators who considered Mary their "American cousin."[62]

Mary's formal presentation to Queen Victoria and British political leaders in 1889 followed shortly after her introduction to Birmingham. Both Queen Victoria and Lord Salisbury found immediate favor with Mary. As dinner invitations continued to arrive by the dozens, Mary handled an overwhelming social schedule with ease. She even managed to win over Lady Dorothy Nevill, who controlled a celebrated social circle in London. Nevill had previously remarked to Chamberlain that she could stand neither America's girls nor its tinned lobster, which did not bode well for Mary.[63] Once again, Mary found a way to charm even the most reluctant of Britons, a skill that continued to amaze her husband. Reflecting on Mary's remarkable abilities, Chamberlain wrote to her mother that his wife was a "charmeuse, as I discovered more than a year ago, and she continues without effort to please all who come near her."[64] Her maternal grandmother also remarked on this trait, reminding Mary that she had "always had a good deal of equanimity and self-possession, and it is evident that you will need it all, to acquit yourself of your part of the duties involved."[65] While most members of British society regarded American girls as ostentatious, Mary's quiet charm and reserved nature provided a distinct contrast to British perception of what America could offer individually and collectively.

Mary spent most of her days running Highbury and responding to the needs of her husband and his children. Soon after her arrival, she began helping the two youngest girls—eighteen-year-old Hilda and sixteen-year-old Ethel—make their way into English society. The majority of her time, however, focused on Chamberlain's political schedule. She almost always traveled with him, though she never spoke publicly. She sat nearby as he crafted speeches, and she offered her support when asked. When her schedule allowed, she attended Parliament and sat in the Ladies' Gallery with the other "ultra-political" ladies, so named by her new friend Lady Randolph Churchill, also American-born and English-wed.[66] The political knowledge that she gained during her childhood and early adult years as the daughter of a man who was a lawyer, a judge, and a cabinet member undoubtedly enabled her to follow the political discussions and debates of the day. As it became more and more popular for political wives, and especially the American wives, to attend parliamentary proceedings, Mary's time and visibility there increased as well.

News of her popularity in England traveled quickly across the Atlantic. Mary received a letter from a family friend who boasted that his "Boston heart swells with pride at the thought of your great success among the Britishers, which, of course, I anticipated from the first."[67] Mary's letters home confirmed her ease in her new homeland. Chamberlain confirmed Mary's acceptance by his fellow Britons in letters to her family as well. Intent on easing any remaining concerns Mary's parents may have had, Chamberlain assured her mother that "your daughter is already as completely one of this family as she is of the other across the water."[68]

Mary dedicated a great deal of her time to her two families throughout her life in England, and she retained close relations with all of Chamberlain's children, especially Austen, as the two were so close in age. He expressed his fondness for Mary to her mother in more than one letter after meeting her family during a three-month visit to the United States in 1890. Upon his return home, he wrote Mrs. Endicott to thank her for "all your kindness during my long visit. I cannot tell you how much I enjoyed it, nor what a pleasure it was to be with Mary in her old home and learn to know all her family." Most appreciative for Mary's presence in their lives, Austen continued: "She plays such a big part in our lives now, interesting herself so much in all we do and helping us so much in everything."[69] Writing to Mrs. Endicott many years later, Austen reiterated the great "happiness she has brought to us all and . . . sympathy and kindness in all that concerns us." He also recalled that he had reacted to the news of his father's engagement as "the best news [*he*] could have brought home . . . and the best of good news it has certainly proved to be."[70]

In addition to her deep commitment to family, Mary cultivated an influential circle of Anglo-Americans in England. Her visiting lists from the 1890s include the names of elites from both sides of the Atlantic—Mr. and Mrs. Whitelaw Reid, the American ambassador to Great Britain; Sen. and Mrs. Henry Cabot Lodge, the American statesman; Mr. and Mrs. William Kissam Vanderbilt, the parents of Consuelo Vanderbilt, who wed the 9th Duke of Manchester; Mr. John Hay, the American secretary of state; Lord and Lady Randolph Churchill; and Mr. and Mrs. Joseph Choate, another American ambassador to Great Britain.[71] Unfortunately, no records of the conversations that took place at these dinners exist, but Mary clearly became an informal ambassador herself by maintaining a demanding political and social schedule that rivaled that of any formal emissary of the period.

Mary's Anglo-American identity and her connections as a "drawing-room diplomat" proved most helpful less than a decade after her marriage, in the mid 1890s, when diplomatic relations between the United States and Britain began to deteriorate due to conflict over Venezuelan borders.[72] The problem took root at the beginning of the century, when Britain acquired Guiana from the Netherlands. By the 1840s, neighboring Venezuela began to express concern over British encroachment on its territory, and by 1876, Venezuela officially broke off diplomatic relations with Great Britain and called on the United States for arbitration, suggesting that the Monroe Doctrine gave the United States some authority in the matter. Although American and English representatives bickered about the boundary for a few decades, the American government did not take a strong interest until 1895, when President Cleveland demanded that Great Britain submit to arbitration in the border dispute.[73] Invoking the Monroe Doctrine, Cleveland threatened to go to war with Great Britain over the issue. In a special message to Congress in December 1895, Cleveland argued that the doctrine was "essential to the integrity of our free institutions and . . . maintenance of our distinctive form of government." With a warning tone, he also maintained that, should Britain contravene boundaries set by arbitration, the United States would regard such action "as a willful aggression upon its rights and interests."[74]

Infuriated by Cleveland's declarations, Mary fired off a letter to her mother demanding to know "what has come over the President? It seems to me almost inconceivable that he should have been in his right mind when he sent that message to Congress."[75] From her perspective, the Venezuela boundary dispute did not fall under the purview of the Monroe Doctrine and certainly did not apply to an area that the English had controlled for years. She felt that the acquisition of new territory was out of the question and voiced the ultimate fear so many observers felt on both sides of the Atlantic: "Think of how terrible it would be for America and England to go to war over a boundary line in Venezuela! And yet how can England be dictated to[?] . . . [T]he position has been made almost intolerable for her. . . . I feel that if [*my two countries*] were to come into conflict it would be a crime against the civilized world."[76]

Justifiably astounded, the British government marveled at why the American government suddenly found this decades-old dispute between England and Venezuela so monumental.[77] The apparently sudden emergence of an aggressive American stand in this quarrel may have been fueled by the depression of 1893, which had weakened the American economy so significantly that many political and business leaders took a new and intense interest in Latin America as an area that could buoy the domestic economy.[78] Relations between the United States and Great Britain became so tense that American-born, British-wed women in London found themselves in an uncomfortable situation. Fearful of what the coming months might bring, many Americans withdrew to continental Europe or returned to the United States for an indefinite period. As the wife of the new colonial secretary, Mary did not have the luxury of retreating to the United States, nor would she have entertained such a thought due to her devotion to her husband's career and family.

In the midst of this crisis, Lord Salisbury, the prime minister who had originally sent Chamberlain to the United States in 1887, again dispatched Chamberlain to Washington to settle the dispute. The fact that Chamberlain's wife was an American enhanced his ability to know, understand, and work with the Americans to find an acceptable compromise. Chamberlain had already met Secretary of State Richard Olney, a Bostonian, while visiting Mary's family two years earlier, and of course Mary's personal connection with President Cleveland could be helpful too. In such a diplomatic situation, the personal and political cannot be divided.

During this time, Mary and fellow Anglo-American bride Lady Jennie Churchill utilized their central position in London's political and social circles, hosting quiet but frequent dinner parties for the most socially influential persons in London. In 1895 alone, the Chamberlains dined with Secretary and Mrs. Olney more than half a dozen times, while Mary lunched with Mrs. Olney on several occasions.[79] After observing the ongoing efforts in England, one U.S. general reported to the American press on

> true daughters of the United States, who are working quietly and mightily to prevent war between the two countries that are looking at each other in a sinister way. For these women, the war means a thousand times as much as it does to other Americans; and they have untold power of international arbitration. . . . These particular ten are so situated that they are in the midst of the greatest powers that rule England today. Their influence, thrown upon the scales, would turn it whichever way they bent themselves.[80]

Their labors did not go unrewarded. For the first time, Mary recognized the undeniable influence of her Anglo-American marriage. Chamberlain attributed the final settlement to his personal discussions with Olney, but Mary's gentle prodding for an Anglo-American accord arguably influenced her husband to some degree.[81] Her efforts had an undeniable and significant calming effect on the situation, which both countries noticed. Partially due to Mary's efforts, as well as the work of the nine other daughters of America, the United States and Great Britain avoided war over Venezuela.[82]

As soon as one crisis was resolved, another took its place. With the advent of the Spanish-American War in 1898, Mary carefully monitored the perspectives of both her countries. Horrified at the fact that American men were fighting in Cuba, Mary's American family assured her that "we never dreamed another war would come, and everyone is outraged at it. The people do not want it. It is Congress that has *insisted* on it!"[83] Although Spain requested support from England, a letter to the United States from the colonial secretary stated that no such help would be forthcoming. Using a speech that he gave in Birmingham on May 13 as an opportunity to promote his now well-rehearsed theme of Anglo-American cooperation, Chamberlain announced that as "terrible as war may be, even war itself would be cheaply purchased if in a great and noble cause the Stars and Stripes and the Union Jack should wave together over an Anglo-Saxon alliance."[84]

The American press wasted no time in attributing Chamberlain's words to the influence of his American wife: "A woman is the power that has stirred [*Chamberlain*] to come out so boldly. It is a little Boston girl . . . who has succeeded in upheaving all the power of Europe." Declaring her the "most talked about woman in England today," the *Boston Herald* article credited Chamberlain's political success to "the Puritan girl." Specific to Britain's position regarding the Spanish-American War, the piece argued that "her husband would do what she wanted. She went to him. A word from him would swing millions. English money, English commerce, English interests of all kinds were with the United States."[85]

As Chamberlain's "admirable helpmate," Mary's success in all things domestic and diplomatic did not go unnoticed in England.[86] Mary's capital with Queen Victoria continued to increase as the monarch attributed Mary's "savoir faire and self possession" to her experience "as one of the cabinet ladies at Washington during her father's term" as secretary of state, which "has had the effect of considerably altering the ideas of Her Majesty with regard to the etiquette and social ethics that prevail at the White House."[87] So impressed was Queen Victoria with Mary that she presented her with the diamond jubilee medal in 1895, a recognition generally reserved for reigning house members and foreign service families. As "a particular favorite" of Queen Victoria, Mary was one of the very few "non-royal" individuals to receive a gold rather than a silver medal.[88]

Consequently, Mary's fellow Americans felt "a certain degree of pride in the fact that a Salem woman stands so high in court circles."[89] But it was Queen Victoria's son, King Edward VII, who bestowed upon Mary the title of Viscountess of Highbury in 1904, which made her a member of the British peerage.[90] Chamberlain had refused any equivalent title for himself, but he noted her command of British political life and her worthiness of such an honor.[91] Chamberlain fully acknowledged that "Her kindness, sympathy and interest made friends where I might have failed."[92] Recognizing that Mary was unlike many other Anglo-American wives, the press relished the fact that she became a peeress in her own right, unlike the "scores of 'princesses,' 'duchesses,' 'countesses,' and 'marquises.' . . . [T]hese American girls wear their title only by the courtesy of heraldry. They gain them because they were the rich daughters of rich fathers."[93] Mary, on the other hand, was described as "no social upstart" and the "real power behind the throne. [*She understands*] the affairs of world-wide importance in which her husband is one of the leading figures [*and has*] an intelligent grasp of the political situation in Europe."[94] Mary's heritage as an "American aristocrat" and her "quiet dignity" immediately challenged the "dollar princesses" stereotype. Instead, according to the American press, her English compatriots saw her not as a "'tuft hunting' American girl" or a "flaunting daughter of the 'noveau riche'" but rather as "a young woman who felt as deep a pride in her ancestry as did the princesses of the blood royal, and who bore herself on all occasions with a modesty, a reserve, and yet a hauteur that made a good many of the English nobility feel a little cheap in her presence."[95]

Mary continued as Chamberlain's unofficial but principal political secretary. As his health declined with advancing age, his family begged him to slow down and temper his devotion to public service. In typical Chamberlain fashion, he responded, "I must either do my utmost or stop altogether and though I know the risks I prefer to take them." In the summer of 1906, he suffered a stroke that left him an invalid until his death eight years later. Always politically astute, Mary withheld the news of the stroke from everyone but her immediate English family, and she canceled all of Chamberlain's commitments by explaining that she was ill.[96] Even Mary's American family did not know of Chamberlain's true condition. A later diagnosis of gout was announced, which provided some time for Chamberlain to make a partial recovery. Instead, Chamberlain's decline was slow and painful. He had resigned from his cabinet post shortly before the stroke and later decided not to stand for re-election in 1914. Six months after that decision, he suffered a heart attack. Mary rarely left his side, and she read all the political news to him in the hope that he would recover. As she was recounting the assassination of Franz Ferdinand, Chamberlain stopped her from finishing the article. Later that day, he suffered a final heart attack. Writing in her diary, Mary simply stated, "At 10.15 my darling died quite peacefully in my arms."[97] Commenting upon Mary's grace and calming influence, Austen reflected that "to have seen her at my father's bedside and since is to have known faith so beautiful and courage so serene, that, once known, they can never be forgotten. I have never imagined any so holy."[98]

Following Chamberlain's memorial service on July 6, Mary felt unusually detached from politics. A smattering of letters flowed across the Atlantic expressing great sadness at Chamberlain's death. Writing to one of Mary's dear friends in Boston, Austen summarized the close relationships forged by his father's Anglo-American marriage more than twenty years before based on "all we have in common of past memories on both sides of the Atlantic, and of present interests and affections. Nothing that affects Mary can be strange or without interests . . . to us." Thankful for what Mary meant to the entire Chamberlain family, he continued, "If it were not for Mary and all that she has brought into my life, I do not think I could go on."[99]

Mary's correspondence during this period focused on the rising tensions in Europe. Mere months after Mary had become a widow, her uncle George Peabody feared that the "whole future of England hangs in the balance."[100] A friend described all Americans and "this country [*living*] in suspense."[101] A cousin asserted that "the loyalty of the colonies, shown in the contributions

William Hartley Carnegie Photograph by Swaine, London, 1923. Photo 53.2, Colonial Society Photograph Collection, MHS.

of ships and money and men, is due in large measure to the inspirations of your husband."[102] The English press seemed to speak to Mary's American family almost specifically when it declared that the "Allies should be more grateful than ever for the clear-sighted sympathy of the American public."[103]

In the midst of war, Mary found love again, albeit in a bit of an odd coincidence, since her new spouse was the man who had conducted her late husband's memorial service. Rev. William Hartley Carnegie and the former Mrs. Chamberlain married on August 3, 1916. Mary had the blessing of her English family and was given away by Austen, who was so pleased with the union that he telegraphed Mary's sister-in law Louise Thoron Endicott with the message that "Mary married in bright sunshine to light her new happiness."[104] Mary's family expanded with the addition of Carnegie's five daughters, which extended her Anglo-American influence all the more.

Mary's new union certainly brought happiness into her life, and she quickly resumed her informal political and social activities. She and her second husband were summoned to Windsor to dine with Prince Edward and Queen Mary, who were most interested in hearing more about the United States and the perspective of its citizens. Mary reported that they desired to know about "the Americans now here, and wanted to be told all I could about them and their point of view." The king confided in Mary that "one of the dreams of his life was accomplished in seeing the [*United States and England*] side by side, fighting the greatest causes in the name of liberty and justice and humanity."[105] Supporting the monarchy's desire for stronger U.S.–U.K. relations and his wife's position as an intermediary of Anglo-American relations, Carnegie maintained that "it is a truism to say that the world's progress depends mainly on the extent to which America and the British Empire cooperate with each other on terms of mutual confidence and cordiality."[106]

As evidence of their wishes for positive Anglo-American relations, Mary hosted numerous teas and dinners following the United States' entry into the war in 1917 for Red Cross nurses, Allied officers, and American students from overseas, as well as many members of Parliament. Her husband's parish, St. Margaret's, was generally considered the "Abbey for Americans" abroad.[107] Reflecting on a particular group of American students who attended one of her teas and then enjoyed a personal tour of the Abbey, Mary suspected that it made them conscious of a "common heritage" and hoped "their first experience of the 'allies' will be a happy omen. . . . [B]ehind it is the call of the blood which differentiates them from all the others."[108] Mary's marriage to Carnegie reinforced both her ties to the United States and her desire for Anglo-American unity.

As the war continued, Mary reflected that "these last weeks have been filled with heartfelt rejoicing that at last the beloved land of my birth is ranged side by side with [*Britain*]." Mary anticipated greatness from this union: "I cannot but feel that to have America & England fighting in a common cause is fraught with great things for the future—better understanding, closer relations must be the outcome—a friendship sealed in blood between blood relations must mean a different attitude each toward the other in the days to come."[109] When the war ended, Mary encouraged her husband to hold regular memorial services at St. Margaret's for American officers and soldiers who were buried in the British Isles.

Mary's second marriage did not last as long as the first. Carnegie died in 1936, the same year as Mary's brother, William, and her beloved Austen died less than six months later. Shaken by the loss of so many in such a short time, Mary turned to her Anglo-American correspondence for comfort. Writing to Louise Endicott in the United States, Mary confided that she had always "been so accustomed all my life to find men [*with*] stimulus and purpose . . . [*men*] who have been so close to me in both countries." In a moment of candor, Mary lamented the "loss of the three who have shared most closely everything, in the three periods of which my life has been made up, so near together in five short months," concluding that she felt "like a ship without a rudder."[110]

Even as Mary mourned her loss, she celebrated Neville's ascension to the prime ministry in 1937. With Mary, and partially due to her influence in his life, Neville shared a desire for closer Anglo-American relations, an alliance critical for Britain on the eve of World War II. In private correspondence, he pledged to "promote Anglo-American understanding and cooperation. Not because I want or expect America to pull our chestnuts out of the fire for us; in any cooperation we shall always do our part and perhaps more than our share." Based on a lifetime of interaction with Mary and her American family and friends, he believed "that Americans and Britain want the same fundamental things in the world—peace, liberty, order, respect for international obligations, freedom for every country." Above all, he deemed that the "U.S.A. and U.K. in combination represent a force so overwhelming that the mere hint of the possibility of it was so sufficient to make the most powerful of dictators pause." In his estimation, Neville considered "cooperation between our two countries . . . the greatest instrument in the world for the preservation of peace and the attainment of those objects of which I spoke just now."[111]

When war broke out once again in Europe, Mary proudly pronounced that "England will give a good account of herself, with the Empire at her back and the co-operation of America in hastening the much-needed supplies." Specific to the war cause, England was most appreciative of the "ambulances, on their mission of mercy, [*as*] proof of the interest and sympathy which comes to our aide in Old England from New England."[112] Relaying information to her family in Boston, she reported that her fellow Britons were "tremendously touched by the great hospitality . . . offered [*by*] friends and relations and from strangers in America."[113] Gratefully, she noted the Americans' sympathies for England evident in the daily papers: "now I think the people of my Native Land are thoroughly roused." Longing for her two countries to fight again side by side, she pressed for the United States to enter the war and reasoned that American involvement "cannot afford to be postponed."[114]

Following the attack on Pearl Harbor and America's entry into the war, Mary seemed almost giddy with excitement: "In one sense the Japanese could not have rendered a greater service had they tried to than their treacherous attack, for it is wonderful how absolutely it consolidated everybody to rally to the defence of the country."[115] As the war progressed, Mary was "more proud than words can say of the part my two countries have been playing."[116] Moved by Anglo-American military cooperation, Mary hosted a Christmas party for American officers and guests in 1942, which was "but one of thousands and thousands . . . which were given throughout England, and I hear the Americans are very much touched by the hospitality which they have received." She noted their generous gifts of "money and goods and sweets and entertainments for British children. . . . Christmas trees, and the warmth of their kindly feeling has been greatly appreciated" by English citizens.[117]

As the war continued, Mary enjoyed observing "American soldiers, R.A.F. in their grey-blue uniforms, sailors of all nationalities of the Allies, overseas troops, and of course a good sprinkling of British troops" at St. Margaret's on Sundays. Most pleased to hear of the British and American "successes in Normandy of the combined forces and the commendation of the fighting qualities which have been so well displayed by the U.S. Army," Mary felt "very proud of my countrymen."[118] She passed along the words of one soldier, a friend's son, who had been on the front lines at D-Day: "he could not say enough of the co-operation and untiring energy of the American troops on his flank . . . [*and*] spoke of their readiness to help." According to this unnamed Englishman, "when one asked [*the Americans*] to do something, they did it, and without delay."[119] Once the war ended, Mary was determined to mark the occasion. Despite continued rationing, food from the United States enabled Mary to host a truly Anglo-American dinner: turkey, cranberry sauce, plum pudding, and mince pies.[120]

Mary celebrated her ninetieth birthday in 1954 in London with her families from both sides of the Atlantic. Encapsulating her Anglo-American life, her cousin George Peabody Gardner posed a somewhat rhetorical question: "How is it that she is able to bind to her with ever strengthening bonds the ever increasing members of her various families?" Considering her Endicott, Chamberlain, and Carnegie kin, maintaining timely correspondence proved a demanding task! Gardner also noted not only her devotion to her three families but also their reciprocal devotion to one another regardless of the ocean between them: "Not only that but by what ledger does she make these families feel such a strong bond with each other?" He postulated that Mary "may have some secret process or weapon but I think it is accomplished by the bounteous love she bestows on all of us and the great love we all feel for her."[121] Such love was a reflection of Mary's dedication to her Anglo-American identity and the transatlantic life she had lived for some seven decades.

Mary Endicott Chamberlain Carnegie died in her sleep on May 17, 1957, at the age of ninety-three. Like her husbands before her, she was memorialized in a service at St. Margaret's. She was buried next to Reverend Carnegie, just feet away from a bust of her first husband. Newspapers on both sides of the Atlantic evoked her several identities as they discussed her passing: Miss Endicott; Mrs. Chamberlain, the widow of Joseph Chamberlain; and the great hostess, Mrs. Carnegie. According to the *New York Times*, "no American woman married to an Englishman succeeded in winning the good-will of Great Britain as Mrs. Chamberlain." As a testament to her life, her portrait was hung in the National Gallery in Washington, D.C., after her death.[122]

Upon her passing, the London *Times* noted that Mary "represented a link, spanning five generations, between London and American circles."[123] Obituaries described Mary as a "remarkable person" who would be "remembered in particular as being one of the great hostesses of her day."[124] But Mary's life was much more than simply that of an American who married well and spent her life giving parties and attending dinners. Her identity as an Anglo-American and her commitment to both of her countries made Mary such a successful drawing-room diplomat. As an informal ambassador for both the United States and Great Britain, Mary was "able to play a special, though she preferred it to be a modest, role in British-American affairs."[125]

Given her elite families, the status of her politically powerful friends, and her uniquely transatlantic life, Mary was asked on more than one occasion when she planned to write her memoirs. Scoffing at the idea, Mary replied that "if I spent all my time looking backwards at the past, I'd have no time for living in the present and future."[126] Although she personally had no interest in reflecting on her life and the role she had created for herself as a true Anglo-American, historians should consider the contributions of these influential women who married into British political and social circles at the turn of the twentieth century. Rather than living a life betwixt and between the United States and Great Britain, Mary and the other American-born, British-wed women like her created new dual identities. In their countless conversations, dinners, teas, and daily interactions with Britons, they created an Anglo-American network that spanned decades. They willingly engaged in the traditional activities expected of international ambassadors—and thus implicitly acted as such. By doing so, they played an important, albeit informal, role in the strengthening relations between the two countries, helping create an environment that would move the United States and Great Britain toward the "special relationship."

Notes

1. While many historians have noted these marriages in passing, they have largely been dismissed as a mere a marital trend that existed over a century ago. Charles S. Campbell and Bradford Perkins, preeminent Anglo-American historians, have debated the significance of these marriages. Campbell described these unions as "the age of trans-Atlantic marriages in high places." According to his calculations, more than 70 American women had married British peers by 1903 and more than 130 by 1914. Based on the number of marriages, Campbell contends that "such trans-

Atlantic unions doubtless had wide influence on policy." He describes these unions as "an extraordinary galaxy of American women married to British governmental leaders. One might almost stop with that in explaining the rise of friendly feelings between America and Britain." Perkins takes a different view of such nuptials. He argues that these were strategic marriages, focused on social and economic union, rather than a fulfillment of the romanticized Anglo-American alliance. He asserts that the "political importance of these marriages was not great, for in very few cases—[*Joseph*] Chamberlain, [*Sir William*] Harcourt, Randolph Churchill, and [*George Nathaniel*] Curzon are the leading exceptions—did the husband gain a leading position. Still, they did foster contact between upper levels of society on both sides of the Atlantic and reaffirm the respect many Americans had for England." Thus a clear debate exists regarding the influence of Anglo-American marriages. See Charles S. Campbell, *Anglo-American Understanding, 1898–1903* (Baltimore, 1957), and Bradford Perkins, *The Great Rapprochement: England and the United States, 1895–1914* (New York, 1968).

Undoubtedly, a plethora of literature exists regarding transatlantic marriages: Gail MacColl and Carol McD. Wallace's *To Marry an English Lord* (1989), Maureen E. Montgomery's *Gilded Prostitution: Status, Money, and Transatlantic Marriages, 1870–1914* (1989), and Candice Lewis Bredbenner's *A Nationality of Her Own: Women, Marriage, and the Law of Citizenship* (1998) are but a few examples of scholarship that discusses Anglo-American marriages. Cynthia Enloe's *Bananas, Beaches and Bases: Making Feminist Sense of International Politics* (1990), Laura Wexler's *Tender Violence: Domestic Visions in an Age of U.S. Imperialism* (2000), and Kristin L. Hoganson's *Consumers' Imperium: The Global Production of American Domesticity* (2007) contribute to the study of international relations, femininity, and domesticity on a broader level. To date, however, no study exists that examines these marriages in the framework of Anglo-American relations or diplomatic history.

2. Diana Whitehill Laing, *Mistress of Herself* (Barre, Mass., 1965), 78.
3. All of the husbands of the aforementioned American brides—Lord Randolph Churchill, George Nathaniel Curzon, and William Waldorf Astor—were members of the Conservative Party.
4. Please note that the case study approach of American-born, English-wed women is an examination of foreign *relations*, not foreign *policy*, a distinction that is slight and subtle but critical.
5. Biographical Sketches, Endicott Family Papers 1612–1958 (hereafter EFP), Guide to the Collection, Collections Guides online, Massachusetts Historical Society (hereafter MHS), accessed Jan. 12, 2010, www.masshist.org/findingaids.
6. *Boston Daily Globe*, Nov. 11, 1888.
7. Laing, *Mistress of Herself*, 21.
8. Laing, *Mistress of Herself*, 19.
9. Mary C. Endicott (hereafter MCE), scrapbook, 1876–1881, EFP.
10. Laing, *Mistress of Herself*, 23.
11. Laing, *Mistress of Herself*, 23.
12. Laing, *Mistress of Herself*, 24.

13. MCE, diary, July 5, 1882, EFP.
14. MCE, diary, July 5, 1882, EFP.
15. MCE, diary, July 5, 1882, EFP.
16. MCE, diary, Apr. 27, 1883, EFP.
17. MCE, diary, May 25, 1883, EFP.
18. MCE, diary, July 21, 1883, EFP.
19. MCE, diary, Sept. 5, 1883, EFP.
20. Laing, *Mistress of Herself*, 33. Also notable is the fact that both of Secretary Whitney's daughters married British men. In 1895, his first daughter, Pauline Payne Whitney, married Almeric Hugh Paget, who later became Baron Queenborough. His second daughter, Dorothy Payne Whitney, married Leonard Knight Elmhirst in 1925, some years after the death of her first husband.
21. Laing, *Mistress of Herself*, 34.
22. MCE, diary, Apr. 11, 1885, EFP.
23. Laing, *Mistress of Herself*, 34; MCE, diary, Apr. 11, 1885, EFP.
24. MCE, April 1885, EFP.
25. Laing, *Mistress of Herself*, 14, 36; *London Times*, Mar. 21, 1933.
26. Though dated, D. C. Watt's article provides a political theory foundation for British political activities and diplomatic relationships overall, and Chamberlain specifically, in the United States during a critical period in Anglo-American relations. D. C. Watt, "America and the British Foreign Policy–Making Elite, from Joseph Chamberlain to Anthony Eden, 1895–1956," *Review of Politics* 25(1963):3–33.
27. Untitled, *Town Topics: The Journal of Society*, Nov. 15, 1888.
28. Joseph Chamberlain to Beatrice Chamberlain, Dec. 9, 1887, AC 1/4/5/41, Cadbury Research Library: Special Collections, University of Birmingham (hereafter UB).
29. MCE, diary, December 1887, EFP.
30. Joseph Chamberlain, quoted in Sir Maycock Willoughby, *With Mr. Chamberlain in the United States and Canada, 1887–88* (London, 1914), 87.
31. Relatively little is known about Chamberlain's earlier marriages. His first marriage in 1861 to Harriet Kenrick ended after only two years. She gave birth to Beatrice in 1862 and Joseph Austen in 1863, who later served as chancellor of the exchequer and foreign secretary, but she died three days after her son's birth. Chamberlain's second marriage in 1868 to Florence Kenrick, a cousin of Harriet's, lasted seven years and produced five children, though his wife and last child, also named Florence, died shortly after birth. Upon his engagement to Mary, Chamberlain burned all his correspondence with his second wife at Mary's request. Peter T. Marsh, *Joseph Chamberlain: Entrepreneur in Politics* (New Haven, 1994), 32.
32. At the time of his engagement to Mary, Chamberlain's six children ranged from ages fifteen to twenty-six. Beatrice and Austen, his children from his first marriage, were older than his fiancée. Laing, *Mistress of Herself*, 14.
33. Laing, *Mistress of Herself*, 15; Marsh, *Joseph Chamberlain*, 289.
34. Marsh, *Joseph Chamberlain*, 289.
35. Joseph Chamberlain to MCE, July 18, 1888, JC 28/A1/39, Cadbury Research Library: Special Collections, UB.

36. Joseph Chamberlain to MCE, Apr. 28, 1888, JC 28/A1/16, Cadbury Research Library: Special Collections, UB.
37. Joseph Chamberlain to MCE, June 21, 1888, JC 28/A1/31, Cadbury Research Library: Special Collections, UB.
38. MCE to Joseph Chamberlain, July 18, 1888, JC 28/B1/36, Cadbury Research Library: Special Collections, UB.
39. Marsh, *Joseph Chamberlain*, 289.
40. MCE to Fanny Peabody Mason, Dec. 27, 1887, EFP.
41. *Boston Daily Globe*, Nov. 15, 1888.
42. Joseph Chamberlain to MCE, Feb. 11, 1888, JC 28/A2/1/5 Cadbury Research Library: Special Collections, UB.
43. MCE to Joseph Chamberlain, July 18, Sept. 28, 1888, JC 28/B1/57, Cadbury Research Library: Special Collections, UB.
44. Joseph Chamberlain to MCE, Feb. 12, 1888, JC 28/A2/1/6, Cadbury Research Library: Special Collections, UB.
45. Laing, *Mistress of Herself*, 46.
46. Maycock, *With Mr. Chamberlain*, 192.
47. *London Times*, Aug. 23, 1927, Mar. 29, 1933; Marsh, *Joseph Chamberlain*, 298.
48. William C. Endicott, Sr., quoted in unidentified newspaper clipping, 1890, MCE scrapbook, EFP.
49. Joseph Chamberlain to MCE, Mar. 10, 1888, JC 28/A1/5, Cadbury Research Library: Special Collections, UB.
50. Joseph Chamberlain to MCE, July 8, 1888, JC 28/A1/36, Cadbury Research Library: Special Collections, UB.
51. Joseph Chamberlain, "Relations with the United States and the Colonies," in *Mr. Chamberlain's Speeches*, ed. Charles Boyd (1914; New York, 1970), 318.
52. *New York Times*, Nov. 11, 1913.
53. *London Times*, Mar. 29, 1933, Nov. 7, 1888; *Boston Daily Globe*, Nov. 8, 1888. Chamberlain had succeeded in the task of drafting a treaty during the conference, but the U.S. Senate chose not to ratify it.
54. *Boston Daily Globe*, Nov. 16, 1888; *London Times*, Nov. 15, 1888.
55. Austen Chamberlain to MCE, Mar. 11, 1888, EFP.
56. Beatrice Chamberlain to MCE, Mar. 12, 1888, EFP.
57. Neville Chamberlain to MCE, Apr. 9, 1888, EFP.
58. *New York Times*, Nov. 16, 1913.
59. W. Endicott to MCE, Dec. 28, 1888, EFP.
60. Laing, *Mistress of Herself*, 57; Marsh, *Joseph Chamberlain*, 312.
61. William C. Endicott, Jr., to MCE, May 5, June 15, 1890, EFP.
62. Laing, *Mistress of Herself*, 66, 68, 78; *New York World*, Jan. 8, 1889.
63. Dorothy Nevill, *Reminiscences of Lady Dorothy Nevill*, ed. Ralph Nevill (London, 1906), 195.
64. Joseph Chamberlain to Ellen Peabody Endicott, undated, 1889, EFP.
65. Clarissa Endicott Peabody to MCE, Jan. 9, 1889, EFP.
66. Laing, *Mistress of Herself*, 78–79; Jeanette Jerome Randolph Cornwallis-West, *The*

Reminiscences of Lady Randolph Churchill (New York, 1908), 119–120.
67. Sigourney Butler to MCE, Mar. 15, 1889, EFP.
68. Joseph Chamberlain to Ellen Peabody Endicott, Jan. 4, 1889, EFP; Chamberlain, quoted in Laing, *Mistress of Herself*, 64.
69. Austen Chamberlain to Ellen Peabody Endicott, Nov. 6, 1890, Endicott Family Autograph/Special Collection, 1721–1938, MHS.
70. Austen Chamberlain to Ellen Peabody Endicott, Nov. 16, 1896, Endicott Family Autograph/Special Collection, 1721–1938, MHS.
71. MCE, visiting list, 1889, 1891, Miscellaneous, Bound Volumes, 1876–1902, EFP.
72. Laing, *Mistress of Herself*, 120.
73. Lars Schoultz, *Beneath the United States: A History of U.S. Policy toward Latin America* (Cambridge, Mass., 1998), 111.
74. Grover Cleveland, Special Message on the Venezuelan Boundary Dispute, Dec. 17, 1895, in *Letters and Addresses of Grover Cleveland*, ed. Albert Ellery Bergh (New York, 1909), 376–381; Walter LaFeber, "The Background of Cleveland's Venezuelan Policy: A Reinterpretation," *American Historical Review* 66(1961):963.
75. MCE to Ellen Peabody Endicott, Dec. 18, 1895, EFP .
76. MCE to Ellen Peabody Endicott, Dec. 21, 1895, EFP.
77. Joseph Smith, *Historical Dictionary of United States–Latin American Relations* (Lanham, Mass., 2007), 222.
78. LaFeber, "Background of Cleveland's Venezuelan Policy," 947.
79. MCE, diary, 1895, EFP.
80. Unnamed American general, quoted in Ralph G. Martin, *Jennie: The Life of Lady Randolph Churchill* (Englewood Cliffs, N.J., 1971), 2:74. By 1895, numerous American-born, British-wed women were living in Great Britain. It is difficult for historians today to identify definitively the American women this particular newspaper article referred to, but Mary Endicott Chamberlain, Lady Randolph Churchill, her sister Clara Frewen, her youngest sister, Leonie Leslie, Consuelo Yznaga (the Duchess of Manchester), Pauline Payne Whitney Paget, Lily Hammersley, Mrs. A. A. Blow, Fanny Reynolds, and Cornelia Adair were prime candidates.
81. Laing, *Mistress of Herself*, 101.
82. For more on the efforts of American-born, British-wed women, see Dana Cooper, "Country by Birth, Country by Marriage: American Women's Transnational War Efforts in Great Britain, 1895–1918," in *Women and Transnational Activism in Historical Perspective*, ed. Kimberly Jensen and Erika Kuhlman (Dordrecht, The Netherlands, 2009), 37–62.
83. Clara Endicott Sears to MCE, Apr. 24, 1898, EFP.
84. J. L. Garvin, *The Life of Joseph Chamberlain, Volume III, 1895–1900: Empire and World Policy* (London, 1934), 302; Joseph Chamberlain, quoted in "For Anglo-Saxon Unity," *New York Times*, May 14, 1898.
85. *Boston Herald*, May 22, 1899.
86. Unheaded newspaper clipping, Family Correspondence, EFP.
87. *Salem News*, Aug. 23, 1895.
88. *New York Times*, July 4, 1914.

89. *Salem News*, Aug. 23, 1895.
90. *Boston Sunday Post*, May 1, 1904.
91. *Boston Globe*, Mar. 2, 1904.
92. *Boston Sunday Post*, May 1, 1904.
93. *Boston Sunday Post*, May 1, 1904.
94. *Boston Sunday Post*, May 1, 1904.
95. *Boston Daily Globe*, July 5, 1914.
96. Marsh, *Joseph Chamberlain*, 627, 647; Richard Cavendish, "Joseph Chamberlain Resigns as Colonial Secretary," *History Today* 53, no. 9 (Sept. 2003):54–66.
97. MCE, diary, July 2, 1914, EFP.
98. Austen Chamberlain to Fanny P. Mason, July 20, 1914, EFP.
99. Austen Chamberlain to Fanny P. Mason, Nov. 1, 1906, EFP.
100. George Augustus Peabody to MCE, Nov. 23, 1914, EFP
101. J. P. Franks to MCE, June 3, 1915, EFP.
102. Endicott Peabody to MCE, Dec. 14, 1914, EFP.
103. *London Times*, Aug. 2, 1915.
104. *Boston Herald*, Aug. 4, 1916.
105. MCE to George Augustus Peabody, Jan. 20, 1919, EFP.
106. *New York Times*, Oct. 20, 1936.
107. Laing, *Mistress of Herself*, 192.
108. MCE to Fanny P. Mason, July 15, 1917, EFP.
109. MCE to Fanny P. Mason, Apr. 18, 1917, EFP.
110. MCE to Louise Endicott, Mar. 30, 1937, EFP.
111. Neville Chamberlain to Fanny P. Mason, Jan. 16, 1938, EFP.
112. MCE to Fanny P. Mason, July 22, 1940, EFP.
113. MCE to Fanny P. Mason, July 10, 1940, EFP.
114. MCE to Fanny P. Mason, Sept. 26, 1940, EFP.
115. MCE to Fanny P. Mason, Jan. 2, 1942, EFP.
116. MCE to Fanny P. Mason, Dec. 1, 1942, EFP.
117. MCE to Fanny P. Mason, Jan. 7, 1943, EFP.
118. MCE to Fanny P. Mason, July 19, 1944, EFP.
119. MCE to Fanny P. Mason, Sept. 28, 1944, EFP.
120. Laing, *Mistress of Herself*, 219.
121. G. Peabody Gardner, "A Toast by G. Peabody Gardner to Mary Endicott Carnegie on Her Ninetieth Birthday," Mar. 16, 1954, EFP.
122. Laing, *Mistress of Herself*, 226; *London Times*, May 25, 1957; *New York Times*, July 13, 1916.
123. *London Times*, May 25, 1957.
124. *London Times*, May 25, 1957.
125. *London Times*, May 25, 1957.
126. Laing, *Mistress of Herself*, 226.

PROFILE

Three Lives of an African American Pioneer

William Henry Lewis (1868–1949)

EVAN J. ALBRIGHT

"THERE ARE NO SECOND ACTS IN AMERICAN LIVES," F. Scott Fitzgerald once observed, but the life of William Henry Lewis had three: sports, public service, and the law. Even more remarkable, Lewis was an African American born during Reconstruction, and his accomplishments over an eighty-year lifespan extended through the Jim Crow era and then concluded at the emergence of the modern Civil Rights movement.

Although Lewis was one of the most accomplished and well-known African Americans of his generation, little has been written about him since his death. Perhaps this is because his achievements had been overshadowed by those of his contemporaries, men such as W. E. B. Du Bois, Booker T. Washington, and William Monroe Trotter. Lewis knew all of them well. He counted among his supporters and patrons Presidents Theodore Roosevelt, William Howard Taft, and Calvin Coolidge. Given his accomplishments and his place in African American history, it is perplexing that there has been so little scholarship about him.

It is not because his life contained no drama. From the beginning, Lewis lived all the classic elements of the Horatio Alger stories that were popular in his youth: a poor and disadvantaged child who, through pluck and luck, finds success and fame. He was born November 28, 1868, in Berkley, Virginia, a mixed-raced village wedged between Portsmouth and Norfolk and buffered from both cities by the east and south branches of the Elizabeth River. His

---

EVAN J. ALBRIGHT is a writer on Cape Cod.

father, Ashley Henry Lewis, was a former slave who had been a sergeant in Company B of Virginia's First Regiment Cavalry, U.S. Colored Troops, during the Civil War. Ashley mustered out in Norfolk in 1866 and the following year married another former slave, Josephine Baker. Lewis's father began as a laborer on the docks, but because he could read and write, he had an opportunity to advance. "Most of our people who could receive some little education became teachers and preachers," wrote Booker T. Washington about the Reconstruction period. Ashley was no different, and two years later he moved to Portsmouth, where he eventually rose through the ranks of the Ebenezer Baptist Church to become its minister.[1]

According to Lewis, his interest in the law had been nurtured in Portsmouth. As a little boy he would flee his chores to observe lawyers as they dueled in the Norfolk County courthouse, a few blocks from his home. "A murder trial is not, perhaps, the best sort of amusement for a boy, but the excitement of these murder trials, in which some of the keenest minds in the state were pitted against each other, provided a kind of stuff to kindle the imagination of an impressionable boy," wrote Washington in a 1913 profile of Lewis.[2]

As a teenager, Lewis attended the state's first college for African Americans, the Virginia Normal and Collegiate Institute in Petersburg. There he came under the influence of the institution's president, John Mercer Langston, the famous abolitionist and lawyer who would later become the first African American U.S. Representative from Virginia.[3] Langston helped Lewis win enrollment to Amherst College in western Massachusetts in the fall of 1888. Here he took up the game of football. Lewis played center, but at 170 pounds he was lighter than most men at that position. This led him to develop a roving style of play that allowed him to take advantage of his speed, agility, and intelligence. He also proved to be a natural leader, and his teammates elected him captain in his final year. After graduation, Lewis entered Harvard Law School. At Harvard he continued his football career and went on to become the first African American college football player named to the all-American Team—not once, but twice—in 1892 and 1893.[4]

After completing his education, Lewis remained in Cambridge and began his legal practice. He entered politics, starting with election in 1898 to the Cambridge Common Council, the lower body of the city government. He won election to the Massachusetts state legislature in 1901 from a predominantly white district. He would be the last African American to be elected to that body for decades.[5] In 1903, Pres. Theodore Roosevelt appointed Lewis an assistant U.S. attorney for Boston. Eight years later, Pres. William Howard

Taft appointed him assistant attorney general of the United States—at the time the highest federal office ever held by an African American and a high-water mark that no other black man would surpass for almost fifty years.

Lewis left public office in 1913 and entered the practice of law full-time, concentrating almost entirely on criminal law. His client list included some of the most notorious criminals in New England, such as Charles Ponzi, the famous swindler. Lewis appeared more than a dozen times before the U.S. Supreme Court; he won his first case before that body in 1930.

William Lewis lived a full life that was remarkable in its list of achievements and its longevity. He was still winning accolades for his legal acumen up to his death at age eighty. Perhaps, the best place to begin his story is at the end . . .

Looking Back

In late November 1948, Yale University announced that Levi Jackson would become the first African American to captain the Bulldog football team. "Excuse Harvard men for yawning," wrote *Boston Globe* sports columnist Harold Kaese. "Fifty-five years ago Harvard had a Negro captain, one who was as good a football player as Jackson is now." William Henry Lewis, the all-American center, captained one game in 1893 when he was asked to lead the Harvard Crimson against the University of Pennsylvania.[6]

College football in 1893 was dramatically different from 1948. There were no substitutions allowed, save for injury, so players were required to play the entire game at both offense and defense. Equipment offered little in the way of protection. There were no helmets and little padding. Some players wore an odd-looking protector for the nose that hung from the forehead by a band around the head. Some grew their hair long, thinking it added protection for the skull. Football was extremely dangerous, but that was what made it so attractive. Lewis's generation had been weaned on exploits from the Civil War related by their fathers and grandfathers. Football gave each man the chance to prove himself on the field of battle, even if the objective was only to move an oblong sphere, not preserve the Union.[7]

The college powerhouses in the 1890s were Yale, Princeton, and Harvard. The University of Pennsylvania was about to break into those ranks, and a victory over the Harvard Crimson would cement its place as one of college's great teams. Harvard in 1893 had a record of 11–1 going into the Penn game. Until their loss to Yale, no other team had scored against them (and Yale had won by scoring a single touchdown). Harvard's captain had been injured in the Yale match, and Lewis was called upon to head the team in what would be his final game as a player. Unlike today, coaches were not permitted to interfere once the game was underway, therefore the responsibility of calling plays and leading the team fell to the captain or quarterback. Thanks to Lewis's play calling, the Crimson crushed the University of Pennsylvania, 26–4. Some wondered why Harvard had not put up such a spirited game against Yale. The reason was clear—the Crimson had not had Lewis as its captain. No one would say that openly, especially not Lewis, even after more than fifty years had passed.[8]

Lewis in 1948 deflected any attempt to match his accomplishments with Yale's new captain, Levi Jackson. "Don't go comparing him with me," he said. "He's alive and I'm practically dead."[9] Lewis was not exaggerating. While his health probably was better than that of most eighty-year-olds, he had been forced to give up many of his passions. He had been involved in politics most of his life, but he suffered from heart trouble. A lifelong Republican, Lewis supported Thomas E. Dewey in the 1948 presidential election, but his poor health kept him sidelined during the campaign. After the election was over, Lewis shared his regrets over the result with another African American Republican stalwart, Roscoe Conkling Simmons of Chicago. "It is probably the last Presidential election I shall witness or still vote in," he wrote.[10]

While football was a distant memory and politics was out of the picture, William Lewis still had the law, and he continued to practice up to the end. Only a few days before he died, he was involved in a major trial in which he proved once again that he was one of the best criminal defense lawyers in New England. His client, Benjamin Siegel, was a real estate broker who had been charged with bribing several members of the city council in Revere, a city perched on the shore just north of Boston. Siegel was tried in Suffolk Superior Court in Boston in the late fall of 1948—along with the city councilmen whose favorable votes he had allegedly procured for a few hundred dollars. The "Revere Bribery Case," as it came to be known, was splashed across the front pages of Boston's newspapers every day. The case had such a high profile that the attorney general of the Commonwealth of Massachusetts, Clarence Barnes, prosecuted the trial himself.[11]

Prior to entering the courtroom, the attorney general and his staff must have felt their case was a strong one. They had persuaded one of the councilors, Leonard Ginsburg, to plead guilty and turn state's evidence. Ginsburg was going to testify that Siegel had offered him five hundred dollars and a "good job" if he would cast a vote in favor of Siegel's housing project.[12]

Siegel's selection of Lewis as defense counsel may have appeared to the casual observer to be an odd one. Lewis, after all, was of an advanced age and an African American. But if Siegel was concerned about his lawyer, he never showed it. In retrospect, it turned out to be the best investment of his career.

Even at eighty, Lewis radiated energy. His grandson, who only knew him in those later years, described him as a "cannonball." Lewis had a large (some said overlarge) head that sat on his shoulders like a cauldron atop a tea table. His skin was bronze, which many described as more American Indian than African. He spoke with a stentorian baritone, a voice that "you could hear from the parking lot," but one that was more importantly always intelligible, even when he whispered in a noisy, crowded courtroom.[13]

Those who attended the trial all remember the same thing—Lewis's closing argument. "The whole of this case is Ginsburg—Leonard Ginsburg—and nothing else," Lewis told the jury, speaking very slowly and deliberately. "When I saw Leonard Ginsburg on that witness stand, I wondered where I had seen that face before. Then I remembered. I remember a famous painting by Leonardo—a man standing with his hand out—Judas!"[14]

It was audacious to use an anti-Semitic canard of the lowest order: linking the Jewish Ginsburg to the betrayer of the King of the Jews. But it was even more daring if not bold when one considers that Lewis's client was Jewish, as were several other defendants. Yet his strategy made twisted sense. At the outset of the trial, Lewis had challenged the jury because no Jews had been seated. The prosecutors had removed anyone they had suspected of having Jewish heritage through peremptory challenges.[15]

Newspapers used words such as "dramatic" and "impressive" when describing Lewis. The one word they did not use was "Negro"—newspapers rarely, if ever, mentioned his race. Articles about the trial quoted extensively from his closing argument, at the expense of his fellow defense attorneys who were usually limited to the bounds of a single paragraph. Lewis's remarks also impressed the jury, for the twelve white men acquitted Siegel and all his codefendants.[16]

At the time of the Revere bribery trial, Lewis reflected on his long legal career: "Life with me has been a great venture, and the law something more than motions and pleadings." While politics and football may have been important in his past, he continued to practice law to the end. A few days after the conclusion of the Revere trial, Lewis announced he was working up motions to the Massachusetts Supreme Judicial Court (SJC) on behalf of three Pittsfield men he claimed had been wrongfully convicted of rape. Forty-eight hours later he was dead.[17]

He suffered a fatal heart attack in his Back Bay apartment. His obituary appeared on the front page of Boston newspapers and in *Time* magazine. More than a thousand mourners turned out for his funeral Mass (he had converted to Catholicism following the death of his wife in 1943), including Gov. Robert Bradford, Governor-elect Paul Dever, and former governor (and infamous Boston mayor) James Michael Curley—impressive company considering his humble roots.[18]

Act One: Football Hero

Lewis's first triumph was in football. Amherst College believed that students must be strong of body as well as mind and required that all of its students participate in athletics. Lewis had never played an organized sport, but in the fall of his freshman year he tried out for football. "I didn't have any uniform, and wore my street clothes," he later recalled. "That first day I got my clothes all torn off and my feet stepped on. The next day they gave me a uniform."[19]

Despite his awkward beginning, Lewis discovered he had a knack for the game, and he went on to become, arguably, the best center in college football. His teammates named him captain. His academic performance was equally impressive. At his graduation in 1892, Lewis was tapped to give the class oration. W. E. B. Du Bois, then a Harvard doctoral candidate, attended the commencement exercises, joining a party that included a beautiful young woman from Cambridge, Elizabeth "Bessie" Baker. Du Bois was suitably impressed with Lewis, but Baker was smitten.[20]

Baker and Lewis began a courtship, which undoubtedly influenced Lewis's decision to enter Harvard Law School, only a few blocks from her home, in the fall of 1892. He also joined the Harvard football team as eligibility rules in the early 1890s permitted graduate students to participate. During his two years at Harvard, the team was more famous for its innovations than its play. Although they lost only one game each year, the loss was to arch-rival Yale, which in the end meant the season was unsuccessful. But each of those years saw Harvard unveil an innovation that changed football: the flying wedge and the leather uniform.

The flying wedge was the brainchild of Lorin Deland, a Harvard alum who had never played the game but had an intellect for strategy and tactics. Deland introduced the play in the Harvard-Yale contest of 1892, and by the next year football teams across the nation had copied it. Under the rules at that time, halves began with a kickoff, but a team did not have to kick to its competitor. Fake kicks were common. The kicker would tap the ball with his

Harvard University Varsity Football team, 1892.
Lewis is seated third from the right on the lower row. Courtesy Harvard University Archives, UAV 170.270.2.

Yale-Harvard football game, 1905.
Digital ID: cph 3c25359. Reproduction number: LC-USZ62–12539 DLC. Courtesy of the Library of Congress Prints and Photographs Division.

toe and then throw it back to another player to run it up the field. Harvard rolled out the new play during the second half kickoff. Harvard captain Bernard Trafford stood alone with the ball at midfield. The other ten men were twenty yards behind him in two lines, each forty-five degrees from the ball and sidelines, with Art Brewer, the halfback, alone between the two lines. Trafford then signaled his men to begin running toward him. When they reached him, he put the ball in play by tapping it with his toe, then picked it up and threw it to Brewer, who was running full speed behind a wedge formed by the two converging lines. "By the time they arrived at the ball, they had worked up a stupendous mass momentum, and the interference they gave for the runner was something wonderful to behold, and terrible to stop," wrote John W. Heisman, the namesake of thc today's trophy for best college player, who was a longtime coach (for Clemson, Georgia Tech, and the University of Pennsylvania, among other schools) and former player (for Brown University and the University of Pennsylvania). This "flying wedge" crashed into the Yale line for a gain of twenty-five yards. Had Brewer not lost his footing, many felt Harvard would have scored. Instead the team was stopped by the Elis, who later went on to win by a single touchdown, 6–0. The play revolutionized football, but only for a short time, as it was banned after the 1893 season.[21]

The following year, Harvard showed up for the Yale game wearing suits made of leather instead of the traditional canvas and moleskin. Each reportedly cost $125. The new uniforms were supposed to be less absorbent so that when wet they would not weigh a player down. They were also more slippery, which Harvard strategists felt would make their men harder to tackle. According to some reports, Yale players countered this by coating their hands with sticky resin. The suits did not give Harvard enough of an advantage, for the Crimson fell again, 6–0. Lewis liked his so well, though, that he wore it for many years as a Harvard coach during practices.[22]

At the end of both his Harvard seasons, Lewis was rewarded with all-American nods. In those years, the all-American team (at least the one recognized today) was selected by Caspar Whitney, sports columnist for *Harper's Weekly*. Whitney chose Lewis in 1892 "for his greater ability as a tackler" and his superior skills, even against opponents who outweighed him by thirty pounds. Usually a center on defense would spend the duration of the play battling the center or tackles on offense, but according to Whitney, Lewis was "astonishing and he was often through on the runner as soon as the [*defensive*] tackles." By the following year, Whitney believed Lewis to be the best center ever. "There can be no two opinions as to the choice of centre," he wrote. "Lewis has proved himself to be not only the best centre of this year, but the best all-round centre that has ever put on a football jacket."[23]

Lewis graduated from Harvard Law School in 1895. The latter half of the 1890s were heady days for the young Lewis, at least on a personal level. He married Bessie Baker in 1896, and their first child, Dorothy, was born in 1897, followed by Elizabeth in 1900 and William Henry, Jr., in 1902. He also kept his hand in Harvard football. His leadership ability on the gridiron translated well to the sidelines. Because of eligibility rules, he was not allowed to play his final year at Harvard Law School, so he coached instead and kept coaching every season through 1906. Head coaches during this period changed every two or three seasons, but assistant coaches, such as Lewis, provided consistency year after year. Coaches, who almost always came from the alumni, were expected to be volunteers, but in 1901, Lewis became the first paid coach in Harvard history, earning $500 per year (in 1904 increased to $1,000 per year).[24]

In 1898, Lewis mentored some of the best players ever to wear the crimson, including four future Harvard head coaches. Not only did they beat Yale that year, but they slaughtered a team considered a juggernaut, the University of Pennsylvania. Newspapers and football insiders credited Lewis with devising the miracle play that stopped the supposedly unstoppable, Penn's famous "guard's back" offense. At the annual football banquet at the end of the season, the evening's program recognized Lewis by having his name on the cover next to that of the official head coach, Cameron Forbes. When he arrived in the hall, Lewis got an even bigger cheer than the featured speaker, Governor-elect Theodore Roosevelt of New York. Cornell University was so impressed that they offered Lewis a professorship if he would coach their football team. Lewis declined; he wanted to stick with the practice of law.[25]

In 1896, Lewis wrote *A Primer of College Football*, one of the first books about the sport. The book was serialized throughout September in *Harper's Round Table*, the young people's edition of *Harper's Weekly*. A few years later, Walter Camp, the "Father of American Football," asked Lewis to contribute a chapter on defense for his wide-selling bible of the sport, *Spalding's How to Play Football*.[26]

Lewis succeeded in football in spite of omnipresent racism. Sometime after the 1892 football season, a Cambridge barbershop denied Lewis service because of his race. Lewis's classmates at Harvard, some of them descendants of abolitionists, launched a boycott against the establishment.[27] "Any man who is worthy to represent the university in a great athletic event and to eat at the same table with other members of the team, is worthy of indiscriminate treatment by a Cambridge tradesman," opined the student newspaper, the *Harvard Crimson*.

> But when such a man can command the respect of all who know him, whose character has always been borne out by his conduct, he deserves the impartial treatment of the students themselves. We have little to say of a man who will deny this. We are glad that in Harvard there is a just appreciation of a person's worth. When an insult is offered to a colored man of Lewis character, the whole university is broad enough and generous enough to rise up in indignation that any one should infer by his conduct, that so contemptible a spirit of snobbishness is in the university and must be catered to.[28]

The barber, Lewis was surprised to learn, had broken no laws despite the fact that Massachusetts had some of the strongest statutes in the nation prohibiting racial discrimination. Lewis heeded the words of the old Civil Rights warhorse Frederick Douglass, who told his brothers and sisters to "keep their grievances before the people and make every organized protest against the wrongs inflicted upon them with their power." Lewis joined forces with Rep. George Meyer, a Boston legislator who offered a bill that would ban discrimination by any business that catered to the public. It took two years, but the state legislature passed the bill and the governor signed it into law.[29]

There was also occasional racism within the Harvard team. Harry Kersberg, a member of the 1905 team, remembered how Lewis had gotten in the face of his teammate Francis "Hooks" Burr, who had been consistently beaten in the Brown University game by an African American player, Albert Fletcher. Kersberg recalled his coach telling Burr, "That guard on the Brown team 'smeared' you," and he demanded to know why. "'I don't know what was the matter with me," Burr replied. "I used my hands on that nigger's head and body all through the game but it didn't seem to do any good." There was an awkward silence. Then Lewis roared, "Why the devil didn't you kick him in the shins?"[30]

Lewis came away from his days playing and coaching football with two important life lessons he would use the rest of his life. First, there was no escaping racism, and in this the gridiron was like the real world. Playing and coaching football at Harvard taught Lewis "to regard with indifference trifling insults," he wrote near the end of his life. "There I learned to consider even severe physical hurts but slight wounds to be endured."[31]

The other lesson he learned, which he applied directly to his career with the law, was to win by any means necessary. This included cheating. During one of the Yale games, for example, Lewis secretly kicked the ball out of the hands of the Eli center. The officials thought the center had snapped the ball too early, and the play eventually resulted in a turnover for Harvard. Even Theodore Roosevelt knew Lewis liked to bend the rules in football, for he had taught some of his tricks to the president's son during an impromptu coaching session at the Groton School. These shenanigans were also practiced in the courtroom, if not by Lewis then by other lawyers he worked with. According to Matthew McGrath, Jr., son of Lewis's longtime law partner, during the Revere bribery trial one of the lawyers stole the attorney general's briefcase. In describing the legal tactics that Lewis, his father, and their peers used, McGrath concluded, "They'd steal dinner from a dog."[32]

Lewis left a little-known legacy to the sport of football. The sport's bloody violence had made it a target for reform, and in 1905, Harvard president Charles William Eliot and the Harvard Corporation voted secretly to ban football. Members of the coaching staff caught wind of the vote, and as a preemptive measure, Lewis joined Coach Bill Reid and other Harvard alumni who called for rules changes to make the game safer. Lewis proposed a "neutral zone" rule, which required teams to be kept apart by the width of the football before the start of each play. Once in effect, players no longer could crowd the imaginary, hair-thin line of scrimmage that supposedly separated the teams but in truth hid a lot of slugging and holding from the officials. Lewis also proposed the rule preventing interference with the center until after the ball is snapped. In 1906, college football enacted the neutral zone rule.[33]

The new rule, along with other changes such as the introduction of the forward pass, transformed football. The adjustments "saved the game and vastly improved it," Lewis observed. "The new game is a safe, sane, and wholesome sport." At the same time, the changes ended his football legacy. Two years later, "I was a 'has-been,'" he told a friend.[34] Before the rule changes, Walter Camp had listed Lewis as the greatest college center of all time. But after the rule changes, Lewis fell off Camp's all-time top eleven, replaced by a modern-era player.[35]

Over the years, Lewis's reputation as a football player and coach faded, save for the occasional mention of his achievement as the first black all-American. As other African Americans broke into college and professional football, Lewis's name would occasionally come up in an article or newspaper story. But following the brief flurry of attention he received with the selection of Levi Jackson as Yale's first African American captain (including getting his picture in *Life* magazine four days before he died), mentions became fewer and fewer until he was almost forgotten. Then, in 2009, he was elected to the

College Football Hall of Fame, well over a century after he had played his last game and sixty years after his death.[36]

Act Two: Political Animal and Public Servant

Lewis began his foray into politics before he left Virginia for Massachusetts. Most published profiles of Lewis's life mention that he attended the Virginia Normal and Collegiate Institute. Few, if any, say why he left. The institute had been founded during the tenure of a Republican governor and legislature. In the fall of 1887, the Democrats in Virginia rose to power and replaced the institute's board of visitors, which oversaw the college, with their own appointees. The new board immediately engaged in a power struggle with the institute's president, John Mercer Langston, a dedicated Republican. In late 1887, Langston learned his appointment as college president would not be renewed in the new year. Lewis, who had just turned nineteen, believed he could petition the governor to overturn Langston's termination. The white South, however, had little tolerance for the so-called "New Negro." According to historian Leon Litwack, many believed this first generation of post-slavery African Americans "was devoid of the habits of diligence, order, faithfulness, and morality that had been taught their elders; young blacks possessed neither the temperament, demeanor, nor humility of former slaves, and they were said to be more restless, less deferential, and, still worse, less fearful of whites."[37]

On November 25, 1887, Lewis and five other students took a train to the state capital to meet with Virginia's governor, Fitzhugh Lee, who granted them an audience. When the students returned to the institute, they were called before a meeting of the faculty and threatened with expulsion. On December 5 and 6, the board of visitors held a hearing on the matter and heard testimony from Prof. William Smith that Lewis and the others were "disorderly students" and that Langston had condoned their behavior. Langston acquitted the students, but the board voted to censure the college president, his staff, and the six students. Shortly before the Christmas break, Langston announced he would leave the post of president.[38]

At a farewell dinner for Langston, Lewis praised his mentor by saying,

> He has given permanent shape and character to the only true and great ideal of African American education, which comprehends the whole field of learning, touching the very dome of thought.
>
> In his lectures . . . he has impressed upon the Negro youth gathered around him the sanctity of the obligations incumbent upon them as

> American citizens, and all their rights, privileges and immunities connected therewith. . . . And I thank God that I have received a goodly portion of that spirit. I swear it now upon the altar of truth, that it shall follow me to the end of my career; for upon it depends all that I am, and all that I may hope to be in this life.[39]

Lewis and the others failed to save their mentor, and for their efforts, they would no longer find the Virginia Normal and Collegiate Institute a welcome haven. Following the removal of Langston, Lewis left the school. According to one news report, the senior class "refused to recite" before Professor Smith. Upon being warned they would be suspended, the seniors "left the college." Langston went on, after a contentious and controversial election, to win a seat in the U.S. House of Representatives from Virginia.[40]

His protégé Lewis would also throw his hat into the political ring. His election to the Cambridge Common Council in 1899 was universally heralded. But by the time he entered the state legislature, his image had begun to tarnish, at least among some of the Civil Rights leaders of Boston. When Pres. Theodore Roosevelt appointed Lewis an assistant U.S. attorney for Boston, the negative attitudes turned to outright hostility.[41] The reason was that many of Boston's African Americans believed Lewis, who was one of the up-and-coming stars of the Civil Rights movement, made a Faustian bargain with Booker T. Washington and exchanged his principles for a paycheck.

In the first few years of the twentieth century, the hearts and minds of black America could be divided into two camps: those who supported Booker T. Washington and those who did not. The latter camp was a small but vocal minority, the most famous members being W. E. B. Du Bois, then a professor at Atlanta University and later editor of the NAACP's house organ, the *Crisis*, and William Monroe Trotter, publisher of an African American newspaper, the *Boston Guardian*.

How big was Booker Washington? Du Bois called him "the most distinguished Southerner since Jefferson Davis, and the one with the largest personal following."[42] Washington rose to national prominence in 1895, a few months after the death of Frederick Douglass. Washington, the founder and principal of a school for African Americans in Tuskegee, Alabama, gave a powerful speech before an unusual, mixed-race audience at the Atlanta Cotton States and International Exposition in which he advocated that African Americans should take advantage of the opportunities in the South to work and acquire property and that southern whites should look no further than the African American race to work their farms and factories. Washington went on to say, "the wisest among my race understand that the agitation of questions of social equality is the extremest folly, and that progress in the enjoyment of all the privileges that will come to us must be the result of severe and constant struggle rather than of artificial forcing." Later he said, "In all things that are purely social we can be as separate as the fingers, yet one as the hand in all things essential to mutual progress."[43]

Booker T. Washington, frontispiece from The Negro Problem, *by Washington et al. (New York, 1903).*

The address, as Washington saw it, "was the first time in the history of the Negro race that a member of my race had been asked to speak from the same platform with white Southern men and women on any important National occasion."[44] Criticism of Washington's Atlanta Exposition speech was scarce in 1895. Washington's words were widely quoted across the country and with great praise. Though later critical of what he derisively called the "Atlanta Compromise," W. E. B. Du Bois initially congratulated Washington "upon your phenomenal success at Atlanta—it was a word fitly spoken."[45] The one place where his speech did not sit well was among the black intelligentsia of Boston. The rancor grew to such proportions that T. Thomas Fortune, editor of the predominant African American newspaper of the day, the *New York Age*, arranged for Washington to meet his New England critics at a dinner held at Young's Hotel in Boston in the spring of 1898. Fortune's account of the dinner went as follows:

> At the proper time, when the coffee and cigars were served, I arose and told the diners that Dr. Washington had desired to meet them at the banquet table and at the proper time to have each of them express freely his opinion of the race question, and how best the race could be served in the delicate crisis through which it was then passing. Each of the speakers launched into a tirade against Dr. Washington and his policies and methods, many of them in lofty flights of speech they had learned at Harvard University. The atmosphere was dense with discontent and denunciation.

> The climax was reached when William H. Lewis, the famous Harvard football coach, told Dr. Washington to go back South, and attend to his work of educating the Negro and "leave to us the matters political affecting the race."[46]

But at some point Lewis changed sides. "This same Mr. Lewis a few years ago was a rabid anti-Washington man and wanted to 'burn down Tuskegee,'" Du Bois wrote Oswald Garrison Villard, the famous social reformer and editor of the *Nation*, in 1905. He continued,

> I labored with him and Trotter and Forbes in past years and was instrumental in getting Mr. Washington and Mr. Lewis together at a small luncheon so that they might understand each other. They evidently came to understand each other so well that Mr. Lewis got a political appointment and turning around proceeded to abuse his former comrades—a conversion in which I had as little faith as I had in his former radical stand.[47]

Did Lewis switch his allegiance to Booker T. Washington in exchange for a job in the Boston U.S. attorney's office, as Du Bois and others believed? The letters of Booker T. Washington and Theodore Roosevelt reveal that, if anyone should be accused of selling out, it should probably be Booker T. Washington. Roosevelt and Lewis had known each other for years. Roosevelt, an avid football fan (specifically Harvard football), had been a longtime admirer of Lewis and his "smash-mouth" approach to the game. The two men had at times appeared on the same speaking platform (always in relation to Harvard football). Lewis had visited Roosevelt at the governor's mansion in Albany and only a few months before winning the appointment had spent time with the new president at Oyster Bay on Long Island.[48] Lewis, in fact, may have had Roosevelt's ear more than Booker Washington did. A few days after winning election as vice president in 1900, Roosevelt replied to

W. E. B. DuBois from The Negro Problem, *by Booker T. Washington et al. (New York, 1903), facing page 32.*

Theodore Roosevelt, frontispiece from his The Strenuous Life *(New York, 1902).*

Washington's congratulatory telegram by talking almost entirely about Lewis. "I have had some long talks recently with my friend Lewis of Harvard," Roosevelt wrote. "There are points where I do not entirely agree with him and I want to consult you about them."[49]

It is not known whether Roosevelt ever had that conversation with Washington. Perhaps because Roosevelt had just been elected to one of the most notorious non-offices in American government—the vice presidency—there was little urgency on Washington's part to discuss the ideas of a potential political rival. All that changed on September 6, 1901, when Pres. William McKinley was gunned down while shaking hands in Buffalo, New York. Eight days later he was dead and Theodore Roosevelt was president. Within a fortnight, Washington extended the olive branch to the Lewis. In a letter to the Boston attorney, Washington wrote,

> The main point of this letter is to say I believe that both you and I are going to be in a position in the future to serve the race effectually, and while it is very probably that we shall always differ as to detailed methods of lifting up the race it seems to me that if we agree in each doing his best to lift it up the main point will have been gained, and I am sure that in our anxiety to better the condition of the race there is no difference between us, and I shall be delighted to work in hearty cooperation with you.[50]

Roosevelt must have told the two men to play nice together. Washington mailed his letter of rapprochement only a few days after he had met with the president in the nation's capital.[51] Lewis, in response to Washington, indicated that he had sent a similar letter that crossed in the mail: "I am delighted to know that our minds were working in the same direction, as you had intended writing me before receiving mine of recent date. I cannot tell you how pleased

I am to know of your continued interest and good will. I agree with you that we can both work for the common end effectually, and without friction."[52]

In December 1902, Lewis visited Roosevelt at the White House. In a subsequent letter to Washington, Lewis wrote that Roosevelt "said, among other things, he was very glad that I was more in unison with you than formerly." Despite being "more in unison," Lewis did not pledge blanket loyalty to Washington's agenda. He explained that

> I told [*Roosevelt*], of course, there were many things about which we might differ, but that we had the same aims and the same end in view. [*Roosevelt*] used a very happy illustration when he replied, saying, "Of course, Mr. Lewis, if another man and myself are working in the same field, whether ploughing or hoeing or reaping, I had much prefer to have him work my way, but it did not matter so much as long as he was working and working toward the same end."[53]

Lewis's letter cannot be construed as groveling for Washington's favor to obtain a high position, as Du Bois characterized it. At that same meeting, Lewis and Roosevelt briefly discussed a political appointment, an ambition to which Washington was clearly privy. Lewis went on to write that Roosevelt "said that he wanted to do something for me and something here in Boston, having the same idea in view which he expressed to you." For Lewis to win such an appointment and for Washington to cement a place as the leading political figure among African Americans, the president of the United States expected cooperation; Lewis, rather than meekly comply, told the president that there were areas where the two men would never agree but that they would cooperate for the good of the overall cause. [54]

Over time Lewis came more and more to Washington's approach and point of view. On many occasions he explained his "conversion" to Booker T. Washington. In a statement to author John Daniels published in 1914, he said,

> For a time after leaving Law School I was counted as one of the radicals and agitators, but I found so many good people who approved Dr. Washington's course and who were just as sincere in their advocacy of human rights and Negro rights as I myself, that I began to ask myself if they were wholly wrong and myself wholly right. I came to believe that they were more right than I, and so I decided that I should not make the business of my life the pulling down of some other men or slinging mud at a real worker.[55]

One reason for Lewis's growing loyalty to Washington and his efforts may have been similarity of background. Unlike Trotter or Du Bois, Lewis was a product of the south, like Washington. Washington had been a slave, as had both of Lewis's parents. Lewis had seen firsthand the challenges of an African American reformer in the South, and although he was living in the North, almost all of his siblings continued to live in Virginia and its environs.

Lewis remained loyal to Booker T. Washington, although he always maintained his independence. As Bookerite Ralph Tyler described it,

> At one time [*Lewis*] fought the industrial propaganda of the late Dr. Washington— he never acknowledged it as THE ONE and only panacea for all our ills. He, later, because he is too big to be narrow and selfish, gave the late Dr. Washington credit for work he was doing, and became a friend of his—each, however, declining to sacrifice or yield views each believed best.[56]

There were those who were suspicious of Lewis and his motives even before the supposed conversion to Bookerism. From the beginning, Monroe Trotter's *Boston Guardian* was openly suspicious of Lewis's intentions. Lewis's picture adorned the front page of the first issue of the publication in 1901, accompanied by an article about his election to the state House of Representatives. Inside, the editors described Lewis as "a young man of some parts and possibilities as long as fortune enables him to take the tide at the flood, but if for any reason the tide is out, or seems setting the other way, much assistance must not be expected from him in stemming it."[57]

Trotter's suspicion turned to outright hostility as a result of the watershed moment of the Civil Rights movement at the turn of the century, hyperbolically called "The Boston Riot." According to historian David Levering Lewis, "If the impact of *The Souls of Black Folk* [*W. E. B. Du Bois's masterful book of essays published in 1903*] on civil rights was like that of *Uncle Tom's Cabin* on slavery, then Trotter's Boston 'Riot' had its civil rights analogue in John Brown's raid on Harper's Ferry."[58] The Boston Riot occurred in July 1903. Booker T. Washington came to Boston to speak before the National Negro Business League, and Lewis emceed the event. A few weeks earlier, Washington had politically crushed William Monroe Trotter when the latter had tried to wrest control of the national Afro American Council at its annual meeting in Louisville, Kentucky. Embarrassed and angry, Trotter planned to turn the tables on Washington by standing up to the "Wizard of Tuskegee" during his speech in Boston.[59]

The Boston African Methodist Episcopal Zion Church on Columbus Avenue was packed with an audience estimated at two thousand. Trotter's plan, apparently, was to demand from the floor that Washington answer nine pointed questions; even if the Wizard demurred, the newspapers would print the questions and bring the conflict with Washington out into the open. Regardless of what Trotter's intention had been, the meeting instead disintegrated into a melee, according to newspaper descriptions across the nation. Trotter and his sister (who supposedly jabbed a hatpin into a police officer), among others, were arrested. Once the room was cleared of the protesters, Washington was able to give his speech without further incident.[60]

At the trial that followed, Lewis was the chief witness against Trotter. Trotter was found guilty of disturbing a public meeting and sentenced to thirty days in the Charles Street Jail.[61] "As for Lewis, he is the dirtiest cur in this case," Trotter wrote a friend from jail.[62] Du Bois, even though he had not been present, believed that the manner in which Lewis had chaired the meeting had caused it to go out of control.[63]

Trotter's criticism of Lewis escalated a few years later following an incident at Brownsville, Texas. In August 1906, a band of African American soldiers quartered nearby at Fort Brown allegedly went on a shooting rampage, killing one white man and wounding two others. After a three-month investigation that produced questionable evidence and no confessions, President Roosevelt ordered that all the African American soldiers stationed at the fort be expelled from the army.[64] Historian August Meier called the Brownsville incident "the grossest single racial injustice of that so-called Progressive Era."[65] African American leaders across the country were outraged. White soldiers never would have been treated that way, they said. One African American leader did rise to support the president. Assistant U.S. Attorney William Lewis declared Roosevelt had made the right decision. His stance caused the *Boston Guardian* to charge that Lewis had "repeatedly and flagrantly sold his honor and sold out his race in order to get a political position with a salary which he has seemed unable to earn at the law."[66] During the presidential election year of 1908, Trotter published large photographs of the Brownsville soldiers accompanied by a photo of William Lewis and quotations from the assistant U.S. attorney expressing approval of Roosevelt's actions. Whenever the *Boston Guardian* ran a story that mentioned William Lewis, Trotter would run his picture with a caption such as "Worst traitor to race in its history" or "Lewis disgraced race."[67] Lewis explained his support of President Roosevelt thus: "I yield to no man in admiration for Colonel Roosevelt. He was my friend and my idol. He appointed me assistant United States attorney in Massachusetts, and in return I defended the discharge of the Brownsville soldiers, a thing no other colored Federal office-holder did."[68]

And what was Lewis's supposed payoff for his loyalty to Roosevelt? Just before the Brownsville incident, newspapers reported that Roosevelt was considering Lewis to be assistant attorney general of the United States, which would have been the highest federal office ever attained by an African American. After Brownsville, he instead gave Lewis the position of assistant U.S. attorney for immigration and naturalization, a job with a much lower profile.[69]

Lewis would not be appointed assistant attorney general until 1910, when Pres. William Howard Taft was under attack by the nation's black press for removing African Americans from federal jobs in the South and replacing them with whites. Taft had promised to appoint African Americans in commensurate positions in the North, but after two years had still done nothing. While Washington was on a tour of Europe, Lewis apparently took it upon himself to write Charles D. Norton, Taft's secretary, to urge the president to move quickly to make northern appointments, which would silence black critics and repair the damage in time for the mid-term elections of 1910.[70] Taft apparently waited until the last minute; in late October 1910, he announced that he would appoint Lewis assistant attorney general. Although Washington clearly was not the instigator of the appointment, he supported it and lent his considerable political resources to the effort to secure Lewis the job. "If I could lift Lewis, I knew Lewis would lift us all," Washington reportedly said.[71] Lewis took office in March 1911, but the appointment still needed ratification by the Senate. For weeks his nomination languished in a subcommittee where it was opposed by Sen. Augustus O. Bacon of Georgia. While Bacon and other senators from southern states had some success stalling the vote, Lewis was confirmed June 14. "[M]any thanks," he telegrammed Washington, "am very happy."[72]

Within days of winning the job, Lewis received a letter from the American Bar Association, which only recently had given him membership. Because the assistant attorney general had not told the nominating committee his race—probably because they never asked—the association requested his resignation, along with those of two other African American lawyers. Lewis refused. Attorney General George Wickersham threatened to resign from the bar association if Lewis was expelled. In August, the bar association voted to retain Lewis and the other two lawyers but with the caveat that all future applicants for membership must state their race.[73]

As an assistant attorney general, Lewis did not have a lot to do. He was in charge of the defense of Indian depredation claims, a legal mechanism whereby victims of conflicts involving American Indians could get reparations. All of these claims had been filed by the early 1890s, and most had been adjudicated by the time Lewis came on board. There was always the chance that Congress would change the laws regarding these claims (as it did in 1915, reopening hundreds that had previously been denied), but until that happened, Lewis was left primarily to his own devices. He attended parties and functions where he was feted as the first African American appointed to a subcabinet post. He became part of what was known as "the Black Cabinet," a group of African American office holders who met daily to discuss how the federal government could improve conditions for the race and, when asked, to present recommendations to President Taft.

If Taft's record on race is any indication, the Black Cabinet was less than effective. One small victory was influencing Taft not to nominate Judge William C. Hook for the U.S. Supreme Court. Hook, according to his biographer, may have come "closer to an appointment to the United States supreme court than almost any man in history who was not appointed, and not only once, but twice." The first time his name came up, Taft at first promised to nominate him but then gave the nod to Judge Willis H. Van Devanter of Wyoming, reportedly because of the influence of both of Wyoming's long-term senators. When Associate Supreme Court Justice John Harlan died in 1911, Taft announced his intention to nominate Hook. A few days before he was to submit Hook's name to the Senate, Taft met with the Black Cabinet over two evenings. At those meetings, Lewis made the president aware of a case that had come before Hook's Eighth Circuit Court that upheld an Oklahoma law allowing separate "Jim Crow" cars for African Americans on trains. The next week Taft submitted the name of Mahlon Pitney of New Jersey to be the new associate justice.[74]

Derailing the Hook nomination may well have been Lewis's only substantial achievement during his two years in the Taft administration. He did, however, make several important speeches during his tenure in the U.S. Department of Justice. A few weeks before Woodrow Wilson's inauguration, Assistant Attorney General Lewis gave a hard-hitting address to the Massachusetts General Court commemorating the fiftieth anniversary of the Emancipation Proclamation. "Are we of this generation worthy descendants of tea spillers and abolitionists?" Lewis asked rhetorically.

> I have observed with aching heart and agonizing spirit during the last 20 years not only the growing coldness and indifference on the part of our people to the fate of the Negro elsewhere; but here in our own city. . . . I have watched the spirit of race prejudice raise its sinister shape in the labor market, in the business house, the real estate exchange, in public places, and even in our schools, colleges and churches.[75]

One month later Lewis became one of the first casualties of the new Wilson administration, asked to turn in his resignation within days of the inauguration. Even though other assistant attorneys general were Republican, Lewis was the only one fired.[76]

After losing his job, Lewis kept his hand in politics, but now from the outside. He used his influence to support various causes, such as the battle in 1915 over the movie *The Birth of a Nation*. D. W. Griffith's epic revolutionized filmmaking, and it would become at the time of its release the most popular movie ever made. Because it made heroes of the Ku Klux Klan, the film drew large protests from the African American community in Boston. In an unprecedented demonstration of unity, Lewis, Boston's NAACP secretary Butler Wilson, and Monroe Trotter joined forces to prevent *Birth of a Nation* from being shown in the enlightened Hub of the Universe. They were thwarted by Boston's mayor, James Michael Curley, who refused to ban the movie even after Lewis and Wilson had managed to convince the state legislature to give the mayor the power to do so.[77]

A few weeks after the battle over *Birth of a Nation* came the unexpected death of Booker T. Washington. The Wizard of Tuskegee's passing allowed Trotter and Lewis to put aside their differences and end their feud. Lewis attended a fifteenth-anniversary dinner honoring the *Boston Guardian* in 1916. In a speech, Lewis claimed to be "a sort of Godfather to the *Guardian*, but the infant grew too lusty for me, kicked, squirmed and cried out on every occasion. I abandoned the child; and I think the *Guardian* abandoned me."[78]

In the spring of 1921, the Shubert Theatre announced that *Birth of a Nation* was returning to Boston. Once again Lewis, Trotter, and Wilson joined forces to prevent its showing. Lewis and company succeeded this time in getting the film banned. By that time, Lewis was fully engaged in the third act of his life, the law.[79]

Act Three: The Law, Always the Law

One of Lewis's first cases after his appointment as assistant U.S. attorney in 1903 was a small political corruption case. Two up-and-coming Irish politicians from Boston's Ward Seventeen allegedly had defrauded the federal civil service commission by taking the postal service test for two of their constituents. Lewis knew one of the men, having served with him in the state legislature—James Michael Curley. Their political backgrounds were similar: both had served on the Common Council, Lewis in Cambridge and Curley in Boston; both had been elected to the state legislature in 1901. Unlike Lewis,

Curley had been re-elected in 1902. When he surrendered to a U.S. marshal on February 25, 1903, Curley became the first member of the Massachusetts General Court to submit to criminal arrest while in office.[80]

Lewis handled much of the legwork for the case, and his hard work paid off. At Curley's trial in September, the jury only deliberated for ninety minutes before returning with a guilty verdict. The conviction added to Curley's notoriety but had little impact on his future political career. Curley embraced the slogan "I did it for a friend," when referring to the case. It even helped him win election to the Boston Common Council while he was serving his sentence in the Charles Street Jail.[81] Curley went on to become mayor and eventually governor of the Commonwealth. He apparently did not hold a grudge, for he was one of the honorary pallbearers at Lewis's funeral in 1949.

Although Lewis did not practice much law as assistant attorney general, an earlier post, though unheralded at the time, established him in an area that he would later turn into a lucrative private practice. In 1907 he was appointed head of Immigration and Naturalization for the Department of Justice for the six New England states. Lewis was responsible for the entire office, which was first in Boston's Sears Building, then later in the Old South Building, where he would also locate the offices of his private practice for the last thirty years of his life. As the attorney in charge, Lewis supervised a staff of seven, all white, that was responsible for prosecution of U.S. immigration laws. Years later, when he returned to private practice, Lewis regularly defended those charged with immigration and naturalization violations.[82]

After his dismissal from the Justice Department, Lewis returned to Boston, where he became a successful private attorney. He joined forces with a former U.S.-marshal-turned-lawyer, Matthew McGrath, and their practice consisted almost solely of defending alleged criminals in the federal courts. No other firm in Boston even came close to Lewis & McGrath in defending the number of bootleggers they represented.[83] "During the 1920s they had great success making money," recalled McGrath's son, Matthew McGrath, Jr. "They both became very wealthy."[84]

Lewis's reputation as a defense lawyer grew; he appeared more than a dozen times before the Supreme Court. He won his first case there in 1930, when the nation's highest court upheld a lower court's ruling in favor of Lewis's client James Farrar. Farrar had been convicted of violating the Volstead Act, the federal legislation behind Prohibition. Lewis's argument before the Supreme Court won freedom for his client.[85] One of those impressed with the attorney's acumen before the highest court in the land was Thurgood Marshall, who as a young law student at Howard University had seen Lewis in action: "[*Lewis*] would tell us about how to try a lawsuit; and how to argue with the judges; because he was a master of it. And we would run to the Supreme Court and hear him argue."[86]

Lewis defended African Americans in numerous high-profile criminal cases. In 1916 he represented three African Americans in Providence, Rhode Island, accused of conspiring with a white woman to murder her husband. The all-white jury acquitted the wife, but it convicted the African Americans. Lewis managed to persuade the judge to sentence them to life in prison instead of giving them the death sentence, as was common in such cases.[87]

The summer of 1919 became known as "The Red Summer," as violence erupted in twenty-six race riots across the country. African Americans, many of whom had fought in the war in Europe where they were pronounced as heroes, returned to face unemployment and ever increasing discrimination. Joseph Lomba, son of immigrants from the Cape Verde Islands off the coast of Africa, killed a white man in a street fight in Onset, a vacation resort near Cape Cod. The incident provoked a mini-race riot in what was normally a quiet, seaside community. Charged with manslaughter, Lomba faced several years in prison. In the winter of 1920, Lewis negotiated a plea bargain with the district attorney—his client would admit guilt and pay a two hundred dollar fine. The district attorney, who may have been preoccupied with another murder case involving two Italian anarchists named Sacco and Vanzetti, agreed.[88]

The next year, William Lewis defended another Cape Verdean man from Onset, John Dias, who, along with two accomplices, stood accused of kidnapping a white woman and her escort, and then raping her while the man was held at gunpoint. Mobs had gathered on two separate occasions to attempt to lynch the eighteen-year-old Dias, but those guarding the jail managed to drive off the attackers with shotguns. Gov. Channing Cox had to issue a public plea for residents to stay calm and let the law take its course, and the Massachusetts National Guard was called in to protect the three defendants.[89]

Lewis and two other lawyers petitioned the court to move the trial. The lynch mobs and the newspaper stories had made a fair trial impossible, they argued. Never before had a lawyer in the history of Massachusetts won a change of venue in a criminal case. But in a landmark ruling, Judge Henry Lummus of the Massachusetts Superior Court agreed to remove the trial to New Bedford, the former whaling capital, some forty miles away.[90]

Lewis once again was on the front page for his legal abilities. Despite a spirited defense, the all-white jury found Dias and his codefendants guilty. Lummus sentenced the men to twenty to twenty-five years in the state prison. Lewis never forgot the case, and he worked for years—for no fee—to free

Dias. He appealed the verdict and lost, then took it to the SJC. When Massachusetts's highest court rejected the appeal in 1924, Lewis made noises about appealing the case to the U.S. Supreme Court.[91]

The year 1924 weighed heavily on Lewis. The Ku Klux Klan, which had witnessed a rebirth thanks in part to the widespread success and acceptance of *Birth of a Nation,* now was a political power to be reckoned with, exerting its control at the Republican National Convention and over Republican politics. The presidential candidate that year was Calvin Coolidge, Lewis's fellow Amherst College alum and former Massachusetts governor. Despite repeated appeals by Lewis, Coolidge declined to denounce the Klan publicly, though his secretary, Bascom Slemp, stated that Coolidge opposed the organization. A few days before the presidential election, Lewis asked, "When did the President whisper this into Mr. Slemp's ear? Is Mr. Slemp betraying a secret? Why doesn't the President speak for himself? Is it because the Republican party today is the Ku Klux party?"[92]

Lewis made what must have been the hardest political decision of his life. "If I consulted my own selfish interests, if I thought of today only, and not of tomorrow, and those who are to come after me, I could probably get more out of the Republican organization than any colored man in America," he said. Lewis had been a loyal Republican his entire life, but for president he endorsed the only candidate who had stood up to the Klan, Democrat John Davis. Lewis issued a scathing attack on the Republican Party that ran some fifteen pages, which was then picked up by the *New York Times* and other publications. To his fellow African American Republicans, he said, "We owe the Republican party nothing. We have long since repaid our debt of gratitude." Later, he said,

> I am opposing the Republican administration not only because of broken promises, and political cowardice; I am opposing it because of a reversal of its whole attitude toward people of color. Segregation still rules in the Government offices in Washington; a whole colored section in the Registry of the Treasury; exclusion from restaurants and rest-rooms run by the Government, when by a stroke of the pen the President might put an end to it.

He later added, "You point . . . to the fine words of President Coolidge. I tell you that fine words butter no parsnips. What we need is more patronage, and less patronizing during the campaign season. I see no hope in Coolidge and Slemp. I prefer to take my chance with Davis and Bryan." Lewis's words were spread across the country. On the front page of the *New York Times*, Lewis urged all African Americans to abandon the Republican ship.[93]

Lewis had been involved in various Civil Rights activities and movements since 1887. In the 1920s, he volunteered his time as a lawyer to numerous civil rights legal challenges, and as late as January 1926, he was working with the NAACP, joining a legal team that argued before the U.S. Supreme Court in a case involving racial restrictions on property sales.[94] But his involvement in Civil Rights affairs evaporated overnight. The reason appears to have been quite personal. Lewis's children were now grown. His eldest daughter, Dorothy, was living in Paris and was engaged to marry a Belgian nobleman. His son, William, Jr., was at Harvard. His second daughter, Elizabeth, had recently graduated from Radcliffe and was teaching French at her former high school, Cambridge High and Latin School. Of all his children, Elizabeth seemed to have the hardest time in life.[95]

On March 13, 1926, some friends visited Elizabeth at her parents' Cambridge home. She excused herself, saying she was tired. When she did not come down for dinner, her father went to her room to get her. He found Elizabeth hanging from a belt in her closet.[96]

According to newspapers, Elizabeth had been in ill health and had experienced a breakdown several months ago, the result of "overstudy and because of her devotion to her duties at school." None of the reporters were able to find anyone who thought she had been despondent or depressed before her death, and at least one acquaintance said she seemed in good spirits.[97] The reason for her suicide may have been related to stress at work, but the timing of her death and its impact on her father seem to indicate other reasons. Elizabeth ended her life just as her sister was in France wedding Pierre Vercken de Vreuschman.[98]

Belmira Nunes, a classmate of Elizabeth's at Radcliffe, believed the reasons for her suicide were tied to race. She recalled Elizabeth as someone who "never associated with blacks, and she looked like her father, brown-skinned with nice curly black hair, but she never, never could have been taken for white. Her sister could have been." Nunes theorized that Elizabeth had found it difficult to adjust to the attitudes about race in the United States, particularly since she had spent much time herself in France, and that this was the reason why she killed herself.[99]

After Elizabeth's death, her father rarely involved himself in Civil Rights issues or legal cases. There were rumors that his wife had demanded he cease these activities, as if, perhaps, they were somehow to blame for their daughter's death. There were other changes as well. Cambridge had been his home since 1892, but not long after Elizabeth's suicide, Lewis moved to the Boston suburb of Dedham. He, his wife, and his son left Cambridge and—one would believe—the terrible memories of Elizabeth's suicide behind.

Lewis tried to curtail his Civil Rights activities and was almost successful—almost. He could not leave the past behind so easily. Lewis continued to be haunted by John Dias and his rape conviction. As he said later, every few weeks his thoughts returned to "those boys," who he believed had been wrongfully incarcerated.[100]

In February 1932, Lewis applied for a pardon on behalf of John Dias, Joseph Andrews, and Benjamin Gomes. It was the first time in his long career as a legal defense attorney that he had ever made such a petition. He received a hearing before a subcommittee of the Governor's Council that September in the Charlestown Prison. Lewis produced a letter from Judge Henry Lummus, the man who had imposed the twenty-to-twenty-five-year sentence on Dias, Andrews, and Gomes. Lummus, whose distinguished career as a jurist recently won him appointment to the SJC, gave Lewis the ammunition he needed. The judge wrote that he believed the three men had received a fair trial, "Yet I cannot say that my mind is free from doubt as to whether the true story has ever been revealed."[101]

Before the subcommittee, Lewis recounted the entire case—the alleged rape, the lynch mobs, all the way through the trial. He revealed how he had learned the alleged victim had been a prostitute, and the escort, her pimp. He said that the woman had concocted the story of the kidnapping and rape to hide from her parents why she had been out all night.[102]

"Gentlemen, I am asking that you recommend to his Excellency, a pardon for these three unfortunate boys—a full, fair and free pardon," Lewis said in his summation.

> Send them out into the world as far as may be purged of this offence. Give them a chance to hold up their heads and to go straight and become useful citizens, so that whenever the finger of scorn is pointed at them, or whenever their past is raised against them, they can say, "Yes, I have paid the penalty of ten or eleven years, but I have received a full and free pardon of the governor of the commonwealth."[103]

In April 1933, the council voted to grant a "pardon with parole conditions" to each of the three Onset men. On May 3, Governor Ely signed the pardons. After almost twelve years in jail, they were free at last.[104]

Lewis was sixty-four in 1933. Although he remained professionally active for the rest of his life, he appeared to stay away from Civil Rights. His most influential contemporaries also became less involved. In the next year, W. E. B.

Du Bois would be forced out as editor of the magazine he had started for the NAACP, the *Crisis*. He continued to be a darling of the American Left, but his ability to influence national or African American affairs had faded. William Monroe Trotter died in 1934 after falling from his roof. Lewis had continued to lend support to his former foe; in 1924, Lewis sent a letter on behalf of Trotter to help collect delinquent subscriptions.[105]

Through the 1930s and 1940s, Lewis continued to make headlines with his legal work. He defended Daniel Coakley, an Irish politician, at his impeachment trial before the Massachusetts Senate. He appeared again before the U.S. Supreme Court in 1944, defending a man who had been convicted of violating the Emergency Price Control Act during World War II. Lewis lost the case; the decision was written by Chief Justice Harlan Stone—Lewis had coached Stone at Amherst College some fifty years earlier.

Curtain Call

After his death, Lewis and his legacy simply faded away—though not for lack of trying. One reason that writing his biography has proved so difficult is that no one has been able to find his personal papers. For years, what papers there were resided with his son, who tried many times to interest potential biographers. When his son died in the mid 1980s, his grandson threw away his father's files, but he is certain there were few, if any, papers belonging to his grandfather. Another reason is that in the latter half of the twentieth century many prominent historians dismissed Booker T. Washington for his political machinations and what they perceived as his accommodationist philosophies. For Lewis, it was guilt by association. Worse, many historians used him as an example of Washington's political power, painting him as the "radical" who switched allegiances. In recent years, historians have begun to revisit Lewis, Washington, and their contemporaries with a new appreciation.[106]

While Lewis's achievements are notable, his legacy has been a mixed bag. In all three acts of his life he helped and inspired many. In football, he touched the lives of men of all races, especially through his coaching. He also encouraged other African Americans to take up the sport and offered assistance when he could. The all-American Fritz Pollard, who later went into professional football, sought Lewis's help in his early college career.[107] With regard to politics and public service, he was a mentor to many and an inspiration to even more. His appointment as assistant attorney general certainly was a remarkable achievement for its time. James Weldon Johnson, future executive secretary of the NAACP, described his reaction in 1912:

> I remember calling on some English friends here and picking up an *Illustrated London Magazine.* I saw a picture of Lewis and an account of his appointment as Assistant Attorney General of the United States; can you imagine the effect of that on the public opinion of the world? I knew that my friends had seen and read, and, as a result, they could not help but have a higher opinion of me and of the race at home on account of my own position.[108]

Lastly, when it came to the law, his skill, experience, and reputation were highly regarded and influential. It would fall to Thurgood Marshall, who during his university days had run to hear Lewis argue before the Supreme Court, and his colleagues at the Legal Defense Fund of the NAACP to overturn the "separate but equal" provision of *Plessy v. Ferguson.* The court had decided on *Plessy* the year after Lewis graduated from Harvard Law School, during his "radical phase," and *Brown v. Board of Education* would not overturn the precedent until five years after his death.[109]

But his impact, considering his achievements, was no doubt less than Lewis himself had hoped. As Johnson observed, there should have been more William Lewises, "not only because it is our right as citizens to participate in the government and that it gives the race a standing in the eyes of the world at large, but it opens up opportunities to convince the other fellow; he must come into contact and that gives the chance. Think of the opportunities given to Lewis."[110]

As William Lewis pushed open the doors of opportunity, they shut behind him and locked. In truth, Lewis could accomplish little because no African American could. Civil rights for blacks did not rest in the hands of Lewis's generation. Washington, Du Bois, and Trotter never managed to see their programs or strategies reach fruition. Instead, it fell to men and women in later decades, who had been inspired by their achievements.

Lewis knew that his life had been a blend of success and failure. "As I look back, life with me has been more than an experience," he wrote shortly before he died. "I would not call it a triumph, but it has been doubt and faith, shadows and sun, labor and reward."[111]

Notes

1. U.S. Census for Virginia, Washington Township, Norfolk County, June 16, 1870; Ashley H. Lewis (Sgt., Co. B, U.S. Colored Volunteer Cavalry, Civil War), pension application no. 331,026, Case Files of Approved Pension Applications, 1861–

1934, Civil War and Later Pension Files, Department of Veterans Affairs, Record Group 15, National Archives and Record Administration Building, Washington, D.C.; Ashley H. Lewis and Josephine Baker marriage license, City of Portsmouth, Aug. 21, 1867; "William H. Lewis, Noted Attorney, Stricken Fatally," *Boston Sunday Globe*, Jan. 2, 1949, p. 2; Booker T. Washington, *Up From Slavery* (1901; New York, 1970), 57; U.S. Census for 1880 (Portsmouth, Va., June 7, 1880).

2. Booker T. Washington, "William Henry Lewis," *American Magazine*, June 1913, pp. 34–37, republished in *The Booker T. Washington Papers*, ed. Louis Harlan and Raymond Smock (Urbana, Ill., 1972–1989), 12:223.
3. John Mercer Langston, *From the Virginia Plantation to the National Capitol, or The First and Only Negro Representative in Congress from the Old Dominion* (Hartford, Conn., 1894), 409–436, 498.
4. Langston, *From the Virginia Plantation to the National Capitol,* 435; Caspar Whitney, "Amateur Sport," *Harper's Weekly* 36(1892):1199; 1893 results quoted in Bob Royce, "All America Bill Lewis," *College Football Historical Society Newsletter*, 2(August 1989):8.
5. "William H. Lewis, Biographical Record of Graduates and Former Students, 1920," William H. Lewis (AC 1892) Alumni Biographical File, Amherst College Archives and Special Collections, Amherst College Library. The next African American elected to the legislature after Lewis was Lawrence Banks, a Republican from Ward Nine, in 1946. Adelaide M. Cromwell, *The Other Brahmins: Boston's Black Upper Class 1750–1950* (Fayetteville, Ark., 1994), 267; "Negro Wins in Bay State," *Nevada State Journal*, Dec. 15, 1946, p. 15.
6. Harold Kaese, "Bill Lewis, Great Negro Center, Recalls Day He Captained Harvard vs. Penn in '93," *Boston Globe,* Nov. 28, 1948, p. 35; Morris A. Bealle, *The History of Football at Harvard* (Washington, D.C., 1948), 534–536.
7. Parke H. Davis, *Football: The American Intercollegiate Game* (New York, 1911), 92; Walter Camp and Lorin F. Deland, *Football* (Boston, 1896), 27, 42–46.
8. Bealle, *History of Football at Harvard*, 91–96. The Harvard contest would be the last game Pennsylvania would lose for almost three years. The Quakers went undefeated in 1894 and 1895 and would not lose until the ninth game of the 1896 season, after which they began another undefeated streak that continued until they faced Harvard in 1898. L. H. Baker, *Football: Facts and Figures* (New York, 1945), 247–254.
9. Kaese, "Bill Lewis, Great Negro Center, Recalls Day He Captained Harvard vs. Penn in '93," 35.
10. "Oath Given to Wm. H. Lewis, Jr.," unidentified newspaper clipping, Nov. 13, 1931, author's files; "Following Paternal Footsteps Proved Wise Choice for Trial Lawyer," *Daily Transcript* (Dedham, Mass.), Oct. 30, 1975; Roscoe Conklin Simmons, "The Untold Story," *Chicago Tribune*, Nov. 28, 1948, p. 55.
11. *Boston Daily Globe, Boston Evening Globe*, Nov. 29, 1948–Dec. 3, 1949.
12. "Ginsburg Feared Vengeance," *Boston Daily Globe*, Dec. 3, 1948.
13. Interview with Matthew McGrath, Jr., Mar. 11, 1997.
14. *Boston Post*, Dec. 18, 1948.

15. I am grateful to the readers of *Amherst Magazine*, who pointed out Lewis's anti-Semitic subtext in response to an article I wrote about Lewis, "Blazing the Trail," *Amherst Magazine,* Winter 2007. See Patti Parson, "Coming to Terms," letter to the editor, *Amherst Magazine*, Spring 2007, retrieved from the *Amherst Magazine* website at www.amherst.edu/aboutamherst/magazine/issues/2007_spring/letters on June 14, 2010.
16. *Boston Post*, Dec. 18, 1948; *Boston Globe*, Dec. 18, 1948, p. 5; "Jury Finds Five in Revere Not Guilty," *Boston Post*, Dec. 20, 1948, p. 1.
17. Simmons, "Untold Story," *Chicago Tribune*, Nov. 28, 1948, p. 55; "Rape Case Appeal to Be Presented in February," *Berkshire Evening Eagle* (Pittsfield, Mass.), Dec. 30, 1948, p. 7.
18. "William H. Lewis, Noted Attorney, Stricken Fatally," 1; "Milestones, January 10, 1949," *Time*, Jan. 10, 1949; "Lewis Rites Attended by Many Officials," *Boston Herald*, Jan. 5, 1949.
19. Edgar Toppin, *Loyal Sons and Daughters: Virginia State University, 1882 to 1992* (Norfolk, Va., 1992), 62; Langston, *From the Virginia Plantation to the National Capitol,* 435; *Boston Herald,* Oct. 24, 1926.
20. W. E. B. Du Bois, *The Autobiography of W. E. B. Du Bois: A Soliloquy on Viewing My Life from the Last Decade of Its First Century* (New York, 1968), 138.
21. Frank G. Menke, *The Encyclopedia of Sports,* 5th ed., rev. Suzanne Treat (New York, 1975), 408; Thomas G. Bergin, *The Game: The Harvard-Yale Football Rivalry, 1875–1983* (New Haven, 1984), 48–50; Scott A. McQuilken and Ronald A. Smith, "The Rise and Fall of the Flying Wedge: Football's Most Controversial Play," *Journal of Sport History* 20(1993):57–59, 64.
22. Bergin, *The Game,* 52–53.
23. Whitney, "Amateur Sport," 1199; 1893 results quoted in Royce, "All America Bill Lewis," 8.
24. William H. Lewis, Biographical Record of Graduates and Former Students, 1920, William H. Lewis (AC 1892) Alumni Biographical File, Amherst College Archives and Special Collections, Amherst College Library. Ronald A. Smith, ed., *Big-Time Football at Harvard, 1905: The Diary of Coach Bill Reid* (Urbana, Ill., 1994), 102. Smith believes that Lewis was the first African American intercollegiate coach of any sport in the United States.
25. The four future coaches were Benjamin Diblee, William Reid, J. W. Farley, and Percy Haughton. *Boston Herald,* Oct. 24, 1926; "Crimson Is Honored," *Philadelphia Inquirer,* Dec. 4, 1898; C. G. Contee, "Historically Speaking: W. H. Lewis," *Black Sports* 2(1973):11.
26. William H. Lewis, *A Primer of College Foot Ball* (New York, 1896); Lewis, "The Science of Football," *Harper's Round Table*, Sept. 8–29, 1896; Lewis, "Defence," in *Spalding's How to Play Football,* ed. Walter Camp (New York, 1904), 97–102.
27. "Center Rush Lewis," *Boston Daily Globe*, Dec. 12, 1893. Also, reminiscence of E. Carroll Taber, who wrote, "There was so much adverse comment about this incident that the shop inserted a notice in the *Harvard Crimson* saying they were ready to serve 'all students.'" E. Carroll Taber to Westbrook Pegler, Feb. 17, 1949,

Herbert Hoover Presidential Library, Westbrook Pegler Papers, William H. Lewis folder, Box 45, 1949.

28. *Harvard Crimson,* May 26, 1893.

29. Frederick Douglass, "Address before the National Convention of Colored Men," Sept. 24, 1883, in Diane Ravitch, *The American Reader: Words that Moved a Nation* (New York, 1990), 297; "Treat All Alike," *Boston Daily Globe*, May 26, 1893; John A. Garraty and Edward T. James, eds., *Dictionary of American Biography, Supplement IV, 1946–1950* (New York, 1974), s.v. "William Henry Lewis."

30. William H. Edwards, *Football Days: Memories of the Game and of the Men behind the Ball* (New York, 1916), 155–156; "Harvard 10 Brown 0," *Harvard Crimson*, Oct. 30, 1905.

31. Roscoe Conkling Simmons, "The Untold Story," *Chicago Tribune*, Dec. 5, 1948, p. s2.

32. "Blue again on Top," *Boston Sunday Herald*, Nov. 20, 1892, p. 4; "Blue again on Top," *Boston Sunday Globe,* p. 4; Smith, *Big-Time Football at Harvard 1905*, 194; interview with Matthew McGrath, Jr., Mar. 11, 1997.

33. Undated clipping (ca. 1908–1916) from unidentified newspaper, William H. Lewis file, *Boston Herald* Newspaper Morgue, Pickering Educational Resources Library, Boston University. Lewis wrote the article sometime between 1908 and 1916, as he mentions Percy D. Haughton as the current football coach of Harvard.

34. Undated clipping (ca. 1908–1916) from unidentified newspaper, William H. Lewis file, *Boston Herald* Newspaper Morgue, Pickering Educational Resources Library, Boston University.

35. Walter Camp, "The Eleven Greatest Football Players of America," *Independent*, Oct. 27, 1904, p. 954; Walter Camp, *The Book of Foot-Ball* (New York, 1910), 361. Camp replaced Lewis with Adolph Schultz of the University of Michigan (1905–1908). Lewis, however, was selected as a member of the "third team" because he was "a player of the olden day, but one who would be of importance to any team today." Camp described Lewis as "Powerful and untiring, and with a good head, he always fed his quarter-back well, and was wonderfully active on the defense."

36. "Letters to the Editors," *Life*, Dec. 27, 1948, p. 4; College Football Hall of Fame website, "2010 Enshrinement Class," retrieved Sept. 4, 2010 from http://collegefootball.org/enshrinement/news_article.php?id=4. More than a dozen of Lewis's contemporaries, that is, men he played against or with, are enshrined in the College Football Hall of Fame. None of his generation have been added since 1971. Similarly, all other black all-Americans through 1950, save one, have been enshrined, and the lone exception had a relatively short career.

37. Leon F. Litwack, *Trouble in Mind: Black Southerners in the Age of Jim Crow* (New York, 1998), 198.

38. Toppin, *Loyal Sons and Daughters,* 16, 19, 62; "The Trouble at the VA. N. & C.I.," *Daily Index-Appeal* (Petersburg, Va.), Dec. 6, 1887; "Professor Langston Removed," *Daily Index-Appeal,* Dec. 7, 1887. Professor Smith was not speaking about the students' visit to the capital but of an earlier boycott of his classes because of a student's accusation that the professor had made improper advances. The Associ-

ated Press on Dec. 7 issued the following item: "Professor Langston was yesterday removed from the presidency of the Virginia Normal Institute on charges of inciting a riot at the institute when some of the faculty undertook to correct some students for insubordination," "Langston's Removal," *Cleveland Gazette,* Dec. 17, 1887, p. 2); Langston, *From the Virginia Plantation to the National Capitol,* 430–431.

39. Langston, *From the Virginia Plantation to the National Capitol,* 430–431.
40. *Elyria (Ohio) Democrat*, Jan. 12, 1888. In the days following Langston's resignation, there were news reports that twelve men formed a "vigilance committee" and ordered Professor Smith to leave town. Though it is unlikely Lewis was among them, it was in this atmosphere that he left Virginia for Massachusetts. "Given Five Days to Leave," *Fitchburg [Mass.] Sentinel*, Dec. 13, 1887.
41. "William H. Lewis, Noted Attorney, Stricken Fatally," p. 2.
42. W. E. B. Du Bois, *The Souls of Black Folk* (Chicago, 1903), 42.
43. Booker T. Washington, *Up From Slavery: An Autobiography* (New York, 1907), 239–241.
44. Booker T. Washington, *Up From Slavery* (1907), 211.
45. Du Bois, *The Souls of Black Folk,* 41–59; W. E. B. Du Bois to Booker T. Washington, Sept. 24, 1895, in *African American Political Thought, 1890–1930: Washington, Du Bois, Garvey, and Randolph*, ed. Cary Wintz (Armonk, N.Y., 1996), 98–102.
46. Emmett J. Scott and Lyman Beecher Stowe, *Booker T. Washington: Builder of a Civilization* (New York, 1917), 314–315.
47. William Edward Burghardt Du Bois to Oswald Garrison Villard, Mar. 24, 1905, Booker T. Washington Papers, Library of Congress, Washington, D.C. (hereafter Booker T. Washington Papers). Du Bois is probably misattributing "burn down Tuskegee" to Lewis. According to a Washington supporter in Boston, Dr. Samuel Courteney, it was George W. Forbes, a classmate of Lewis's at Amherst and coeditor of the *Boston Guardian* with Trotter, who became so excited at an indignation meeting that he said something along the lines of, "It would be a blessing to the race if the Tuskegee school should burn down." Samuel Courteney to Booker T. Washington, Oct. 27, 1901, Booker T. Washington Papers.
48. "Last Football Talk," *Harvard Crimson,* Mar. 24, 1896; Louis Harlan, *Booker T. Washington: The Wizard of Tuskegee, 1901–1915* (New York, 1983), 16; "New Plum for Lewis," *Boston Herald*, Jan. 13, 1903.
49. Theodore Roosevelt to Booker T. Washington, Nov. 10, 1900, in *Booker T. Washington Papers*, 5:673. Washington's assistant, Emmett Scott, scrawled a quick note on the letter, "You have him sure!" referring, I believe, to Roosevelt and not Lewis.
50. Booker T. Washington to William Lewis, Oct. 1, 1901, quoted in Scott and Stowe, *Booker T. Washington*, 316. This letter apparently does not exist in the Booker T. Washington Papers at the Library of Congress. Its existence, however, is certain because Lewis's response does appear there.
51. Booker T. Washington, *My Larger Education*, 1911, excerpted in *Booker T. Washington Papers*, 1:441.
52. William H. Lewis to Booker T. Washington, Oct.14, 1901, box 13, reel 11, Booker T. Washington Papers.

53. William H. Lewis to Booker T. Washington, Dec. 29, 1902, box 13, reel 11, Booker T. Washington Papers.
54. W. E. B. Du Bois, *Dusk of Dawn: An Essay toward an Autobiography of a Race Concept* (New York, 1940), 77; William H. Lewis to Booker T. Washington, Dec. 29, 1902, box 13, reel 11, Booker T. Washington Papers.
55. John Daniels, *In Freedom's Birthplace* (1914; New York, 1969), 128–129.
56. Ralph Tyler, "Who Shall Be Our Leader? William Lewis Says One," *Cleveland Advocate*, July 5, 1919.
57. *Boston Guardian,* Nov. 9, 1901, quoted in Stephen R. Fox, *The Guardian of Boston: William Monroe Trotter* (New York, 1970), 45.
58. David Levering Lewis, *W. E. B. Du Bois: Biography of a Race, 1868–1919* (New York, 1993), 301.
59. Fox, *Guardian of Boston*, 46–49.
60. Fox, *Guardian of Boston,* 55; "Negroes Make Riotous Scene," *Boston Globe,* July 31, 1903, quoted in *Booker T. Washington Papers*, 7:229–239. William Trotter was charged with disturbing a public meeting. His sister was arrested for assault, through the charges were later dropped.
61. Fox, *Guardian of Boston,* 49–58.
62. William Monroe Trotter to George A. Towns, Oct. 18, 1903, quoted in Fox, *Guardian of Boston*, 57.
63. Lewis, *W. E. B. Du Bois,* 302.
64. Probably the best account of the Brownsville debacle that this author has read is John D. Weaver, *The Brownsville Raid* (1970; College Station, Texas, 1992).
65. Harlan, *Booker T. Washington*, 323.
66. *Boston Guardian,* Oct. 26, 1907, p. 4, quoted in Fox, *Guardian of Boston*, 160.
67. *Boston Guardian,* Feb. 29, 1908, p. 4, Apr. 18, 1908, p. 1.
68. *Boston Evening Transcript,* Sept. 25, 1912, quoted in *The Negro American: A Documentary History*, ed. Leslie H. Fishel and Benjamin Quarles (Glenview, Ill., 1967), 388. This quotation is from a speech Lewis gave in Ohio denouncing Theodore Roosevelt's Bull Moose Party convention, which had excluded African Americans to appease a coalition that included "lily whites" from the South.
69. "High Office for Negro," *New York Times*, Aug. 15, 1906; "Appointed Head of New Bureau," *Boston Herald*, May 21, 1907.
70. William H. Lewis to Emmett Scott, Sept. 15, 1910, quoted in Harlan, *Booker T. Washington,* 348.
71. "High Office for Negro," *Boston Evening Transcript*, Oct. 26, 1910; Booker T. Washington to William Howard Taft, Oct. 27, 1910, in *Booker T. Washington Papers*, 10:426. See also various letters written by Washington between May 29 and June 14, 1911, in *Booker T. Washington Papers,* 11:173–216; Simmons, "Untold Story," *Chicago Tribune*, Nov. 28, 1948, p. 55.
72. Ralph Waldo Tyler to Booker T. Washington, June 4, 1911, and William Henry Lewis to Booker T. Washington, June 14, 1911, in *Booker T. Washington Papers,* 11:190, 216.
73. Various clippings, including "Wickersham Denounces Attempt to Oust Lewis,"

Boston Advertiser, Mar. 1, 1912; "If Lewis Goes He Will Quit," *Boston Globe,* Mar. 5, 1912; "Bar Society Votes to Seat W. H. Lewis," *Boston Herald*, Aug. 28, 1912; "Color Line Up at Milwaukee," *Boston Globe,* Aug. 27, 1912.

74. Ralph Waldo Tyler to Emmett Jay Scott, Jan. 19, 1912, in *Booker T. Washington Papers,* 11:459–460; Thomas Amory Lee, "William C. Hook: Judge of the Eighth Circuit Court of Appeals of the United States," *Kansas Historical Quarterly* 3(1934):68–85. In an appropriately ironic twist, the case that led to the undoing of Judge Hook, *McCabe v. Atchison Topeka & Santa Fe Railway Company* (235 U.S. 151 [1914]), came before the U.S. Supreme Court in 1914. It affirmed the decision of Judge Hook's court. One of the associate justices who affirmed the earlier decision was James C. McReynolds, the former attorney general who fired William Lewis.
75. William H. Lewis, "An Address Delivered before the House of Representatives of Massachusetts," Feb. 12, 1913, in *Masterpieces of Negro Eloquence*, ed. Alice Moore Dunbar (New York, 1914), 414.
76. "Wilson Relieves Clark's Misgivings," *New York Times,* Mar. 11, 1912; William Henry Lewis to Booker T. Washington, Mar. 7, 1913, box 13, reel 11, Booker T. Washington Papers. Although the new attorney general, James C. McReynolds, had a reputation for racial prejudice, Lewis's firing probably had less to do with his race than the fact that he publicly campaigned for Taft.
77. Fox, *Guardian of Boston,* 191–197.
78. *Boston Guardian*, Dec. 2, 1916, quoted in Fox, *Guardian of Boston,* 201.
79. Fox, *Guardian of Boston*, 260–261.
80. Jack Beatty, *The Rascal King: The Life and Times of James Michael Curley, 1874–1958* (Reading, Mass., 1992), 80.
81. Beatty, *Rascal King,* 77–91; Lewis's involvement is not covered in Beatty's book, but his signature and handwriting appears on many of the documents in the case file: *U.S. v. Thomas F. Curley, James J. Hughes, James Michael Curley and Bartholomew Fahy*, 1903, U.S. District Court for Massachusetts, Records of District Courts of the United States, Record Group 21, National Archives and Records Administration—Northeast Region (Boston). Lewis also listed the case in various biographical materials he would write from time to time.
82. File 111256, Department of Justice Central Files, R.G. No. 60, straight numerical files, Box 392, Entry 112, National Archives and Records Administration Building, Washington, D.C.
83. Analysis by author of the docket of criminal cases in U.S. District Court of Massachusetts, 1921–1933.
84. Interview with Matthew McGrath, Jr., Mar. 11, 1997.
85. *United States v. Farrar,* 281 U.S. 624 (1930).
86. Thurgood Marshall, speech given at the installation of Wiley Branton as dean of Howard Law School, Nov. 18, 1978, retrieved from the website for Juan Williams's *Thurgood Marshall: American Revolutionary* (New York, 1998), under "Speeches/Articles, 'The Equality Speech,'" at www.thurgoodmarshall.com/speeches/equality_speech.htm on May 30, 1999.

87. J. Clay Smith, Jr., *Emancipation: The Making of the Black Lawyer, 1844–1944* (Philadelphia, 1993), 107; Peter Shiver, Jr., *Dictionary of American Biography, Supplement IV*, s.v. "William Henry Lewis."
88. "Blow of a Fist Kills Young Man at Onset Wharf," *Brockton Daily Enterprise*, Aug. 26, 1919; "Lomba Fined $200 for Manslaughter," *Boston Daily Globe,* Mar. 4, 1920. For Judge Thayer and District Attorney Katzmann's involvement in the Sacco and Vanzetti case, see Felix Frankfurter, "The Case of Sacco and Vanzetti," *Atlantic*, March 1927.
89. Massachusetts Archives, GC3/series 328, Governor's Council, Council Pardon Files, Box "1933," Benjamin Gomes file, "Hearing on the Petition of Joseph Andrews, John Dies [*sic*], and Benjamin Gomes, held at State Prison, Thursday, Sept. 15, 1932 at 9:30 A.M., before the Advisory Board of Pardons and Board of Parole" (cited hereafter as Mass. Archives, "Hearing on the Petition of Joseph Andrews . . .").
90. "Change of Venue Granted in Butler Case," *New Bedford Evening Standard*, Oct. 19, 1921.
91. Mass. Archives, "Hearing on the Petition of Joseph Andrews . . . ". I have found no record indicating that Lewis appealed the case to the U.S. Supreme Court.
92. "Leader of Negroes to Work for Davis," *New York Times,* Aug. 31, 1924. Coolidge and Lewis shared one year at Amherst (1891–1892), when Lewis was a senior and Coolidge a freshman. See Donald R. McCoy, *Calvin Coolidge: The Quiet President* (New York, 1967), 13–15.
93. For details on the rise of the Ku Klux Klan and its impact on national politics, see Wyn Craig Wade, *The Fiery Cross: The Ku Klux Klan in America* (New York, 1987); William H. Lewis, "Leader of Negroes to Work for Davis," *New York Times,* Aug. 31, 1924.
94. *Corrigan v. Buckley*, 271 U.S. 323 (1926).
95. Maria Luisa Nunes, *A Portuguese Colonial in America—Belmira Nunes Lopes: The Autobiography of a Cape Verdean-American* (Pittsburgh, 1982), 75–76.
96. "Suicide of Girl Hidden," *Boston Post*, Mar. 24, 1926.
97. "Admit Teacher Took Own Life," *Boston Herald,* Mar. 24, 1926.
98. "Admit Teacher Took Own Life," *Boston Herald,* Mar. 24, 1926.
99. Nunes, *Portuguese Colonial in America,* 75–76.
100. Mass. Archives, "Hearing on the Petition of Joseph Andrews . . .".
101. Mass. Archives, "Hearing on the Petition of Joseph Andrews . . .".
102. Mass. Archives, "Hearing on the Petition of Joseph Andrews . . .".
103. Mass. Archives, "Hearing on the Petition of Joseph Andrews . . .".
104. "Onset Men Set Free after Pardon by Ely," *Boston Daily Globe,* May 4, 1933, p. 9.
105. Ridgely Torrence, *The Story of John Hope* (1948; New York, 1969), 247; Fox, *Guardian of Boston*, 272.
106. For examples of Lewis as Washington's pawn, see Fox, *Guardian of Boston*, 44–45; Lewis, *W. E. B. Du Bois,* 300; and August Meier, *Negro Thought in America, 1880–1915* (1963; Ann Arbor, Mich., 1988), 244. For examples of new appreciation for Lewis and Washington, see Gregory Bond, "The Strange Career of William Henry

Lewis," in *Out of the Shadows: A Biographical History of African Americans,* ed. David K. Wiggins (Fayetteville, Ark., 2006), 39–57; and Robert J. Norrell, *Up From History: The Life of Booker T. Washington* (Cambridge, Mass., 2009).

107. John M. Carroll, *Fritz Pollard: Pioneer in Racial Advancement* (Urbana, Ill., 1992), 53–55.
108. James Weldon Johnson to George A. Towns, June 26, 1912, quoted in Miles M. Jackson, "Letters to a Friend: The Correspondence of James Weldon Johnson to George A. Towns," *Phylon* 29(1968):188.
109. Speech given by Thurgood Marshall, Nov. 18, 1978, at the installation ceremony of Wiley Branton as Howard Law School dean, retrieved from the website for Juan Williams's *Thurgood Marshall: American Revolutionary* (New York, 1998), under "Speeches/Articles, 'The Equality Speech,'" at www.thurgoodmarshall.com/speeches/equality_speech.htm on May 30, 1999.
110. James Weldon Johnson to George A. Towns, June 26, 1912.
111. Simmons, "Untold Story," *Chicago Tribune,* Nov. 28, 1948, p. 55.

REVIEW ESSAY

Nature's Place in the Modern City

Two Stories of Changing Boston-Area Landscapes

STROTHER E. ROBERTS

Michael Rawson, Eden on the Charles: The Making of Boston. *Harvard University Press, 2010.*

Jill Sinclair, Fresh Pond: The History of a Cambridge Landscape. *MIT Press, 2009.*

THOUGH THEY TRACE VERY SIMILAR SETS of historical changes within the land- and waterscapes of the Boston area, *Eden on the Charles* and *Fresh Pond* will appeal to very different audiences. A finalist for the 2011 Pulitzer Prize in History, the prior title is more ambitious in its geographic focus; its historical gaze incorporates not just Boston proper but also the suburbs and towns along its periphery. It is also the more scholarly endeavor and engages far more extensively with existing literature in urban and environmental history. *Fresh Pond*, by contrast, cannot truly even be said to be an environmental history of Cambridge, much less the larger Boston area. Instead, the volume concentrates its attention on its own eponymous natural feature and the lands immediately surrounding it. The result is a work in which distinct personalities, particular events, and specific debates about the pond's future present themselves in vibrant detail.

Eden on the Charles is, at its heart, a study of urban politics. Its pages do not so much present a tale of humanity's transformation of the natural world, though this is certainly an important subtheme, as tell a story of city dwellers

STROTHER E. ROBERTS is a visiting assistant professor of history at Bowdoin College. His current work examines the impact of transatlantic markets on the natural environment of the colonial Connecticut Valley. In 2008–2009, he received a New England Regional Fellowship Consortium award, which supported his research at the Massachusetts Historical Society and other archival institutions in the region.

and suburbanites contending among themselves over nature's proper place within an expanding urban landscape. It is the story of a city, of Boston, but it is also a story of "the American city," with Boston serving as a representative case study of the major trends shaping contemporary urban centers throughout the nation. *Eden on the Charles* belongs to a growing body of environmental history that seeks to counterweight earlier scholars' obsession with "wilderness" by drawing attention to how Americans interacted with their natural landscape not just at the periphery of settlement but in the very heart of burgeoning urban centers. Like the authors of many such histories, Michael Rawson devotes the lion's share of his attention to the nineteenth century, a period that witnessed the explosive growth of American cities and the expansion of their governing powers and responsibilities. The class tensions that surrounded the transformation of Boston's lands provide the book with its human drama.

That is not to say, however, that Rawson overlooks the profound changes taking place in Boston's physical landscape during the nineteenth century. Rather, the natural features that most interest Rawson are those that have been most clearly affected by the prevailing ideals of contemporary Bostonians. Echoing other environmental historians (most notably William Cronon), Rawson reminds his readers that "'[n]ature' . . . is neither wholly cultural nor wholly physical, but almost always both" (x). It is the "infrastructure" of the city—its parks, waterworks, sewers, residential suburbs, harbor facilities, and suburban forest preserves—that most intimately connects Bostonians to their natural surroundings, "governing how the two spheres of city and nature interact" (vii). It is unfortunate that this well-nuanced definition of the natural world sometimes gets lost amid Rawson's prose, where "nature" sometimes serves as a stand-in for mere greenery and at others as shorthand to describe those landscapes produced during the colonial period that later reformers wished to replace. All too often, the book's focus on the environmental changes that took place during the 1800s obscures the centuries of human environmental action that formed Boston's turn-of-the-nineteenth-century landscape. Thankfully, Rawson clarifies his intended definition of "nature" in his final chapter, correcting any misconceptions readers may have gleaned from earlier pages.

Five thematic chapters explore Boston's transformation from a colonial port town that was, in many ways, still very rural in character to a burgeoning metropolis that epitomized the social and cultural trends that, by the early twentieth century, gave birth to the modern American city. The first chapter follows the transition of Boston Common from cow pasture to urban park. Rawson uses this example to highlight the growing disconnect between the productive activities of the country and a newly distinct realm of urban life. Shifting middle-class perceptions of nature as a site for genteel "leisure" rather than "labor" drove this transition, eventually overcoming the protests of those who advocated other options, some wishing to see the Common remain as pasture and others urging that the new park be opened up to the raucous entertainments of the working class. Middle-class reformers continue to play the antagonist in the book's second chapter, on the establishment of Boston's metropolitan water supply. In this case, claims that clean water would improve civic health and might also uplift the moral character of the poor stymied proponents of what Rawson calls "the culture of privatism"—the pursuit of personal wealth and individual interest at the expense of community-oriented goals.

Chapter Three follows the struggle over the fate of Boston's suburbs—a struggle beginning in the 1840s that distilled into a debate over whether they should be incorporated into the city to provide housing for the working class or remain a part of the "country" to provide homes for affluent Bostonians who wished to enjoy a respite from the unpleasantness of the city by finding peace amid the beauty of a more natural landscape. A fourth chapter, dedicated to the city's efforts to drain wetlands and deposit landfill along sections of the shoreline, follows the many debates that raged over what this might do to the harbor that had "made" Boston and helped it to become a thriving commercial center. The final chapter draws on earlier themes in its examination of the late-nineteenth-century push to establish forest preserves along Boston's expanding urban fringes. Though many advocates realized that these "wilderness" lands actually bore the marks of more than two centuries of Euro-American settlement, the growing scarcity of open woodlands in the urban landscape combined with a national fervor for conservation activity. The result was green spaces where trees would clean the city's polluted air and Bostonians could seek solace from their urban lives amid the glory of a "nature" that had been carefully created for them.

The author of *Fresh Pond* presents less a history than an impressively detailed and exhaustively researched chronicle of the major events and actors that have shaped the pond since the mid seventeenth century. The archival work that has gone into recreating the many stories that lie behind this landscape is truly impressive, though it must be said that the book's illustrations often steal the show. Sifted, no doubt painstakingly, from the detritus of the ages, scores of historical maps, drawings, paintings, and photographs trace the changing features of Fresh Pond and the people who populated its shores.

This book's seven chapters rely far more heavily on chronology than do those in *Eden on the Charles*. After a brief, self-consciously presentist introduction offering a preview of the story to come, the book plunges back in time to the last ice age when glacial advance carved the bed of the future Fresh Pond. From there, the book's second chapter follows the pond's life up through the colonial period, when its waters and surrounding marshes provided fish, waterfowl, and hay for early settlers, to the early nineteenth century when the pond became a popular destination for Harvard students and members of Boston's working class out for a day of ice-skating or general alcohol-fueled revelry. The chapter ends with the pond's decline as a recreational destination in the late nineteenth century, a shift that is never properly explained. Chapter Three explores how local icehouses and brick makers harvested the waters and mud of the pond to meet the demands of both local and distant markets, thereby tying Fresh Pond to a broader world and often remaking its banks and shallows in the process.

It is in Chapter Four that Jill Sinclair most directly engages some of the same questions raised by Rawson. The book's last four chapters describe the pond's late-nineteenth-century transformation into a reservoir for Cambridge's municipal water supply. They also follow the shifting uses of the parkland created along the pond's shores as, from the 1880s to the end of the twentieth century, city bureaucrats sought to balance the demands of water quality with calls for leisure space for middle- and working-class visitors. Sinclair concludes with an insightful paean to the historical significance of Fresh Pond, only briefly bemoaning the site's rejection for a spot on the National Register of Historic Places in 1982. She points out that although the Massachusetts Historical Commission rejected Fresh Pond precisely because of the many alterations made to its landscape over the course of the last three and a half centuries—the Commission argued that the site had lost its "historical integrity"—these very changes were, in fact, what make Fresh Pond such a representative and compelling artifact of American history.

Both of these titles should appeal to their respective audiences. *Eden on the Charles* ably integrates urban and environmental history; in so doing, it offers new insights for scholars in those fields and for anyone seeking to understand the development of the nineteenth-century United States. *Fresh Pond* deserves a place both on the bookshelf of the serious researcher and on the coffee table of anyone with an antiquarian interest in the New England landscape.

Index

Index